FANDOM IS UGLY

CRITICAL CULTURAL COMMUNICATION

General Editors: Jonathan Gray, Aswin Punathambekar, Adrienne Shaw
Founding Editors: Sarah Banet-Weiser and Kent A. Ono

Fandom Is Ugly

*Networked Harassment
in Participatory Culture*

Mel Stanfill

NEW YORK UNIVERSITY PRESS

New York

NEW YORK UNIVERSITY PRESS
New York
www.nyupress.org

References to Internet websites (URLs) were accurate at the time of writing. Neither the author nor New York University Press is responsible for URLs that may have expired or changed since the manuscript was prepared.

Library of Congress Cataloging-in-Publication Data
Names: Stanfill, Mel, 1983– author.
Title: Fandom is ugly : networked harassment in participatory culture / Mel Stanfill.
Description: New York : New York University Press, [2024] |
Series: Critical cultural communication | Includes bibliographical references and index.
Identifiers: LCCN 2023040746 (print) | LCCN 2023040747 (ebook) |
ISBN 9781479824953 (hardback) | ISBN 9781479824960 (paperback) |
ISBN 9781479824977 (ebook) | ISBN 9781479824984 (ebook other)
Subjects: LCSH: Fans (Persons) | Social media. | Harassment. | Mass media and culture.
Classification: LCC P94.5.F36 S73 2024 (print) | LCC P94.5.F36 (ebook) |
DDC 306/.1—dc23/eng/20231206
LC record available at https://lccn.loc.gov/2023040746
LC ebook record available at https://lccn.loc.gov/2023040747

New York University Press books are printed on acid-free paper, and their binding materials are chosen for strength and durability. We strive to use environmentally responsible suppliers and materials to the greatest extent possible in publishing our books.

Manufactured in the United States of America

10 9 8 7 6 5 4 3 2 1

Also available as an ebook

CONTENTS

Introduction

Toward a Theory of Fandom Ugliness

Recent years have seen repeated ugly moments in US public culture. In 2014, video game–based antifeminist harassment campaign Gamergate was both horrifying enough and intense enough to attract mainstream attention.[1] In 2017 came the deadly Unite the Right rally in Charlottesville, Virginia, which was driven in large part by desires to protect and celebrate Confederate monuments.[2] The following year, *Star Wars: The Last Jedi* actress Kelly Marie Tran was subjected to relentless racist and sexist harassment until she left social media.[3] These various incidents are quite different, but this book argues that they are usefully thought about together—and, specifically, usefully thought about together through the lens of fandom. In each of these cases, participants have intense affective attachments to the texts and people that they organize communities about online. Community members talk about interpretations together, and many of them create and circulate their own texts, from art to memes, forging ties between them that enable taking collective action, at times even offline. These are, I argue, fannish behaviors and fannish affects. Since the late 1980s, the field of fan studies has taken seriously these forms of attachment and participation in the realm of media, and my argument is that fan studies can help us make sense of the incidents referenced in this paragraph, and the others I talk about in this book, even—or especially—those that do not seem to have much to do with fans.

At first glance, it might seem inappropriate to talk about reactionary culture, and its "excessively threatening, violent, or sexually violent rhetoric; attempts to incite violence or criminal action in the real world; and/or the causing of harm to 'ordinary' people or vulnerable groups," in terms of fandom; framing such actions in terms of fans can downplay the seriousness of harmful behavior, which is why Emma Jane argues that it is ethically questionable to do so.[4] Resistance to linking disturbing

1

public behavior to fandom comes from two directions: on one hand, media and consumption and pleasure continue to be seen as frivolous and unimportant, both unworthy of study and irrelevant to topics like electoral politics and hate movements; on the other hand, the people who do think fans are worthy of study have operated from a longstanding and widespread assumption that fandom is progressive.[5] This book seeks to disrupt both of these assumptions.

Why "Fandom Is Ugly"?

On one level, calling this book "Fandom Is Ugly" is intended to echo and contrast with the shorthanding of early, celebratory fan studies as "Fandom Is Beautiful" by Jonathan Gray, Cornel Sandvoss, and C. Lee Harrington, who identified this as a simplistic and superseded approach in their 2007 history of fan studies—though much study of fans remains celebratory.[6] However, the value of saying that fandom is ugly goes beyond simple symmetry. The "Fandom Is Ugly" framework helps distinguish this project from concepts that already exist but do not do the work I contend is needed. Why not "toxic fandom," as proposed by William Proctor and Bridget Kies?[7] Why not "antifandom," as coined by Jonathan Gray and taken up by many since?[8] Why not "reactionary fandom," my own term from an earlier project?[9] To begin with the last of these, reactionary fandom is specifically about the intersection of fans or fannish behaviors and reactionary politics—politics that seek to roll back social and cultural change, and particularly to revitalize the racism, sexism, and homophobia that became less socially acceptable over the course of the late twentieth century. Reactionary politics are certainly part of the ugliness this book examines, particularly in chapters 1, 6, and 7, but this concept is insufficient to my purposes here: there is also nonreactionary ugliness that needs interrogation.

"Toxic fandom" also has limitations as a term. First, it doesn't have a clear definition, but nevertheless circulates as if everyone knows what it means. Scholarship that engages with toxic fandom demonstrates an emergent consensus that toxicity involves nasty behavior, such as "rude language" or "harsh criticism,"[10] "consciously and spectacularly abusive, disrespectful behaviour,"[11] or "coordinated harassment."[12] There is also a strong sense that, like other "toxic technocultures," it maps onto "retrograde ideas of gender, sexual identity, sexuality, and race."[13] There is nevertheless an enduring fuzziness to the term. Proctor and Kies contend that there is such a thing as "progressive toxicity," which seems to violate the second agreed-upon characteristic of toxic fandom as politically conservative.[14] This is not to say that progressive positions are not sometimes labeled toxic. As Jessica O'Donnell points out, "Gamergate represents a focused, organised backlash against feminism, which was repeatedly referred to by Gamergaters as being a toxic influence."[15] Moreover, feminists were not only victims of being labeled "toxic" but also perpetrators: as Caitlin Lawson notes, "Digital feminism can reproduce the failings of previous waves of feminism by excluding women of color and even labeling them 'toxic' when they call out their marginalization."[16] These examples begin to suggest that "toxic" tends to mean anything the beholder doesn't like. Perhaps, as Matt Hills contends, toxicity is best understood as an eruption of orthodoxy in the face of change.[17] But as Suzanne Scott points out, toxicity is often "positioned as an invasive and poisonous force" in a way that lets fandom writ large off the hook.[18] The ways "toxic fandom" brackets off a set of negatively valued behaviors as something separable from fans or fannish behavior as a whole is, to my mind, its greatest weakness, which is then compounded by being a floating signifier masquerading as a known concept.

Then why not "antifandom"? As defined by Gray, antifans are "those who hate or dislike a given text, personality, or genre."[19] Antifans feel strongly enough about the object they oppose to do things like create hate sites or hate blogs.[20] Certainly, fannish ugliness includes all of that. Bethan Jones argues that "much as fandom has become a recognized state of being in our daily lives [. . .], so too does antifandom permeate our politics, interactions, and affective engagements, and recognizing it as such informs the ways in which the 'darker underbelly' of antifandom can be engaged with, examined, and pushed back against."[21] Jones is quite correct to identify antifandom as pervasive, and so too is fandom's underbelly, but I would argue that they are not quite the same thing. As Jane notes, "Anti-fan discourse is increasingly being used as a sort of metaphorical fig leaf for preexisting prejudice and bigotry," a usage I am not eager to replicate.[22] Antifandom is a useful concept, but using it to cover any and all kinds of opposition to mediated objects risks flattening out a wide spectrum from dislike to violence.

Ultimately, "fandom is ugly" does different work than the other terms do—necessary work. Am I saying that all fandom is ugly? Or merely that fandom *can* be ugly? If readers are familiar with incidents like Gamergate, or the ferocious backlash against the 2016 remake of *Ghostbusters* starring a cast of women that featured intense racist and sexist harassment against actress Leslie Jones, or the racist and sexist fan campaign that chased *Star Wars* actress Tran from social media, it might seem obvious that fandom can be ugly. But neither most readers nor I would want to say that all fandom is ugly. Yet unpacking the #NotAllFans reaction that might arise in response to the title is in fact part of the work this book does—the title is intended to be provocative. Calling fandom "ugly" takes an evaluative stance, as "toxic" does and "anti-" does not. It is expansive, as "toxic" is, but deliberately rather than haphazardly so—it requires specification on its face rather than seeming in any way obvious. And it is broader than reactionary politics alone, though reactionary politics are certainly essential to many of its formations. Ultimately, *Fandom Is Ugly* takes up fandom as both a site of articulation of power and a mode of articulation of power. It asks both how fandom as traditionally understood reflects and refracts broader relations of power—and, specifically, domination—and how we understand those broader relations of power better when we look at them with the tools of fan studies. This is a move to use fandom as a theoretical lens, akin to how queer theory has expanded beyond focusing solely on queer people to examine things like the war on terror and the social construction of disability.[23] In the following sections, I take up two early 2020s moments in US public culture, one very ugly but less legible as fannish, and one very fannish but whose ugliness is less overt, to trace out some of the contours of what it might mean to take seriously that fandom is ugly.

"An Angry Mob of MAGA Fans": January 6 and Fandom Violence

On January 6, 2021, the world watched as a mob broke into the United States Capitol building. Some participants carried zip ties to arrest members of Congress they saw as traitors and wore earpieces to coordinate with one another. Some brought pipe bombs or guns with high-capacity magazines. Some erected gallows out front. Five people died, including a woman shot while breaking into the floor of the House of Representatives. In the days that followed, the group that invaded the Capitol was described as "insurrectionists," "a mob," and "a riot," but also—perhaps most interestingly—as "Trump fans."[24]

What does it mean to talk about a violent attempt to overturn the results of an election in terms of fandom? Certainly, Donald Trump's followers had already been identified as behaving like fans long before they invaded the Capitol.[25] Thinking of January 6 in terms of fandom helps us see that, at a fundamental level, the rioters acted like fans. As Amber Davisson argues in her study of Hillary Clinton fans, "Fandom [. . .] connotes a particular relationship to media content, which is characterized by emotional engagement."[26] The rioters were understood as having an intense emotional attachment to their object of fandom: multiple news sources called them "fervent," as in "records show fervent Trump fans fueled US Capitol takeover."[27] The term "ardent" was also widespread, as in "his most ardent fans strong-armed their way into the People's House."[28] The rioters were not engaging in political persuasion through reasoned argument in favor of their candidate, but very specifically expressing their intense feelings about him, emphasizing the ways in which "contemporary political leaders are often represented and read in ways not dissimilar to celebrities drawn from the world of show business."[29] Indeed, the ways in which many Trump fans had not previously been interested in electoral politics could make these performances "fan-based citizenship," meaning "public engagement that emerges from commitment to a fan-object."[30]

The rioters also went to a physical place to make their fandom material. As fan studies scholar Abby Waysdorf notes, physical fandom spaces and places "are sought out to give a sense of 'reality' to what is only, if vividly, imagined"; she adds that the fact that fans "have been in the same place as the text, or in a place that allows them to be physically immersed in the text, creates a different connection to it than watching does."[31] This different—and more intense—connection helps explain why it was not enough to simply support Trump, but rather some of his fans felt a need to go to the "Save America" rally in support of his false claim that the election had been rigged against him, and then moved the location of that rally to the Capitol building when he urged them to do so, suggesting the kind of intensified connection Waysdorf identifies with more traditional fan travel practices. This was also an intensification of Trump fans' earlier fandom behaviors. On one hand, Trump had been holding regular rallies to bring his fans together in person throughout his presidency and dating back to his candidacy. On the other, as Lucy Miller notes, "As fans, Trump supporters feel the need to defend Trump the man from any perceived attack."[32]

The value placed on going to the important site of the important event with all the other fans explains, in part, why so many of the capitol rioters documented their participation with pictures posted to social media.[33] As CNN anchor Brian Stelter commented, "They wanted to be filmed. They wanted to be seen doing this."[34] Why is that? Much like fan-convention or tourism selfies, these images documented that the fans had been there because that has cultural capital in the group: "The photos of the QAnon Shaman, the photos of the vaping rioter, the photos of the man with his feet on Pelosi's desk [. . .] ricochet in the far-right internet as proof of victory."[35] The documentation that this online-origin event had taken place in the physical world was part of the story, but fans documenting that they, individually, were there is about raising their own status compared to those who did not go, or who did not get as far into the building. This is also why some rioters took souvenirs, such as an envelope from Speaker Nancy Pelosi's office, which is structurally, if not semantically or economically, analogous to buying a t-shirt at a fan convention. That is, the souvenir had meaning in relation to their loyalty to Trump, not because Pelosi's belongings had value to them (as the example of the rioter putting his feet on her desk demonstrates).

The Trump fans at the Capitol also put on often elaborate costumes to take on characters they wished to embody—that is, they engaged in something quite like the fandom practice of cosplay (costume play). As media studies scholars Craig Norris and Jason Bainbridge argue, "In its purest form cosplay is akin to performance art, taking on the habitus of a particular character through costume, accessories, gesture and attitude."[36] There is certainly a gap between traditional cosplay and Trump fan behavior, because Trump fans are not being specific, existing characters. However, despite the divergence from cosplay proper, there are important points of convergence: the Trump fans were in fact trying to use their outward appearance to create a simulacrum of who they wanted to be like. This was as true of those who showed up in homemade military tactical gear as it was of the so-called Q Shaman wearing the pseudo-Norse regalia of a horned helmet and fur. These costumes signaled belonging in broader groups as they situated Trump fandom in both militarized, violent masculinity and white-supremacist symbology.[37]

A great many of the rioters' practices, then, are isomorphic with fan practices. However, because fandom is not often thought of as serious or important, calling them fans may act to downplay the gravity of their actions. When CNN anchor Becky Anderson noted that "investigators are looking at the evidence that this was more than just a group of amped-up Trump fans, turning their anger on lawmakers but rather, a planned attack," the implication was that "just fans" could not have also planned an attack.[38] One journalist distinguished between "loyalists who had come prepared for battle" and "other Trump fans" who were "carried along towards the Capitol" by the speech he gave on that day, seemingly parsing out levels of responsibility for the violence, with the battle-prepared at fault and Trump fans merely in the wrong place at the wrong time.[39]

The varying ways the mob's activities were described show a lack of consensus about what exactly they were doing. One headline discussed "Chaos in the Capitol as Donald Fans Run Riot"; on one hand, this suggests disruption, but on the other, "run riot" is often used figuratively, and by this description the event could have been no different from any boisterous crowd gotten a bit out of hand.[40] If the participants were "angry crowds of Trump fans"[41] or "an angry mob of MAGA fans,"[42] that sounds worse, but still not too bad. Even when they were seen as violent, was it more like a misdemeanor? Was this a case where "fans strong-armed their way into the People's House"[43] as multiple articles termed it? If what they did was just breaking and entering, that is certainly a crime, but not a violent one. Or were they doing something more serious and militaristic? Was it an "assault," an "attack," or a "siege," as various sources labeled it? Did they "storm" the Capitol or Congress, as was the most common phrasing? Recognizing this event as an insurrection or attempted coup designed to overturn an election in favor of an autocratic ruler means the rioters' actions were quite serious, and fandom accordingly tends to drop out of the picture. These were almost never the same sentences that called them "fans"—just 3.5 percent of the violent verbs appear in the same sentences as the word "fan." The through line here is to disarticulate fans from violence, which works to establish fan actions as less serious—in line with traditions of seeing fandom as trivial.

But these were people who loved a celebrity so much that they traveled to an event and showed off that they did so and put on costumes. That is being a fan. And they were violent, and it turns out that that is being a fan too. In such ways, much as fandom helps explain the particular affects and behaviors of the January 6 riots, the January 6 riots highlight some truths about fandom that have not tended to be recognized, particularly the ways in which intense affective attachments to objects of fandom can and do turn violent. This incident also highlights how there is nothing about fandom as a cultural formation that precludes the kinds of attachments to white-supremacist beliefs on display on January 6, from Confederate flags to neo-Nazi tattoos.

"It's a Net Good If It Gets AO3 to Change": Disruptive Use of Fan Fiction Platforms as Noble

In February 2021, a fan fiction story titled *Sexy Times with Wangxian* (*STWW*) broke into wider awareness, attracting news coverage.[44] Though the story had been posted in serialized installments since October 2019, it was not until it reached the point that "its author has linked it to more than 1,700 site tags (and counting)" that it attracted widespread attention.[45] Tags on the fan fiction hosting platform Archive of Our Own (AO3), where *STWW* was posted, are intended, as they are on many sites, as metadata to describe the posts they appear on, but tags also serve a particular role in fan fiction "as both warning and advertising," letting people either stay away from stories with particular features or seek them out.[46] While the *STWW* author insisted in an interview that the tags were genuinely intended to signal relevant information about the story, eventually it was the case that "the tags are so numerous, they can't fit into a single screenshot on a large monitor."[47] This caused significant usability problems on AO3, and users posted videos showing how long it took to scroll past *STWW*. Moreover, the story was tagged with multiple fandoms, such that the problem was not localized to TV series *The Untamed* (Tencent Video, 2019), which gave rise to the "Wangxian" romantic pairing in the story. As Kristina Busse notes, "Overtagging and undertagging can also obfuscate reader searches," making the tags less useful for the purpose of finding or avoiding content.[48] The navigation problems the mega-tagging caused were widely debated in fandom spaces, and several more users subsequently posted stories with massive quantities of tags, such as "fics with the entirety of Kafka's *Metamorphosis* and a chapter of *The Great Gatsby* in their tags."[49] One site of discussion around mega-tagging—and several claims to have posted mega-tagged copycats—was the Fail-FandomAnon (FFA) community, a forum on blogging website Dreamwidth where fans anonymously (and often harshly) comment on current events in fandom.[50]

Some FFA posters freely admitted to adding their own intentionally mega-tagged fan fiction on AO3. One announced, "I tried to post Lolita [in the tags], but it kept crashing Chrome. Womp womp."[51] That poster continued, "I'm actually going to knock it off now, because I keep forgetting to turn my VPN on, and I'll be legit[imately] upset if my main AO3 account gets banned for this." That is, this person, though deliberately attempting to disrupt AO3, was a regular enough user to be upset if posting access was cut off—but did not see any contradiction between that use and plotting to break the site's usability. Posters also discussed strategy for their antics. One asked, "So just . . . do it with a sock?" referring to the common Internet concept of the "sock puppet," or false account that appears to be a different person but is actually controlled by the same person, usually used for the purpose of agreeing with oneself to create the appearance of support.[52] Another asked, "What were the hours and timezones to post it [if] you wanted to stay at the top of the tag again?"

It was not that these fans did not recognize that posting mega-tagged fiction was disruptive to using AO3. Indeed, the harm was the point; they made sense of themselves as activists and their attempts to incapacitate the platform as noble because they were doing so in the name of making AO3 correct what they saw as a design flaw that allowed mega-tagging. One poster claimed, "It's called 'white-hat hacking.' They're trying to drive AO3 to do something about this bullshit." This is not the standard definition of white-hat hacking, which usually refers to working with an organization to find security flaws so that they can be patched, and another poster said as much: "Aggravating an organization into changing an exploit isn't white-hat by any definition." A second pro-mega-tagging poster conceded, "You're right, it's malicious compliance and/or civil disobedience." This explicit mention of a higher purpose or serious activism provoked a strong response: "Fucks sake. You are really not as brave or special as you think you are for fucking up the tags on a fanfic website."

However, this sense that mega-tagged fics constituted collective action in the name of a cause was mentioned by several posters. One compared the effort to "A Modest Proposal," implying that, like Jonathan Swift's satirical 1729 essay that proposed eating poor Irish people's children, mega-tagging could be used to call attention to the failures of existing policy. Another called the posts "tag limit demonstrations," which could simply mean demonstrating the limits (or unfortunate lack thereof) of the current tag system, but in the context of slippage between mega-tagging and activism invokes "demonstration" as a synonym for "protest." One poster summarized the situation by saying, "It's kind of inevitable that other people would start doing the same, either to try to force AO3's hand or out of malicious intent (which is what the wangxian author is doing at this point). I don't even think it's just the one nonny [anonymous poster] across several accounts, it seems like there's more than one person already trying this out." That idea of "forcing AO3's hand" is important here. The deliberately destructive use of the site, figured as white-hat hacking, civil disobedience, or activism, was understood as disruption in the service of a worthy cause—securing site design changes to prevent future mega-tagging.

On the other hand, some posters pointed out that breaking AO3 to show its flaws caused collateral damage. One contended that "just because one person is annoying you, I don't get the point of being an asshole to the entire rest of the user base." Another argued that, more than simple annoyance, "the sheer number of tags on some pages is too much for several users and causes their browser to crash," making the site literally rather than figuratively unusable. One user put in, "Damn, just say you hate visually impaired people and move on." That is, any user employing a screen reader would have to sit through each of the dozens or hundreds or thousands of tags being read aloud, rendering the site especially unusable for them.

One specific objection of those critical of mega-tagging was that AO3 is run by volunteers. Tag problems particularly impact the site's tag wranglers, who "work within the Archive to ensure that the varied forms of user-generated tags are sorted and filterable, without changing any of the specific tags the users choose, so that the archive users have an easier time finding the type of content they are looking for."[53] This role is necessary because AO3 is organized with a "curated folksonomy," meaning that "classificationists manage a large set of user-generated terms to create a navigable thesaurus that combines equivalent terms and creates hierarchical relationships among related terms [. . .] by making links of equivalencies or relationships between tags."[54] The difficulties megatagging caused for the tag wranglers were described by one poster who self-identified as one:

> Tags need to be associated with fandoms if they have fandom-related concepts in them. Stupid useless tags need to be kicked to No Fandom. Tags that mean the same as canonical tags need to be synned to [made synonyms of] the canonical tags. Tags that meet certain criteria need to be made canonical. When the bins get clogged with garbage, it's harder for tag wranglers to do the work needed on the non-garbage tags. And it doesn't matter if the garbage comes from one troll work with 1000 tags, or 1000 troll works with a single tag each, so tag limits have nothing to do with this issue. /wrangler nonnie

According to this user, it is the use of meaningless new tags they have to try to make meaning of that creates the intensive labor. Tag wranglers, then, are on the front lines of turning mega-tagging into usable metadata, and deliberately mega-tagging, one user argued, "is just flinging shit on people who had nothing to do with policy and who don't have any power to put pressure on/change the OTW's minds." That is, policy (and design) decisions are made by the AO3's parent nonprofit organization, the Organization for Transformative Works, not the people having to clean up the tags.

Tag wranglers were not the only volunteers affected, however. As another user pointed out, there was a flaw in mega-taggers' logic: "It's cute that you think causing volunteers to spend their time taking down works for things that are already in violation of the terms of service is going to somehow give other volunteers the time to create and implement new features." That is, what the previous commenter called "troll works" were also flooding the site's Policy & Abuse Committee—who "handle any complaints that come in about content uploaded to the Archive of Our

Own. The team determines if complaints are about legitimate violations of the Terms of Service, and what to do about them if they are"[55]—with problems to solve. This does nothing to provide resources for changing the site's design. The spillover to multiple areas of the site's volunteer structure was explicitly discussed on FFA:

A: "Literally all this is doing is distracting volunteers from trying to do their actual fucking work."
B: "Is this about the wranglers, or?"
C: "I imagine it also takes up abuse's time."
D: "Your imagining is correct."[56]

At a broad level, posting mega-tagged works in protest of *STWW* was often disputed as a tactic. One poster said, "I hate this framing of the volunteers as the ordinary users' enemies, who must be bullied into useful work." Another commenter sarcastically noted, "Yeah, this is just how you get change. Just like how you scream at a grocery store checker because you don't like the store's coupon policy." But a poster in favor of trolling AO3 to cause policy change pushed back: "It's more like if a grocery store refused to ban screaming so a bunch of people just stood around screaming in the kumquat [a]isle." The idea that one should do the obnoxious thing to get someone else to prevent the obnoxious thing is, at least, consistent.[57]

In addition to the more apparent usability questions, the incident was also linked into broader fights over the AO3. One user connected the incident to AO3's general policy to not restrict content beyond the bare minimum required by law: "I know AO3 is all 'artistic freedom' but this illustrates how people doing this can make the site damn near unusable when all the searches come up with shitp[o]sts and not what the person is searching for, and that is something I'm sure concerns them." That is, the tagging showed the limits of the hands-off approach. Moreover, a body of fans often known as "antis," who had long critiqued AO3's permissive approach to content, rejoiced at the site's struggles.[58] One FFA poster pointed out, "The dickheads think you're on their side." Another replied, "Lol, yeah, the twitter thread also has antis celebrating it because any disruption to Ao3 is a plus for them. Congrats." The specific Tumblr post I found directly linked from FFA has since been deleted (though it lives on in reblogs), but several posts on both Tumblr and Twitter expressed similar sentiments: that those AO3 users who were calling for changes of the site's policy to prevent mega-tagging were hypocritical because such people typically also defend the platform's hands-off approach to the content of stories, however objectionable. Through this incident and the ways in which some fans were fully prepared to attack something important to them to force it to be the way they wanted, we can begin to see a kinship with things like storming the Capitol. While the two clearly still diverge in terms of actual violence and the scale of the harm, the similarities of the structure of engagement suggest the value of putting them into conversation.

Toward a Full-Spectrum Fan Studies

Juxtaposing these two cases hopefully begins to suggest the need for cross-pollination between research on one mediated phenomenon and research on the other. To understand cultures organized around reactionary politics, we need fan studies. And to understand media fandoms, we need the insights of research on reactionary cultures.

To begin with the former, links between reactionary cultures and fandoms are immanent in multiple cases. A significant portion of the research on Gamergate has examined how this fan-backlash incident has significant links to what would later become broadly known as the alt-right.[59] Similarly, research has shown that the harassment campaign against Leslie Jones, which was ostensibly about fans of the *Ghostbusters* franchise feeling that the 2016 remake featuring a cast of women impinged on their fandom, also had deep ties to the alt-right,[60] and not simply because Breitbart writer Milo Yiannopoulos "acts as a node between the two communities," though Yiannopoulos's platform was essential to the speed and size of the campaign.[61]

Such connections have also been found outside of these specifically popular culture–based campaigns. In their study of far-right media manipulation, Alice Marwick and Rebecca Lewis found linkages of these communities to "radicalization across areas of gaming and fandom."[62] Similarly, Bharath Ganesh identifies what he calls "digital hate cultures" as a potent stew encompassing "the so-called 'manosphere,' an antifeminist coalition of men's rights activists, bloggers, pickup artists, and alleged experts in sexual strategy, and the Red Pill community; gamer and nerd subcultures; and a recently aligned coalition of neo-Nazis, anti-Semites[,] Islamophobes, libertarians, Christians, atheists, conservative nationalists and so-called 'race-realists' who profess a eugenic view of interracial competition."[63] In such ways, then, connections between reactionary cultures and media fandom have been identified, but they largely have not been subject to in-depth examination. One of this book's key contentions is that such in-depth examination is necessary to fully understand these social phenomena.

At a fundamental level, putting reactionary culture into conversation with fandom calls attention to the ways contemporary far-right politics is a mediated, participatory community. Jessie Daniels was an early observer of online white supremacists, describing them as forming "knowledge communities where those who oppose racial equality can gather and affirm for each other their shared ideas about white superiority."[64] Similarly, Stephanie Hartzell describes white-nationalist website Storm-front as leveraging the ways white people increasingly "seek affectively positive formations of racial consciousness—ways of acknowledging race, in general, and whiteness, in particular, that feel good."[65] It is essential that we take these forms of affirmation, affect, desire for belonging, and, especially, pleasure seriously; fan studies has demonstrated both the importance of and methods for doing so. While Khadijah Costley White theorizes the Tea Party as a brand rather than a fandom, she explains that this Obama-era reactionary movement "depend[ed] heavily upon the constantly interchangeable roles people play as both consumer and producer."[66] Paying attention to the ways audiences are not passive consumers of media but actively produce not only interpretations but their own texts is rooted in the analytic framework of participatory culture, popularized by fan studies.[67] The active participation and co-construction done by audiences is essential to contemporary reactionary movements, and fan studies work helps illuminate this.

In particular, if, as Bridget Blodgett and Anastasia Salter note, "both fandom toxicity and the rise of the alt-right [feature] heavy deployment of 'us vs them' mentality,"[68] the framework of fandom and antifandom seems productive to make sense of both cultural phenomena. Jane opposes such uses of antifandom, arguing that "it would be both odd and disturbing, for example, if racist hate speech was described as the active audienceship of antifans of African Americans."[69] I agree with Jane that these connections between reactionary cultures and fandom are disturbing, but not that they are inaccurate. For example, Hartzell notes that "Stormfront members emphasize distinctions between racist efforts to hate, dominate, and oppress others (white supremacy) and noble efforts to promote love of white people and protect white interests and culture (white nationalism)."[70] The contrast between the two suggests that cultivating white nationalism as precisely love of white people is intended to distance it from the socially unacceptable connotations of white supremacy as hatred of Black people, Indigenous people, and other people of color. White nationalism is in fact always and inevitably both of these things, but the slipperiness between being for X and against the opposite of X, and the ways they are mutually reinforcing, are known to fan studies but particularly sharply visible here. Dissimulating hatred of X as love for Y is frequently seen in fan contexts, particularly in cases of backlash.

Some work has been done to think about reactionary cultures as fandoms, beyond those cultures explicitly rooted in media objects like the Gamergate or *Ghostbusters* campaigns. Proponents of Donald Trump have been discussed in this way.[71] Clara Juarez Miro similarly engaged with a fan studies approach to right-wing populism in Spain.[72] We need more of this work and a more systematic look across cases. This book undertakes to provide these things. What are the consequences for how we understand participation when a popular cultural form like comics is subsumed into the culture wars and becomes a breeding ground for reactionary politics? What does it mean for political-candidate support to be structured through practices of antifandom, even hatred, for other candidates? How do traditional fandom practices of rallying around the fan object and spending money for support come into play in the building of alt-right social media celebrity? Is white supremacy itself usefully understood as structured like a fandom?

On the other hand, the contemporary moment also demonstrates the limits of fan studies' knowledge. Both early in the history of the field and more recently, scholars have argued that fans are inherently progressive. Fans have also argued this about themselves. Such arguments are rooted in a sense that fandom is resistant—whether to media industries in particular or to norms in general. This resistance is particularly acute around hegemonies of gender and sexuality. This argument is not wrong.

Fans *are* progressive and resistant to various hegemonies. But that is not the entire story—fans are reactionary and shore up hegemony at least as often. Fandom *is* beautiful. But it is also profoundly ugly. Fan studies needs to take the insights of research on reactionary culture seriously and ask some of the same questions about homophobia, misogyny, and especially white supremacy in the context of fandom. Francesca Coppa herself, though a defender of fandom as beautiful overall, acknowledges that that is not the whole story: "I know the evil that fans do. Fandom has all the upsides and the downsides of any other community."[73] Rebecca Tushnet puts a finer point on it, saying, "Fandom is made of people, and people are sometimes awful to each other."[74] Nevertheless, in the field of fan studies we have tended, repeatedly, to forget, coming down on the side of taking a positive view of fandom overall. Given the uphill battle to legitimize both fandom as a culture and studying it, this was likely inevitable. However, it has had some unintended consequences. Treating fans as underdogs in the face of the powerful media industry—which they were, and are, but they are not only that—tends to flatten out internal divisions and inequalities. Moreover, while the construction of fans being marginalized as geeks may historically have been true, increasingly fans are a favored demographic. This embrace has been highly selective and constrained, but it has nevertheless happened in a significant way.[75]

In addition, as Salter and Blodgett point out, while fans have been and continue to be linked to the geek masculinity of lacking physical strength, the aggression and violence constructed as essential to masculinity are still central to this construct, merely computer-mediated through things like social media, video games, etc.[76] Indeed, fans' belief that they are marginalized or even persecuted as fans/geeks/nerds can serve as a radicalization pathway. As Katie Wilson has shown, campaigns from 2013 to 2017 that sought to ensure that "traditional" white and masculinist science fiction won Hugo Awards, mounted by groups known as the Sad Puppies and Rabid Puppies, spoke to fans' sense of being "bullied" because negative stereotypes about fans feminize them, making them ripe for recruitment into men's rights activism.[77] Thus, feelings of being marginalized as fans seem to slide easily into feeling oppressed as men or as white people.

Research in fan studies has begun to do this kind of work in the past ten years or so. In particular, there is a growing awareness that fan studies should not have assumed that fans are progressive. Rukmini Pande is deeply, and rightly, critical of "the dominant view that media fandom spaces are subversive and liberatory by *default* because of their willingness to explore queer sexualities."[78] Moreover, Pande has noted that when fan studies talks about fandom or fangirls, fan studies scholars usually do not actually mean everyone, as "the referents of these terms remain US- or UK-central popular media texts and white, cisgender, middle-class women."[79] Benjamin Woo argues more strongly that "race remains a marked absence in the literature, indicated more by apologies and lampshading than by sustained research or reflection"[80]—and indeed, in revisiting even the recent literature to write this section, I found that race appears more often as part of a seemingly obligatory list of characteristics of fans or their texts than it does as the object of in-depth analysis. These are serious limitations of the field, and ones that have impeded our understanding.

In her landmark 2015 essay, "African American Acafandom and Other Strangers: New Genealogies of Fan Studies," Rebecca Wanzo argued that "if we see attachments to whiteness and xenophobic or racist affect as frequently central to fan practices, then sports fandom ceases to be an outlier."[81] These two patterns—whiteness and racism—are key sources of fandom ugliness, as an increasing area of research has shown.[82] Poe Johnson notes the illogic that was required to conclude that fandom is progressive: "Historically, black people have been denied access to representations that depict their basic humanity. [. . .] There is no reason to suggest that, left to its own devices, fandom would do anything differently."[83] While, as I will discuss next, the racism Johnson highlights is the most urgent concern given historical patterns of neglecting race as an essential power system that structures fandom, his point is also true more broadly: fandom, like Soylent Green, is made of people, who will by default possess the prejudices of their society. Why would we expect them to inherently be better? These patterns recur across fandom, with white fans often treating discussion of race as an intrusion on what they see as a race-free spaces.[84] This sense of fandom as apolitical happens despite the fact that fan works are racist at least as often as the mass media texts they draw from.[85] Indeed, Johnson cautions against simple inclusion as the answer to fandom's whiteness and racism problems; given the prevalence of racism in the broader culture, "when we call for greater inclusion within fan spaces, we must be careful what we are asking for, and from whom we are asking it."[86] That is, simply including more people of color without changing the structuring racism merely puts those people into a racist situation.

While the greatest need for improved understanding of fandom is around race, recent research has also argued that fandom is not as progressive around gender and sexuality as it is often assumed to be, either. With regard to gender, Busse has noted that fannish practices coded as feminine are still often marginalized by other fans.[87] In particular, Scott contends that what she calls "spreadable misogyny" has "flourished in part because the convergence culture industry has rendered fangirls an invisible or undesirable segment of the 'fan' market."[88] These ugly tendencies in fandom, that is, have been reinforced by media-industry market segmentation. As for sexuality, fans might disproportionately write romances between men—56 percent of the one hundred most popular romantic pairings in 2022[89]—but many such writers and readers see queer men more as erotic playthings than as a representation of an actual type of human being.[90] Moreover, there is a tendency to overt homophobia in relation to love stories between women.[91] In such ways, if Pande critiqued the idea that the existence of same-sex romances in fan fiction inherently made fandom progressive from one direction, Julie Levin Russo critiques it from another, questioning the way fan studies "positions not necessarily queer-identified women writing about not necessarily queer-identified men as *more* queer than people who are queer."[92] That is, when fan studies lauds fiction about men who are typically heterosexual in the source text, by women who themselves may or may not be queer, it focuses on risk-free fictional play and transgression at the expense of those who hold marginalized identities.

I undertake a sustained interrogation of fandom here rooted in the insights of research on reactionary culture. In so doing, I take up Cait Coker and Karen Viars's call that "fandom must also be investigated as a troubling and dark space."[93] I also heed Andrew Ryan Rico's insistence that "studies must expand to include challenging and often denigrated fan communities such as that of the Columbine shooters. To better understand Internet fandom, the field of fan studies must be willing to journey deeper into the darkness."[94] In taking this position, I resist the tendency of some scholars to respond to fandom ugliness with declarations that the perpetrators are not really fans but rather "trolls" or (right-wing) culture warriors leveraging the passions of fandom to recruit new participants. Rather than excluding the ugly from fandom, we need to take it seriously. We need more work like that of Jones, who argues that "the fact that Gamergaters seem to be protesting progressive moves toward inclusivity does not make them any less part of a fan community, or their behavior any less antifandom against progressiveness."[95] Wilson's work connecting men's rights activism to fan backlash movements, discussed above, also fits in here.[96] There has also been increased research into "harmful practices driven by fans' feelings of entitlement, possessiveness or superiority, which enable them to make claims about their favourite franchise."[97] This has included research on such practices as cybervigilantism and digital vigilantes.[98] Reckoning explicitly with how these are acts of fandom is essential to understanding them. How has focusing on the presence of queer love in fan fiction suppressed attention to these stories' homonormativity—their white, cisgender, middle-class centers of gravity? How has celebrating queer fans' resistance to media industries encouraged eliding the aggressive, even violent means of that resistance? How does focusing on sexuality as the terrain of debate over acceptable fan fiction crowd out conversations about racism?

Research on fans and research on reactionary culture have primarily been conducted in parallel rather than in conversation. On one hand, this is the case because fan studies continues to be marginalized as unimportant, frivolous, and even self-indulgent, like fandom itself. On the other hand, fan studies has tended to think of fandom as progressive, and so has not recognized its kinship to events occurring in reactionary culture. However, one of the cases I hope to make in this book is that these areas of inquiry need each other.

About This Book

Fandom Is Ugly is divided into three sets of chapters. It includes case studies about groups who are more obviously fans—those who form communities around media texts—as well as about those who are less obviously fans, analyzing communities historically within the orbit of fan studies as well as more broadly interrogating culture using the tools of fan studies, in order to show the interplay of these approaches. My primary objects of analysis are social media posts. In large part, this is the case because much of fandom ugliness *is* social media posts: the anonymity or pseudonymity of platforms, the way they facilitate interconnections between like-minded people, and the ease and speed of communication make it both possible and likely for fan anger to turn into networked harassment. Thus, I draw on content from Twitter, Reddit, Tumblr, and Dreamwidth. These posts are of interest not as evidence of individual bad behavior (and I do not include usernames or any other information about individual posters for the same reason) but as patterns of discourse—meaning power concretized in language. Discourses are ideas with impact, because assumptions about what is true or correct structure thought and action.[99] In the aggregate, across many posts by many different people, a composite picture emerges of the underlying logics of each phenomenon I examine. In a few places, the discourse I draw on is instead news articles about a particular ugly phenomenon. While this adds a layer of mediation, professional journalistic norms that press discussion is supposed to be neutral and balanced[100]—in particular, norms of explaining "both sides" of an issue—mean that these sources typically include the views of the groups in question, serving my purpose of understanding how the participants in the ugly phenomenon I examine make sense of the situation.

To analyze the corpus of discourse in each chapter, I used Analytics-Qualified Qualitative Analysis.[101] This involves, first, a discourse analysis of each body of text. Discourse analysis is a form of close reading that attends to patterns of language use, how ugly behavior was framed, and the underlying relations of power that shaped the discussion. As a second layer of analysis, I used computational digital humanities techniques such as analyzing metadata for distribution of posts over time, calculating word frequency in the corpus using data-mining software Orange,[102] and looking at patterns in categories of fan fiction. These quantitative and computational analyses let me see the big picture of the corpus, triangulating the other observations.

Chapters 1 and 2 consider objects that are both clearly ugly and clearly fannish. Chapter 1, "What Real Fans Want Is Straight White Heroes: Constructing Fandom in Comicsgate," examines the late-2010s Comicsgate movement, which opposes diversity in comics, for its constructs of comics, the industry, and especially fandom. Comicsgate members oppose those who are fans in the wrong way and those who critique comics with respect to social justice. They argue that fans are knowledgeable and should be listened to, that all fans share certain tastes, and that all fans find certain aspects of comics important, constructing a vision of fans as those who share their opinions, much as any other fandom does. Moreover, Comicsgaters, like other reactionary political groups in and out of media fandom, believe they are embattled despite being both socially dominant as straight white men and the core target demographic for nearly all comics-industry products. Seeing themselves as downtrodden when they are actually still quite powerful is about perceiving the diminution of white masculine power relative to that of other groups both as far greater than it actually is and as a fundamental threat to white men, rooted in a notion that white masculinity *should* be powerful and when it is not, something has gone wrong. The tension between thinking of themselves as so central and important and powerful that losing their patronage would devastate the industry and thinking that they are weak and downtrodden in the face of progressives and bad fans getting too much industry attention exemplifies a contradiction fundamental to contemporary reactionary politics.

The second chapter, "'#SenatorKaren Back Stabbed Bernie': Antifandom and Political Engagement on Social Media," uses tweets from antifans of US senator Elizabeth Warren that employ the snake emoji to examine how users construct political fandom. I find that the tweeters engaged in fannish magical and conspiracy thinking about both Warren and fellow senator Bernie Sanders, seeing her as an at times all-powerful enemy and him as the inevitable victor of the 2020 US presidential election if only she had not intervened. Tweeters also argued about whether using the emoji about Warren was sexist. At a broad level, snake emoji users had incoherent politics that were critical of the wealthy yet enamored of Bitcoin, self-identifying as progressive while also using right-wing terminology such as the pejorative "woke." Some tweeters did raise substantive critiques of Warren around broken campaign promises and her spurious claim to be Indigenous, but they were few and far between. Ultimately, I find that, while politics is often imagined to be a site of rational debate about policy, it is in fact a deeply affective space of attachment to candidates in ways that bear little relation to their actual policies, and that, moreover, this attachment may well be negative. That is, posting about how much one dislikes one's opposed candidate or searching that candidate's name on a social platform to find people speaking positively about that person with the purpose of responding negatively are indicative of a profound cathexis that must be reckoned with if we are to understand contemporary patterns of political engagement online.

The next section, chapters 3–5, turns to the traditional terrain of fan studies, queer transformative works–making fandom. Chapter 3 is "On the Homonormativity of Slash, from Curtain Fic to Canonicity." I demonstrate that on some levels fan fiction is indisputably transgressive of heteronormativity: refusing the positioning of heterosexuality as default and normative, imagining otherwise than hegemonic masculinity, and positioning women as agential rather than passive in sex. At the same time, I argue, slash also very often upholds homonormativity through a drive to construct the men in slash as "normal" and reproducing the white supremacy of hegemonic culture through unwillingness to write stories about or have investments in characters of color. Finally, I contend that the contemporary tendency in femslash communities to value only textual inclusion is deeply conservative—in fact, itself a form of homonormativity letting straight norms dictate queer lives and desires.

Chapter 4, "Hell Hath No Fury like a Fan Queerbaited: The Death of Lexa and Fan Vitriol," examines fan activist movements for inclusion and representation—and how they get ugly. It takes as its case study what happened when television show *The 100* (The CW, 2014–2020) killed off lesbian character Lexa in 2016 in a shocking twist after actively encouraging queer fans to engage with the show. I first examine how fans address showrunner Jason Rothenberg through media-industry value systems. Tweets discuss canceling the show, refusing to watch, and unfollowing Rothenberg. Fans also call on the CW network to intervene in the situation. Further, they frequently tag Rothenberg and address him directly as at fault for the negative outcome. Next, I consider how fans frame him as the villain and even include threats. Third, I examine how this behavior is consistent with the ways the fan base had a history of emphasizing only their own marginalization as queer without any critique of the show's racism. Ultimately, I argue that it is important to understand this backlash in relation to other moments of intense social media anger directed at a single figure or particular group. In the end, what the Lexa case shows is how the combination of fans' belief in their own powerlessness in the face of industry and the amplification power of social media facilitates extreme responses, such that the structures of social media reaction make one group of people who are angry on the Internet look much like another.

In chapter 5, "The Anti Wars: Sex Crimes, Free Speech, and Papering Over Racism," I examine an outpost of contemporary intra-progressive culture wars through what I call the "Fandom Anti Wars," analyzing what fans talk about—and don't—under the sign "anti." First, I explain the position of those who self-identify as "antis," including a critique of how the tendency to assume that the fan fiction one writes or reads is a reflection of one's real sexual desires produces an essentialist model of sexuality. Next, I explain how the other side, anti-antis, articulate their opposition to antis through an individualist language of free speech that elides questions of how some speech can chill other speech. Finally, I explore the limits of the ways both sides of the debate leverage a language of progressiveness, arguing that defining the problem of fan fiction as about sexuality forecloses taking a hard look at the costs of stereotyped and dehumanizing representations of people of color.

The third and final part of the book focuses in on clearly ugly phenomena we might be most uncomfortable thinking of as fandoms, but that I contend we need to understand in precisely that way. In chapter 6, "'I Just Joined the #MugClub!': Fan Consumer Activism meets the Culture Wars," I interrogate practices of rallying around a fan object through the case of #VoxAdpocalypse, a hashtag that sprang up in 2019 when right-wing YouTuber Steven Crowder had his account demonetized for repeated harassment of Carlos Maza, a journalist at online outlet *Vox*. The demonetization sparked more than one hundred thousand tweets with the hashtag, primarily from defenders of Crowder's right to racist and homophobic "jokes" about Maza. If political consumption such as boycotting and buycotting is typically understood by its practitioners as a moral act, these fans, too, think of what they are doing as deeply moral. Ultimately, #VoxAdpocalypse is characterized by public performances of financial support for a perceived like-minded community, at the same time that it is deeply enmeshed in contemporary culture-wars discourses and a concept of free speech as a right to get paid. At a fundamental level, the incident turns on questions of identity, in particular tweeters' sense of themselves as victims of marginalized groups they both mock and see as extraordinarily powerful. The construction of group identity around a media object, consolidated through consumption, makes fandom a useful interpretive lens for #VoxAdpocalypse.

Addressing a culture perhaps most unlike that of traditional fandom, chapter 7 is "'Teaching White Kids They're Bad': Antifandom of Critical Race Theory and Fannish Attachment to Whiteness." In it, I argue that the panic around critical race theory (CRT) that began in 2021 is an intense affective relationship to a text—a negative one—and can therefore usefully be thought of through the lens of antifandom. In the panic, CRT is treated as a transmedia text, and particularly one that is modular and can be drawn from selectively to create an everybogeyman. This then recruits intense negative affective attachments to CRT, which enable attachments to whiteness. Seeing the ingroup as an embattled underdog, even when it is not, is a common feature of fandom, and a frequent response to feeling isolated and especially embattled as part of a group is to seek out community. In this way, thinking about the CRT panic alongside fandom helps us make sense of how emotionally intense the panic is, as well as how unmoored it is from the facts of actual CRT scholarship. Through applying the lens of fan studies to something that by most definitions bears little resemblance to a fandom, we see both what the field has to offer and, more importantly, the power of (intense, negative) affect in shaping contemporary culture.

Finally, in the conclusion, "Of Victimhood and Vitriol," I highlight the underlying patterns in beliefs and behavior across types of ugly fandom toward making sense of why it appears where and when and how it does. I show that ugly fandom is rooted in beliefs about fans being victims—whether as fans, as queer people, or as white men; of industry, of other fans, or of social justice. Moreover, ugly fandom responds to actual social structures and situations that have been misunderstood. This is what makes it such an intractable problem, as fans may be misinterpreting what they see, and acting horribly in response, but they are not making it up. It is important to take seriously the deeply affective nature of fan ugliness, and this is why fan studies is such an essential lens on contemporary power relations.

1

What Real Fans Want Is Straight White Heroes

Constructing Fandom in Comicsgate

Beginning in the late 2010s, the Comicsgate movement coalesced in opposition to attempts to increase the prevalence and prominence of people of color, women, and queer people as characters and creators in mainstream superhero comics, characterizing these efforts as attacks on the straight white men characters and creators they love. Like Gamergate before them, members of this group expressed their displeasure through aggressive tactics, including doxing, harassment, and violent threats directed at prominent comics creators.[1] One online hub for Comicsgate is the subreddit r/WerthamInAction, founded in 2015.[2] According to its creator, the "subreddit tracks and discusses attempts to smear, intimidate, censor, culturally appropriate, ethically corrupt, or otherwise harm the comic book industry and culture, specifically such attempts by the SJW hate movement." In addition to listing five different kinds of harm allegedly done to comics as a medium, this comment identifies the enemy—the "SJW," or "social justice warrior." Naming such people, known for promoting racial and gender justice, as a "hate movement" signals Comicsgate's constitutive opposition to such forms of justice, and thus its alignment with right-wing ideologies.

The origins of Comicsgate are somewhat murky. Some trace the movement to 2015, when controversy erupted around a variant cover for an issue of DC's *Batgirl* depicting the titular heroine being abused by the Joker. The publication of the variant cover was eventually canceled at the request of the artist after some feminist critics argued that the art was inappropriate for a book aimed at young girls.[3] However, this decision prompted significant backlash from some comics fans, who complained that a social media campaign against the cover was a call for censorship. Others identify the reactionary backlash as starting earlier, responding to the series of decisions by Marvel to diversify its products by giving new characters a chance to wear the mantle of some classic heroes (an Afro-Latino Spider-Man [2011], a Muslim Ms. Marvel [2013], a woman Thor [2014], and a Black Captain America [2014], oh my!).[4] The movement gained additional mainstream attention when industry professionals were subjected to online harassment under the hashtag #Comicsgate. These professionals included author Chelsea Cain, targeted for posting an image of a superheroine wearing an "Ask Me about My Feminist Agenda" t-shirt in 2016,[5] and Marvel editor Heather Antos, targeted for posting an image of women Marvel employees drinking milkshakes in honor of the passing of comics publisher Flo Steinberg in 2017.[6]

What ultimately unites these flashpoints is desire from a subset of fans to resist what they perceive as "forced diversity" in comics—and indeed "diversity" shows up in 225 comments collected from r/WerthamInAction. "Forced diversity" refers to the idea that storylines featuring non-"straight white men" characters or references to progressive causes are an unwanted intrusion by the forces of political correctness in a space imagined as reserved for apolitical escapist fantasy. As one poster put it, Comicsgate aims for "an end to obsessive no-escapism politics in a majority of titles." According to proponents of this narrative, the kinds of events discussed above were examples of the comic book industry becoming willing to alienate its "loyal fan base"—geeky straight white men—to cater to "outsiders" who wanted to push liberal political agendas. As these centers of gravity in the discourse begin to suggest, Comicsgate is a clear case of what I have elsewhere called "reactionary fandom," describing a formation in which "fandoms overtly embrace reactionary politics and reactionary politics increasingly take fannish forms."[7] This is a position rooted in seeing straight white men as the cultural default and rejecting (often intensely) the inclusion of anyone else within the fannish community or as characters in the fan object, with such inclusion seen as an unwelcome imposition. These fans thus have a (frequently implicit) model of who fans are and should be. It is this construction that this chapter interrogates, asking, How do Comicsgate supporters construct the ideal fan? Conversely, how do they construct illegitimate fans? And how can these constructions of what it means to be a fan help us understand how media fandom is increasingly intertwined with the beliefs and tactics of the far Right?

Comicsgate is a useful case study because it sits at the intersections of multiple trajectories that drive both fandom ugliness and our need for a new approach to it. On one hand, Comcisgate is right at the center of what fan studies has long focused on: fans of geeky media who are in conflict with an industry that fails to meet their needs. On the other hand, the way these fans consider inclusion of outgroup members to be a failure, respond with mass harassment, and see themselves as the victim in the story despite rejecting inclusion and engaging in harassment are recurring patterns across this book. If the first set of factors might traditionally make them sympathetic figures to pro-fan or anti-corporate analysis, the second calls such a move into question—in this case and possibly in others. I began this investigation by scraping the subreddit using the Python Reddit API Wrapper, extracting the complete text of all posts and comments from the first available post on March 21, 2015, to the point of data collection on July 28, 2019, a total of 1,005 posts and 7,141 associated comments from 733 unique users.[8] To concentrate on how Comicsgaters specifically understand who fans are and what they do, I then filtered for posts with the word "fan" using Microsoft Excel, collecting both those specific posts and their surrounding threads in order to retain context, for a total of 2,131 posts and comments in 163 threads from 393 users. As this is 54 percent of all users who posted in the subreddit, it shows how much this topic is on their minds. As a first step in analysis, I filtered for just the posts in which "fan" appears (282 posts). I next used AntConc, a concordance and text-analysis software,[9] to focus in on the specific instances of "fan" and the twenty-five words on either side of its appearance; in this analysis, I included variants like "fans," "fandom," and "fanbase" but excluded words like "fantasy," for a total of 379 instances of "fan." After an initial overview read of this data, I grouped together posts that discussed what Comicsgaters defined as "us" and as "them." Within these groupings, I conducted close reading of the texts in each group for themes in how "good" and "bad" fans were characterized.

Comicsgaters are far from the only fans to police boundaries around what constitutes a good or bad fan, who is in their group and who is outside. Such boundaries are inevitably contested, often sharply so, with Matt Hills noting that "toxicity is, perhaps, necessarily articulated with the matter of fan boundaries and borders—that is, it is inevitably linked to issues of (fan) authenticity as much as indeterminacy."[10] Fans feel intensely about group boundaries, and they often behave accordingly. Moreover, while my focus on Comicsgate and Hills's mention of toxicity might suggest that this is the stuff only of contemporary reactionary movements, Suzanne Scott notes that "boundary policing within fan cultures is not new, or an exclusively masculine pursuit."[11] Indeed, scholars have noted this kind of boundary policing among the women fans often considered progressive.[12] It is also particularly common in sports fandom.[13] However, what is distinctive about boundary policing in Comicsgate is that its connection to reactionary politics is close to the surface, as Comicsgaters directly set themselves up against SJWs and Tumblr users. As Bridget Blodgett and Anastasia Salter note, one commonality between "both fandom toxicity and the rise of the alt-right lies in the heavy deployment of 'us vs them' mentality."[14] However, the way Comicsgaters define "us" and "them" can also not be disentangled from defining "fans" and rejecting those they see as being fans in the wrong way: who like the wrong things; participate in the wrong kinds of practices, such as fan fiction; or are the wrong kind of people, namely, women. Comicsgaters also argue that "real" fans should be listened to and know best for comics, as well as articulate what it means to be a good fan, with a set of likes and dislikes that they assert as universal. Finally, Comicsgaters see themselves as victims specifically as fans. That is, at every turn the fannishness of their complaints comes right along with the political content; if we look only at the reactionary-politics aspect of this phenomenon, we fundamentally cannot understand it, nor similarly ugly movements in contemporary media culture.

Them: Defining Comicsgate's Enemies from SJWs to Fanfic

A key part of Comicsgate's rhetoric of complaint is defining the enemies of what they identify as true fans—enemies who range from bad fans to not fans at all. As the mention of the SJW at the subreddit's founding already begins to suggest, some of the groups Comicsgaters identify as their opposition make their ties to other reactionary movements clear. The SJW is a frequent enemy of reactionary movement Gamergate, as well as of other reactionary fans.[15] Comicsgaters see such people as a significant threat; "SJW" is among the ten most frequent words in the overall data, with 1,618 total mentions. The term "SJW," as Lisa Naka-mura identifies, was "previously used in the mid-2000s by Tumblr and Live Journal bloggers to refer to the struggle against forms of body-based social discrimination such as sexism, racism, ableism, homophobia, and classism," adding that "'social justice' activism online is fundamentally a product of contemporary feminist media theory that evolved in reaction to one of second-wave feminism's greatest weaknesses: its lack of inter-sectionality with other identities."[16] From those sincerely activist origins, the term was coopted in the mid-2010s by reactionaries and began to be "used as a pejorative within these communities to describe individuals who they claim are overly invested in identity politics and political cor-rectness."[17] Adrienne Massanari and Shira Chess report that "according to Google search trends [. . .], 'social justice warrior' reached critical mass beginning in August 2014, right around the time of #Gamergate";[18] using this term so prominently demonstrates Comicsgate's relationship to broader patterns of reactionary backlash.

The pejorative use of "SJW" to describe inappropriate fans is quite prevalent from Comicsgaters. That SJWs are something to avoid is taken as self-evident, as when one commenter offers to another, "Can I interest you in a very impartial and non-SJW fan podcast of the Mar-vel shows instead?" Indeed, the figure of the SJW is powerful enough that it is leveraged in a variety of critiques of "bad fans" even when it is not particularly relevant. One poster complains that "the tumblrinas and SJWs are coming from a land of yaoi and slashfic, where bros can't exist and all the males are secretly gay or bi, so the slightest glance at another man immediately leads to a manly yet passionate make-out session with senpai."[19] There are several things happening here: the poster critiques the tendency of fan fiction stories featuring romance between men to leverage any intimacy into sexual intimacy, collapsing the homosocial ("bros") into the homosexual. Yet along the way, he identifies these misbehaving fans as SJWs and "tumblrinas"—a pejora-tive term for users of microblogging platform Tumblr—when a "manly yet passionate make-out session with senpai" is, at best, tangential to social justice. In such ways, Comicsgate features a mishmash of variet-ies of conservatism, including both those who generally dislike same-sex content and those whose discourse employs far-right Internet bogeymen like the SJW.

Tumblr is in fact frequently thought of across reactionary fandom as a source of, or metonym for, bad fans. "Wertham in Action" itself is a snowclone of earlier anti–social justice subreddits, including Gamergate hub Kotaku in Action (KIA).[20] As Adrienne Massanari explains, "/r/KIA takes its name from yet another subreddit with a strongly anti-feminist bent: /r/TumblrInAction (TIA), and unsurprisingly, they share some of the same moderators. Designed originally to satirize the culture of Tumblr, TIA has since shifted to become a meeting place for Redditors to mock feminism, non-binary and trans* gender identities, and social activism."[21] The "X in Action" formation thus tends to name subreddits that treat SJW politics, and Tumblr, as an ideological enemy. As one commenter says, "The issue that always arises is there's a certain vocal segment of fandom (I hesitate to use that word even, as it's usually Twitter and Tumblr warriors looking for an excuse to be outraged) that opine that diversity for its own sake is the ultimate goal, not good stories and characters, and when others begin to criticize that opinion or its inevitable results (lazy storytelling and faux progressive caricatures), then they're racist, sexist, or anti-diversity." First, this comment suggests that Twitter and Tumblr "warriors" are not true fans. It then goes on to characterize such people not as sincere in their desire for justice but as "looking for an excuse to be outraged," invested in diversity at all costs, and resistant to alternate views—all typical critiques of the SJW.[22] The comment also incorporates the idea that low quality is "inevitable" from inclusive stories, showing the underlying Comicsgate assumption that such content is inherently lesser. Additionally, it treats identifying racism and sexism as name calling rather than substantive critique—as is common from reactionaries (see chapter 7). It thus packages together opposition to diversity and more standard fannish concerns about quality and maintaining community boundaries.

Tumblr fans are also often rejected specifically because they are feminist and/or queer. For example, one comment in response to a headline that read "fans beg for Captain America to come out" said, "I severely doubt ANY significant portion of the fandom is 'begging' for this. A handful of drooling morons on tumblr writing bad slash fiction is not a headline." The poster, first, categorically distinguishes Tumblr users from "the fandom"; he then goes on to reference fan fiction as an illegitimate practice and classify this desire for queer inclusion as "drooling."

As analyzed by Lucy Bennett in the context of R.E.M. fandom, "drool-ing" often operates in fandom as a dismissive way to discuss "extreme levels of adoration and desire" that are considered inappropriate and unserious ways to engage with the object of fandom.[23] In classifying a desire for queer representation as the stuff of droolers and their alleg-edly excessive desire, the comment enacts a common homophobic logic that queer people are inherently sexually explicit, categorizes a practice disproportionately done by women as illegitimate, and classifies such people as not only "morons" and not fans but also not to be listened to. In such ways, Comicsgate is an instance of what Massanari calls "toxic technocultures," which "demonstrate retrograde ideas of gender, sexual identity, sexuality, and race and push against issues of diversity, multi-culturalism, and progressivism."[24]

The construction of the wrong kind of fan as feminist also deploys common reactionary fandom bogeymen. In addition to the SJW, these bogeymen include media critic Anita Sarkeesian. Sarkeesian had previ-ously been targeted by angry gamers for her 2012 "Tropes vs. Women in Video Games" YouTube series critiquing the prevalence of troubling gendered tropes in games, and she was folded into the grievances of Gamergate when it escalated in August 2014.[25] Sometimes, engagement with Sarkeesian uses her exactly as a figure for a threatening outsider, as when one Comicsgater says, "I don't freaking understand these peo-ple. They don't even fucking read comics. They read comics like Anita Sarkeesian plays video games—solely to criticize them for not having a gray-aromantic hogwarts-kin pseudo fairy dragon trans headmate as the heroic lead." That is, Sarkeesian functions as the symbol of a nonfan illegitimately critiquing a media form. The poster then creates a cari-catured, over-the-top version of a request for queer representation in comics, stringing together both real and made-up identities to cast them all as absurd, again both highlighting queer inclusion as what is objec-tionable and tying it to devalued types of fandom (such as Harry Potter fandom).

Thus, while the ostensible purpose of posts on r/WerthamInAction is to complain about current comics storylines, creators, and commenta-tors and/or suggest what the Comicsgaters think should happen instead, in the process they make assertions about comics fans. They define both themselves as appropriate fans (which I will discuss in the next section) and those who are fans in the wrong way: through liking the wrong things, engaging in the wrong practices, or even being the wrong kind of people. First, Comicsgaters are dismissive of fans who like media and merchandise rather than solely or primarily books. As one fan describes, "At my LCS [local comics store], I asked the owners 'have you seen an uptick in new people with the mainstream popularity of comics?' The owner of my local store (whose a woman, BTW) said 'no, not really. There are a lot of new fans and they come in, but they don't buy comics. They want to buy the t-shirts and the toys and stuff, and we've seen a big spike in sales of that, but comics are bought by the same people who always bought them.'" Here, this fan reports (or invents) a conversation that sharply distinguishes "new people" joining comics fandom as he understands it from those interested in "the t-shirts and the toys." Only buying comic books counts as being a comics fan in this worldview, despite "a big spike in sales" for other products.

Another fan is similarly dismissive of wrong kinds of fandom: "Yeah I agree /r/Marvel is terrible, it's MCU [Marvel Cinematic Universe] fans and they're a triggered, circlejerk, o' cancer and that sub has caused me to regret that the movies ever took off." This commenter resents fans of the MCU for their prevalence in the Marvel subreddit, because they are fans of the wrong thing, in the wrong way. Such fans are "triggered," meaning—in the discourse of online reactionaries—that their "emotional and psychological fragility required trigger/content warnings and safe spaces,"[26] and specifically that they take offense with regard to social justice issues. Such fans are also seen as both insufficiently critical of what this poster sees as low quality (collectively masturbating over it instead) and cancerous—a routine, but not particularly well-thought-through metaphor for a notion that some malign influence is continually expanding and must be eradicated. Fundamentally, interest in other uses of comics characters than actual print books is frowned upon as an illegitimate way of being a fan.

Second, bad fans engage in illegitimate practices, particularly fan fiction. Indeed, fan fiction is such a sign of illegitimate engagement with media (a belief not unique to Comicsgate) that it can serve as a shorthand. One Comicsgater uses "fan fiction" to object to the hiring of creators whose work he sees as illegitimate, saying, "Now you have people who make shitty politicized artwork fan fiction on blog websites getting jobs that their shitty politicized fan fiction writer friends hire them for to produce horrendous comics." That is, work that engages questions of social justice is not only politicized but inherently fan fiction rather than legitimate cultural production, both of which the commenter identifies as shitty. The terms are seemingly synonymous in this discussion. This connection of fan fiction to political commentary is axiomatic for these fans who despise both, as when one commenter notes that "SJW-ist opinions dominate the Fanfiction community and find their way into a lot of Fanfic works." The idea of fan fiction as a shorthand for any content they do not like also shows up in objections to the fact that Thor's name was transferred along with his powers in one comics story arc. "Thor: hammer AND fucking name/ taken from him and given to [a] Mary sue who emasculates him." As Kristina Busse notes, "Mary Sue," a term coined by Paula Smith in a 1973 satirical story, mocks "a type of fan fiction where the original female character would be exceptional in background, looks, and accomplishments, often sidelining the canonical characters or achieving a romantic relationship with the protagonist. As authorial self-insert Mary Sue tends to be wish fulfillment."[27] Thus, to say that Jane Foster as Thor is a Mary Sue is to say that she is unreasonably exceptional. One fan contends that "honestly, if they didn't fck around with taking Thor's name/identity, absolutely cucking the shit out of thor as a character and personality and pushing Jane as the bestest mjolnir wielder evar who never loses to anyone or anything . . . it would have been [a] fine arc . . . but nah, what a surprise that stupid SJW politics [are] ruining comics~."[28] The idea of a woman taking Thor's place would have been tolerable, in this view, if not for how it was done, particularly the name transfer, which is figured as "cucking" him. While denotatively this is nonsensical, as there is no cuckoldry involved, the term "cuck" refers, on the reactionary-right Internet, to any insufficiently manly man, through a (seemingly not quite conscious) transitive property wherein lacking the power that straight white men are expected to have is equated to having one's wife-property used by another man. In such ways, fan fiction is consistently overdetermined as illegitimate through its association with SJW politics such as feminism.

Moreover, fans that Comicsgaters construct as the Other are (presumptively heterosexual) women. In discussing women's alleged rejection of the 2017 casting of Jodie Whittaker as the Doctor in *Doctor*

Who, one fan said, "Given the actors they had for the Doctor up until the old guy, it's obvious why the female fans hate it . . . they want to date the Doctor, not be the Doctor."[29] Women's fandom, for this commentator, is inherently or primarily about eroticizing men.[30] Another fan makes an even broader statement, claiming that "many female fans like watching male heroic characters for fanservice reasons. Women's viewing preferences contribute to the predominance of males in leading roles (by the same token, porn for opposite-sex-attracted males almost always features the female in the leading role)." This comment makes several related moves. Like the previous one, it assumes that women's primary relationship to men characters is to eroticize them, both likening this to porn and classifying it as fan service, thus constructing such eroticism as central to fandom in general.[31] It gets stranger from there, arguing that women's attraction to men is a consideration in centering superhero stories on them—as if women are not typically seen as a surplus audience for superhero media,[32] ignoring the fact that conventional wisdom among media makers says that men will not consume media with women as main characters, but not the other way around.[33] Then, in what may seem a tangential comment but is actually quite telling, the poster identifies the sex object of the porn video as its leading role, quite a feat for a figure who, at least in traditional heterosexual porn, has no agency. This inability to tell a subject from an object, or a powerful role from a powerless one, is tremendously consistent across Comicsgate discourse. Overall, the enemies of Comicsgate are both people invested in progressive politics and those who are the wrong kind of fan, who are not always sharply distinguished.

Us: Fans Who Care about the Right Things, in the Right Way

At the same time as Comicsgaters describe a model of their enemies, they also (inevitably) identify the "us." At times, these fans make a conscious argument about what fans *should* be, but usually they make universalizing statements about what fans do that are exclusionary prescriptions, not descriptions. Comicsgaters argue that fans are knowledgeable and should be listened to, that all fans share certain tastes, and that all fans find certain aspects of comics important (and not others). Ultimately, they construct a vision of fans as those who share their (conservative) tastes, the kind of (disproportionately white and masculine) people comics have long served particularly well.

First, Comicsgaters demonstrate a sense that fans should be listened to and know what is best for comics. On one hand, they root this contention in the fact that they have been fans for a long time. Multiple posters mention the length of their tenure to give weight to their critiques of current comics storylines. The structure of such comments carries an argument by concatenation, sticking the fact of being a longtime fan onto the critique without explicitly identifying the relationship between the two statements, as when one post says, "As a 20 years marvel fan I'm really disappointed with the path they choose. A spy, a avengers, a killer trained by Shield, one of the best martial artists of the mArvel universe engaging in feminist rhetoric? Sorry, not convincing. Any suggestions of alternate publishers WITHOUT this PC overwhelming crap?" For this fan, "feminist rhetoric" and "PC crap" do not belong in comics, and he uses his longtime fandom to give himself authority to make that judgment. Even the less overtly reactionary members of the group make the same move and identify the same target of their opposition, with one saying, "I have a lot of grievances against comics. I have been reading them, and a die-hard comics fan since I was a kid, back in the 60's"; to explain those grievances, this poster points to his own comics, which he elsewhere describes as something that "will set off SJWs, and while that is not my intention, it's due to the simple fact that I enjoy comics that explore social and ethical issues." There is nothing about exploring social and ethical issues that would inherently upset an SJW—and indeed, other posters identify social issues as an unwelcome imposition on comics *by* SJWs—which suggests that this poster has a specifically anti–social justice take on those issues. In such ways, then, the real fan and a position opposed to social justice are tightly intertwined in this discourse. Importantly, this is exactly the same formation as other fan-industry conflict, in which fans point to their loyalty to argue that they know better than industry. Fans are often correct that their attention to continuity is superior to that of media makers, but thinking of this through Comicsgate challenges the tendency in fan studies (including my own) to side with fans over industry in such disputes.

On the other hand, Comicsgaters position themselves as authorities because they have specialized knowledge. One fan situates his critique by contending that "most comic fans can name one or two really great arcs. Killing Joke. Death of Superman, etc.," suggesting that knowing these "really great arcs" is standard for fans; he then goes on to argue that Wonder Woman "doesn't have one. She isn't allowed to have a game changing arc, because she needs to stay perfect and flawless so she can beat up ideological strawmen." That is, because Wonder Woman is powerful and an overtly feminist character, this commenter argues that she is not allowed to be flawed and complex, and therefore is uninteresting, an opinion he justifies by contrast to the stories "most comic fans" agree are "great." Similarly, in a thread about an MTV video, *Can You Name 7 Superheroes of Color?*, one commenter rattles off many comics characters who are people of color: "How about : Spawn, Steel, Falcon, Warmachine, Blade, Storm, M.A.N.T.I.S., Kato, Catwoman (Twice!!), Deathlok, Diggle!!, Bishop, Hiemdall, the Human Torch, and finally, the man, the myth, the legend, Nick Fury!"; he adds, "And EVERY single one of those has appeared in live action TV or movies. You don't even need to be a comics fan to name them. [. . .] (Just someone with half a brain who watches genre movies)." This comment does a couple of things. By listing so many characters who are not widely known to people who are not longtime comics fans (and, indeed, who often are not central characters) and insisting that these characters *are* widely known, the commenter implies that anyone who does not know them must not have even "half a brain." At the same time, by saying that "you don't even need to be a comics fan" to know this, the commenter exposes a fundamental assumption that comics fans have extensive knowledge. As Busse notes, this is a broader tendency in fandom: "Forms of possessions and knowledges thus can be used to establish membership; not getting insider jokes, not owning mandatory paraphernalia, or not knowing specific facts may all indicate outsider status."[34] In such ways, Comicsgaters construct the (good) fan as knowledgeable, and those without such a collection of details ready to hand as insufficient.

Additionally, Comicsgaters construct (good) fans through blanket statements about taste that are arguments disguised as descriptions. In this, they replicate Stuart Hall's insight about politics: "Politicians always think they know what people feel. It's a fallacy, because there is no such thing as 'the people.' It is a discursive device for summoning the people that you want. You're constructing the people, you're not reflecting the people."[35] That is, in purporting to describe what "the fans" feel, these reactionary fans construct "the fan" in a particular, interested way. First, fans are defined as people who all appreciate particular things. As Derek Johnson notes, often in fan communities, "'True fan' status necessitated appreciation of one aesthetic, one prescribed evaluative relationship to the text."[36] Thus, one Comicsgater, as part of defending 1987 Alan Moore comic *Watchmen* as "arguably one of the most important pieces of modern American literature [. . .] within the comic book world," argues that "there are few comics that all comic fans are likely to have read and watchmen is one of them."[37] This argument situates *Watchmen*, a Cold War–era series about an aging team of superheroes who confront their own mortality and the inevitability of human conflict, as central to being a comics fan. It is an argument, disguised as a description, that acts to summon the desired fans. Another poster seeks to dismiss the importance of "Cultural Sensitivity" and "Diversity" as "things you don't have to worry about [as a comics creator] if you aren't popular enough to draw notice. When normal people start to notice and care, but not know or care enough to be actual fans, is when you have problems"; in the process of saying that only "normal," nonfan people care about such things, he argues that "the old time fans just want their escapist entertainment, and they don't want to talk about any of the politics of it." Here, "actual fans," unlike more casual consumers, are not interested in cultural sensitivity or diversity, and they *do* want escapist entertainment. In such ways, Comicsgaters assert their personal or subgroup values as characteristic of all comics fans as a group.

In addition to constructing fans as valuing the same things, Comicsgaters posit that fans have shared dislikes. In a thread discussing a comic described as "Victorian, Female Batman," one fan ventriloquizes other fans as supporting his point: "On first glance, I'll say this is a good thing. I often see fans, myself included, saying leave existing characters alone and make new ones." Fans, that is, are people who do not want longstanding characters altered to be more inclusive. Another commenter asserts that "what the comic fandom and the world at large have a problem with is authoritarian moral busybodies who try to destroy anyone who questions their rigid ideology or offer an opposing point of view"; while this poster does not at any point specify what the allegedly rigid ideology is, this complaint is part of arguing that trolling behavior is justified in order "to avoid the consequences that would be imposed on them by self-appointed moral authorities with no tolerance for any deviation from their chosen set of beliefs." This comment reflects a common feeling on the Right that facing backlash for their opinions is harm done to them (as opposed to someone else exercising free speech in return), suggesting that the objection is to so-called SJW beliefs.[38] These fans thus take their own view of what is unacceptable and attribute it to all fans.

Comicsgaters are also defensive about the perception that they dislike certain things, suggesting that they might care more about those "busybodies" than they let on. In particular, there is a tendency to refute accusations in ways that commit the act they mean to deny. Thus, when one poster declares, "Comic book fans don't have a problem with women, minorities, or anybody else. And they never have," again making universalizing statements about all comics fans, he constructs "women" and "minorities" as something to potentially have a problem with—indeed, as something other than comic book fans (and constructs people of color as "minorities"!). The statement thus throws itself into question. Another Comicsgater makes an even clearer move, saying, "Not a fan in the world has a problem with a black Captain America if the story is done right." The construction of being "done right" is quite common in such discussions, and it operates from a premise that a Black Captain America would not inherently be a worthy story, but rather would have to meet some (unspecified) criteria to be acceptable to comics fans. Through making these sorts of moves, Comicsgaters conjure the subset of fans that they then pass off as all fans or, more tellingly, as real fans.

Moreover, Comicsgaters set out what they believe comics fans should and should not care about by identifying what fans allegedly do and do not care about. One fan identifies the proper interest of fans as in the technologies superheroes use: "My interest in black panther was always in the idea of his cool suit, vibranium based tech, advanced nation . . . You know, comic fan stuff." Here, description as argumentation is particularly clear, with the commenter labeling his own interests as universal "comic fan stuff." In doing so, he dismisses the relevance of the specific characteristics of Black Panther, "an extravagantly wealthy monarch and scientific genius" hailing from "the technological utopia

CONSTRUCTING FANDOM IN COMICSGATE | 39

of Wakanda"—located in Africa—whose introduction in 1966 is often understood as "a calling out and subversion of generic (re: racist, colonialist) jungle tales" and "can also be seen to resonate with black power–identified cultural productions."[39] That is, the commenter has to erase the origin and history of the character to make this claim—the same thing Comicsgaters often condemn when characters are reworked to have a different gender or race.

Finally, and related to the idea that fans only care about certain things, there is a construction of fandom as "celebrating the story the way it is," as the vice president for marketing at Lucasfilm infamously defined it in 2002.[40] One poster argues that DC should reintroduce the original white version of a character to "bring their old fans back instead of appealing only to the new spoiled generation of offended by everything." This is a definition by contrast—"old" or original fans are not "offended by everything," and they are not "spoiled," meaning they don't have an expectation that they get their own way—a remarkable claim from someone proposing that comics be made differently in a subreddit that is more or less a collective tantrum from fans not getting their own way. This kind of argument about change as illegitimate is nevertheless common, with another poster contending that "people who're actually fans of something don't demand classic characters be changed or replaced because they're the wrong race, sex, and/or orientation." Here again, wanting change is perceived to be incompatible with being a fan. The idea that fans should like a story the way that it is demonstrates that not critiquing the text is often constructed as the correct way to be a fan.[41] As Henry Jenkins noted more than thirty years ago, this is often a gendered kind of fannish orientation, as it is fans who are men that tend to look for authorial meaning and respect the text as it is, referenced in this comment's commitment to celebrating the classics.[42]

Ultimately, the good fan has been a fan for a long time, has deep knowledge (even, at times, deeper than that of those who actually make the media), has shared taste values about good and bad fannish texts, and supports the object of fandom against perceived attack. Importantly, this is the description of a good fan in virtually every fandom; these are fundamentally fannish concerns and values. While the specific forms these values take are immersed in reactionary politics, as structures they are exactly what any fans do.

They Are Oppressing Us as Fans: Comicsgate's Victim Identity

Given the Comicsgate view of us versus them, they inevitably also theorize the contact and conflict between the groups, and in particular
identify themselves as being persecuted by SJWs and bad fans. This
builds on notions of fans and geeks as marginalized that have become
part of such identities.[43] However, as Scott notes, it is also the case that
the "'myth of nerd oppression' [. . .] is part and parcel of the growing
sociopolitical influence of the alt-right and men's rights movements."[44]
That is, these fans seeing themselves as marginalized is deeply tied into
the upsurge on the far Right of seeing themselves as victims as men,[45]
white people,[46] and white men.[47] This occurs despite the fact that these
groups continue to be socially powerful.[48] As Hamilton Carroll notes,
"White injury is clearly more perception than reality, but it is a perception that has extraordinary sociocultural heft,"[49] and this is also
true of the perception of injury to men. Indeed, the clearest point of
contact between Comicsgate and other reactionary political groups in
and out of media fandom is the ways they believe they are embattled
despite being both socially dominant as straight white men and the
core demographic for nearly all comics industry products. However, it
is also essential to take seriously that Comicsgaters argue that they are
devalued, disrespected, and even subject to attack *as fans*. Comicsgaters
believe, first, that they are seen as expendable or not heeded by industry. There are a few related variations of this claim, as in the notion of
being forgotten or abandoned from one poster: "I don't feel much like
supporting an industry that turned its back on fans like me." Another
commenter figures the divergence between his type of fan and the contemporary industry more negatively: "Why dust off characters and
explore various themes & issues when you can alienate your fanbase[?]"
This version is less an argument that industry is turning away from
fans than it is an argument that industry is pushing away. As we have
seen repeatedly, such comments equate Comicsgaters with fans writ
large, treating a move away from what Comicsgate proponents want as
devaluing the entire fan base. Importantly, Comicsgaters are not wrong
that longtime fans and loyalty are not respected by media industries,
but this is the case because comics, like every business, is pushed by
the financialization of capital to ever more growth, not catering to the

same fixed group, but this is blamed on women, people of color, and queer people.

Additionally, Comicsgaters believe that they are subject to negative responses for their (allegedly superior) tastes, such as being shamed for not liking things or blamed when products do not succeed. One poster paradoxically both presents comics fandom as something to fear ("very vocal," "very rabid") and suggests that fans are going to be mistreated: "All I know is this . . . that when this fails, the same people that decided to radically change a 50 year cultural icon with a very vocal, loyal, and very rabid fan base are going to blame that very loyal and vocal fan base instead of say, themselves." This is, in a sense, the quintessential Comicsgate comment—we are downtrodden, but don't mess with us. These fans also (and ironically, given their complaints about other people's offendedness) find the way industry relates to them offensive, as when one poster says, "More and more marvel titles seem to be insulting the fans that have reservations about where the company is going." Here, moving in new directions is figured as an insult to fans.

At the extreme and hyperbolic end, fans feel hated or even subjected to attack. One commenter titled a post "I'm honestly a bit butthurt about Marvel's naked hatred of their core customers," going on to say, "They don't admit any culpability in their slumping sales, they just blame the RACIST SEXIST SCUM who are their customer base." Although short, this comment is dense. First, it constructs specifically those fans who do not like new directions as the customer base. Second, it treats "racist" and "sexist" as insults. Third, producing products these particular fans do not want to buy and suggesting that prejudice may play a role in their not wanting to buy them is termed "hatred" of such fans. There are also multiple comments that describe things fans dislike in terms of violence: one commenter alleges that Marvel is "kicking long-time fans in the teeth with nonsense like Grrl-Thor and letting democrat party operatives write books like *Captain America*." One wonders what such a person would do if faced with any actual oppression or violence, but what is most telling is the use of the far-right term "Democrat party," again signaling the fluidity between the communities. Fandom is linked to these far-right groups not only because they share politics but also because of active cross-pollination of shared Internet sites and key figures.[50] Overall, what is important here is how much Comicsgaters understand their oppression as being *as fans*. Even as the content of the objections is about race and gender, it is consistently constructed in terms of being undervalued as loyal fans and consumers. The two cannot be peeled apart.

Conclusion: From the Cuck to the Comicsgater

Comicsgate's discourse on Reddit demonstrates an entire cosmology of how they understand comics, the industry, and fandom. They are against those who are fans in the wrong way and those who critique comics with respect to social justice (and may or may not be fans at all). Comicsgaters argue that fans are knowledgeable and should be listened to, that all fans share certain tastes, and that all fans find certain aspects of comics important, constructing a vision of fans as those who share their tastes—the kind of disproportionately straight, white, and masculine people comics have long served particularly well. The clearest point of contact between Comicsgate and other reactionary political groups in and out of media fandom is the ways they believe they are embattled despite both being socially dominant as straight white men and being the core demographic for nearly all comics industry products. Specifically, Comicsgaters argue that they are devalued, disrespected, and even subject to attack. Seeing themselves as downtrodden when they are actually still quite powerful is about perceiving the diminution of white men's power over other groups both as far greater than it actually is and as a fundamental threat to white men. There is a straight line from this to the cuck, the man who does not have the power he ought. This is a notion that white masculinity *should* be centered and powerful and that when it is not, something has gone wrong. The tension between thinking of themselves as so central and important and powerful that losing their patronage would devastate the industry and thinking that they are weak and downtrodden in the face of SJWs and bad fans getting too much industry attention exemplifies a contradiction that is fundamental to contemporary reactionary politics. At the same time, the fact that these feelings about the self are refracted and routed through attachment to some external text—rather than attached directly to identity—is why we need fan studies to understand them.

2

"#SenatorKaren Back Stabbed Bernie"

Antifandom and Political Engagement on Social Media

I hate Bernie Sanders. I think he is a jerk. He thinks he was entitled to win the Democratic primary. He thinks that other candidates who share his politics should have gotten out of his way so that he could win, and that by not doing so they betrayed him and progressive politics generally and stole votes he was entitled to. He thinks that he should have been able to parachute into the Democratic Party for the presidential election and it should have welcomed him taking over with open arms and should not have been wary of him as an outsider who had not ever contributed to building the party but wanted to use its apparatus for his own presidential ambitions. He thinks that the fact that he was not welcomed as some kind of messiah is a sign that the election was rigged against him. He thinks he was entitled to be president of the United States. He thinks that as president he could unilaterally set policy and create the world he wants to see with no obligation for negotiation or pragmatism in interacting with others.

Or maybe none of that is true about Sanders. But claims that he is owed something and was betrayed are certainly frequently pushed by his fans online, and while my above statement is a bit facetious, this narrative did genuinely sour me on him despite my agreeing with most of his policies.

These pushy online fans, often known as "Bernie Bros" (sometimes pejoratively, sometimes reclaimed as a self-identification), and the way they can shape attitudes about the candidates they support, sparked my initial interest in studying political fans behaving badly. In doing so, I build from the small but growing body of work on political fandom. By "political fandom" I refer to times "when a political movement assumes the character of a fandom,"[1] and particularly such movements around electoral politics and politicians. This is to distinguish my object here from what Ashley Hinck calls "fan-based citizenship," meaning "public engagement that emerges from a commitment to a fan object," which flows from media to politics.[2] Those who study politics often reject mixing it with popular culture as unserious, but Liesbet van Zoonen advocates for the usefulness of the popular to politics, identifying popular and traditional modes as "complementary resources for political communication rather than oppositional."[3]

Thinking about electoral politics through the lens of fandom thus helps us see how both are sites of intense emotional attachment.[4] As in Clara Juarez Miro's work on populism, I see political participation "not only as a set of ideas and discursive frames, but also as a networked social movement that involves emotionally complex ties among its members."[5] Both fandom and politics are also spaces currently characterized by (particularly Internet-based) participatory culture, such as blogging,[6] social media participation,[7] and memes,[8] as well as traditional transformative fandom practices like fanvids and fan fiction.[9] In particular, this chapter expands on work examining fandoms that develop around politicians.[10] Some of this work considers positive fannish attachments to broadly progressive objects like Barack Obama and Bernie Sanders.[11] A second group of studies considers fandom around reactionary politics and politicians.[12] I build from this work to consider ugly fan behavior attached to ostensibly progressive objects, which is so far understudied—mirroring the gap in fan studies at large that this book, especially chapters 3–5, takes on. As the opening narrative suggests, it is, at least in part, a chapter about bad behavior from fans of Vermont senator and 2016 and 2020 US presidential candidate Bernie Sanders.

However, it is also a chapter about the intense negative affect that attaches to a fellow progressive politician, Massachusetts senator and 2020 presidential candidate Elizabeth Warren—indeed, it is primarily a chapter about the practice among critics of Warren on Twitter to use a snake emoji when discussing her, which attracted my attention because it was such a frequent behavior that it called out for an analysis.[13] I make sense of snake emoji users as antifans of Warren. "Antifandom," first coined by Jonathan Gray in 2003, refers to "those who strongly dislike a given text or genre, considering it inane, stupid, morally bankrupt and/or aesthetic drivel."[14] Cornel Sandvoss is one of the few who considers political antifandom, arguing that the Tea Party, a right-wing movement that arose in backlash to the election of Barack Obama in 2008, was rooted in "a form of anti-fandom underpinned by a 'politics of against'"—against Obama, against Democrats, and against "the social and cultural change of the postwar era" with respect to gender, race, sexuality, and other systems of power.[15] Sandvoss is in the minority in taking this approach, but I contend that more such analysis is needed, as I found that antifandom of Warren is deeply intertwined with fandom of Sanders. This case study thus provides a view of what happens when there are clear objects of both love and hate, suggesting the value of fan studies to understanding political rivalry. It is an instance of fan bad behavior with high stakes, but also one that is rooted in a misunderstanding of power relations, which this book shows is often central to ugly fandom.

To examine this fandom/antifandom of politicians, I collected tweets, as Twitter is a key site for contemporary political discussion, with many tweets featuring political content and the ones that do getting more retweets.[16] The platform is also known for being a key venue for networked harassment due to the ability of retweets and trending topics to transport posts beyond their original contexts.[17] This combination made it the perfect place to host this particular manifestation of ugly fandom. I used the Twitter Archiving Google Sheet (TAGS) to collect tweets for the search "Warren AND 🌙" from May 1, 2021, to April 8, 2022.[18] This resulted in 3,944 total tweets from 2,289 unique users (2,191 tweets without retweets). To gain an overview of the data, I plotted the tweets on a timeline, locating two peaks of activity, May 7–10, 2021, and October 31, 2021, that significantly exceeded the average number of tweets per day.[19] I took a random sample of one hundred tweets from the May 7–10 period and collected all tweets from October 31 to investigate what was happening during these high-traffic periods. Next, to learn about the major figures in this discourse, I used network-analysis tool Gephi to look for accounts with high in-degree (others tweeted to) and out-degree (tweeted to others),[20] as well as conducting a word-frequency analysis on the username column of the TAGS output using data mining software Orange to find those who sent many tweets.[21] After identifying these accounts, I collected their profiles as of April 15, 2022, to see what kind of persona the account projected. To look at patterns within the text of tweets themselves, I first calculated word frequency, suppressing "Elizabeth" and "Warren," words I knew would be frequent because of the nature of the search and therefore not meaningful, from the calculation. I then examined meaningful words among these most frequent, such as names of politicians ("Bernie," "Liz," "Biden," "Sanders"), political terms ("progressive," "left," "sexist," "sexism," "campaign," "DNC"), and discussions of the emoji use itself ("snake," "snakes," "emojis," "emoji").[22] I used AntConc, a concordance and text-analysis software, to locate the specific instances of these keywords and the twenty-five words on either side of their appearance to focus in on how the term appeared and identify patterns.[23] I closely read this concordance output and the samples from the high-tweet days to look for patterns in the language used and the underlying assumptions to unravel the discursive formation that animates this practice.

This analysis showed that tweets that used the emoji in relation to Warren engaged in fannish magical and conspiracy thinking about both Sanders and Warren, seeing her as an at times all-powerful enemy and him as the inevitable victor if only she had not intervened. Tweeters also argued about whether using the emoji about Warren was sexist. At a broad level, snake emoji users have incoherent politics that were critical of the wealthy yet enamored of Bitcoin, self-identifying as progressive while also using right-wing terminology such as the pejorative "woke." Some tweeters did raise substantive critiques of Warren around broken campaign promises and her spurious claim to be Indigenous, but they were few and far between. Ultimately, I find that, while politics is often imagined to be a site of rational debate about policy, it is—particularly in the United States with its candidate- rather than party-based system—in fact a deeply affective space of attachment to candidates in ways that bear little relation to their actual policies. Moreover, this attachment may well be negative. That is, posting about how much one dislikes one's opposed candidate, "hate-watching" their social media,[24] or searching their name on a social platform to find people speaking positively about them with the purpose of responding negatively are indicative of a profound cathexis that must be reckoned with if we are to understand contemporary patterns of political engagement online.

Warren Antifandom/Sanders Fandom: Politics through Fannish Habits of Thought

While my search term focused on Warren, these tweets were inextricable from conversations about Sanders, with "Bernie" the second most frequent word in the corpus after removing Warren's name, with 666 instances including retweets and 303 without; "Sanders" was ninth most frequent, with 243/75.[25] Despite the centrality of Sanders to the data, it was uncommon for snake emoji users to self-identify as Sanders fans, though it did happen occasionally. Sometimes this self-identification was direct, as in "when Bernie endorses get Elizabeth 🐍 Warren in 2024, how should we Bernie bros respond?" That is, the poster both anticipates Sanders endorsing Warren and has a low opinion of her that they assume their fellow Bernie Bros share, which they experience as creating a tension between following Sanders and hating Warren. Such comments suggest that, "rather than a by-product of the bond to the fan object, the antipathy towards the object of anti-fandom can be self-motivated and on occasion an even stronger factor in users' emotional investment in the electoral process."[26] Hating Warren is more central to this user than loving Sanders, even as the two are inextricable. At other times, the link of the emoji to Sanders fandom is more indirect, identifying emoji users as Sanders supporters without the tweeters naming themselves as such: "She was called a 🐍 by Bernie supporters for a reason!!" However, calling a politician by his first name, as both of these tweets and many, many others do—"Bernie" is between 2.7 and 4 times more frequent than "Sanders" (with and without retweets)—can signal perceived intimacy or friendliness or other positive affective attachment on the part of the tweeter, suggesting a fannish relationship. Thus, while some might, as one tweet does, claim that "most of the Bernie people who called Senator Warren a 🐍 weren't actually Bernie people at all . . . 🫣🫣🫣," the patterns in the data suggest that they were in fact "Bernie people."[27]

This tendency as to who uses the emoji begins to suggest why, for an emoji explicitly about Warren, the discourse centered so significantly on Sanders. Warren's impact on Sanders in the 2020 Democratic Party primary was a consistent topic in the tweets. She was seen as "hurting his chances" or "kneecapping," "undermining," or even "sabotaging" Sand-ers. As one tweeter put it, "The 🐍 stayed in the race to hurt Bernie's chances of becoming president." It is notable here that, though the two were competing in the primary election, the framing is not about Sand-ers becoming the nominee but rather fast-forwards to him becoming president. This is a recurring theme in which snake emoji users ignored the practical specificities of how politics works, which I will discuss in more depth later. More intensely, Warren was often identified as the main reason Sanders failed to secure the nomination. She was described as "instrumental" to his loss or as having "single-handedly" caused it. Electoral political fandom is thus deeply shaped by an "understanding of [fans'] object of fandom as being in competition with others."[28]

This link of Warren and Sanders was consistent. As one tweeter put it, "Elizabeth Warren is a backstabbing 🐍 who single-handedly destroyed Bernie's campaign." As with many of these tweets, this one both figures Warren as tremendously more powerful than she actually is (which could in some sense be flattering) and understands that power solely in relation to Sanders, decentering her from her own political career. Tweeters also alleged that Warren stayed in the race, or even ran in the first place, specifically to hurt Sanders. One tweet claimed that Warren "'persisted' in the 2020 primaries to siphon votes from Bernie Sand-ers." This framing as "siphoning" implies ill-gotten gains, and indeed the idea of vote or support theft shows up repeatedly. In addition to being a critique of Warren, the implication is that the electoral support right-fully belongs to Sanders. The most pointed version of this argument is that Warren's whole candidacy was in opposition to Sanders: "Warren, a candidate who solely existed as a potential spoiler for bernie." This is the edge of the anti-Warren discourse that touches conspiracy theories.

Fundamentally, the conspiracy-theory version of this narrative con-tends that Warren's campaign was orchestrated by others. This theme varies from generalized comments about the power resting with the "establishment" and "elites" to specifically naming the Democratic Na-tional Committee (DNC) or the Democratic Party or former president Barack Obama as the mastermind behind Warren's campaign choices. This stance gives rise to tweets like "she stayed in the race to attempt to derail his campaign, so the party could tamper w/ the election again." This comment has some interesting valences. The party was holding the election to determine its own nominee for president; though of course it was administered by local elections officials, it is fundamentally the party's election. However, the party is figured as an outside, tampering force. The post also signals clearly that Sanders is not part of "the party," and indeed positions him in opposition to it, despite the fact that he was running in its primary election. At times, the arguments reach the level of the unhinged, concocting elaborate, multilayered conspiracies, such as the claim that "the Warren betrayal was choreographed. But she wasn't the only player in that performance. Bernie let it happen, because it was his purpose. They both intended to absorb revolutionary energy and divide leftist votes, blocking change. Both deserve the 🐍, but only Warren gets it." It is not at all clear how this poster thinks change would happen if neither Warren nor Sanders had been in the race for leftists to vote for (as they do not appear to be suggesting that leftists refuse to participate in the electoral process), but there is an implicit contention that revolution would have been possible without them.

Similar to the conspiracy theories about the election, there are also outlandish claims about Warren herself. Some tweeters claim that she is a "white supremacist" (as opposed to someone who benefits from and has not had a good record of trying to dismantle white supremacy, which is true). Others say that she works with or for the CIA. Some even say that, despite generally being seen as a progressive (though this is contested by many anti-Warren tweeters), she was out to defeat the Left, as when one commenter contended, "I'll never forget or forgive Warren for fighting to defeat Bernie & the left from 2016–2020." Overall, then, a significant thread in the conversation is about how Sanders was put upon by everyone and anyone, despite the fact that the data set is comprised of tweets about Warren by those who dislike her.

Alongside this conspiracy theorizing about sinister actions from Warren and others, snake emoji users demonstrate magical, utopian thinking about Sanders's power. There is a recurring idea that "we would have President Bernie Sanders if it weren't for Warren protecting the status quo." This is a claim that Sanders would automatically have become president had Warren not run, or if she had endorsed him, an outcome that would have required winning both the primary and the general election. However, Sanders had less than half the delegates and popular vote as nominee Joe Biden and large swaths of the American public remain deeply suspicious of progressive politics in general and socialism in particular. Sanders as president was in no way a foregone conclusion. Similarly, another commenter argues, "Had she not stayed in to split the vote (because at that point in the race there was a 0% chance of her winning, face it the 🐍 was not competitive at all) Bernie would have overwhelmingly won." Here again, this description is counterfactual to what happened, but it displaces all of Sanders's woes onto Warren. Overall, then, one key thing the snake-emoji tweets show is how tightly antifandom of Warren is intertwined with fandom of Sanders.

Of Snakes and Sexism

There was also a significant strand of argument about whether using the snake emoji was sexist. This debate arose particularly in response to Representative Ro Khanna (D–CA) speaking out against the emojis as sexist, saying, "Enough with the snakes in the comments! Disagree vehemently. But social media should not be a forum for sexism or gratuitous meanness. We need to call that out when we see it. @warren has been a champion for progressive values."[29] At the broadest level, the word "sexist" appeared 103 times, "sexism" 62, and "sexists" two (collectively, approximately 8 percent of all unique tweets). Several posters pointed out, correctly, that it is not inherently sexist to critique Warren as a politician. As one tweet said, "Believe it or not Ro, women can be horrible people and it does not make anyone a sexist for pointing out Warren is a 🐍." The poster is correct that if you find a politician horrible and say so, it is not necessarily sexist. As another astutely noted, "Saying women leaders being criticised is sexism is in itself sexist. They are not infantile children." That is, treating women politicians as fragile, weak, unable to be critiqued, or needing protection is in fact sexist.

It is important to note that many snake emoji users agree with Khanna's underlying position that sexism is unacceptable. Some therefore respond to critiques about sexism by flatly denying that using the emoji is sexist: "Snake emojis are not sexist." There are also instances of posts critiquing the use of direct sexist language, such as using the term "Karen" simply to silence a woman—rather than as a term for a white woman abusing the power of white womanhood. One tweeter contends that "Elon musk calling Warren a Karen because she wants to raise his taxes is blatant sexism and has nothing to do with her other 🐍 like behavior." Others acknowledge that using the emoji is sexist, and that other methods of critiquing Warren are preferred. As one poster pointed out, "Snakes are historically used to symbolize women as 'conniving' in Judeo-Christian cultures, similar to people using Jewish tropes to vilify Bernie, its just wrong in this context to use 🐍. It undermines our critique!" Thus, it is clear that this commenter is not in favor of Warren, but is aware of the implications of the emoji and encourages fellow critics to make less sexist choices. In these ways, then, emoji users tend to agree that sexism is bad regardless of their stance toward the emoji itself.

However, there is nevertheless direct sexist language about Warren. A handful of tweets call her a bitch. In one such use, the poster argues, "Elizabeth Warren is not a good person. in fact, she's a horrible person who deserves to be shamed for the rest of her miserable and hopefully short life. fake ass snake bitch. 🐍🐍🐍." The tweet does not just call Warren a bitch but argues that she deserves to be treated badly and expresses hope that she will die soon. The one instance of "cunt" is similarly dramatically terrible: "Sexism would be if I called her a malignant cunt. As a compromise I use 🐍🐍🐍 instead." The comment is telling; the snake is perceived to be similar in intent to "cunt" but more polite. There are also many tweets calling Warren dismissively by the diminutive "Liz" (129 occurrences, approximately 6 percent of all unique tweets). As opposed to the familiarity of "Bernie," applying a nickname Warren does not herself use professionally in a hostile tweet is clearly about disrespect, echoing Judith Butler's description of people calling them "Judy" in critiques of their work: "There was a certain exasperation in the delivery [. . .], a certain patronizing quality which (re)constituted me as an unruly child, one who needed to be brought to task."[30] This is certainly the subtext of comments like "just sit down, Liz 🐍." This tweet does not engage with Warren's policies or stances; it merely commands her to stop taking up space.

In addition to these overt instances of sexism, there are subtler ones that pervade even seemingly more substantive critiques of Warren. While it is certainly not sexist to critique a politician, that is, the critique frequently took on sexist contours. For example, arguments about

Warren's candidacy harming Sanders sometimes carried an assumption that what she did in her own campaign was all about this man. The instances of framing her as "hurting his chances," "kneecapping," "undermining," and "sabotaging" discussed in the previous section construct her actions as existing only in relation to him. Dislike of Warren is also structured around blame for Sanders's failure to secure the presidential nomination. Tweeters even assume that her running at all was about him. In particular, there was often an implicit or even explicit contention that she should have stepped aside in favor of Sanders or subordinated her ambitions to his. One tweeter argued that "she should of done the right thing and dropped out before super Tuesday and endorse Bernie Sanders. She acted very 🐍 like." This connection is notable—it is failing to get out of Sanders's way, not any of her specific positions or actions, that is "very snakelike." However, if it is sexist to treat Warren as too weak to critique (and it is), it is also sexist to imply that she did not have agency in choosing to run, in choosing to leave the race, and in choosing when she did so. Thus, repeated comments to the effect that Warren "became a DNC pawn," as opposed to simply making strategic choices the poster did not like, are sexist because they deny her agency.

Moreover, some critiques of Warren fall clearly into sexist tropes, ultimately invoking what Karrin Vasby Anderson calls a "narrative of pathological ambition" that has been applied to candidates like Hillary Clinton but not to men.[31] There are multiple criticisms of Warren for caring about her career, such as "Warren is a careerist who betrayed us to stroke her ego." She is also often equated to another seemingly too ambitious woman, Hillary Clinton, whom the popular imaginary saw as having "pathological ambition—ambition that could destroy not only her own campaign but her party as well."[32] Multiple commenters were critical of the fact that Warren "stayed in the race for weeks after she had no chance of winning." Yet Sanders did the same in 2016 and 2020, saying during the latter campaign that "while Vice President Biden will be the nominee, we must continue working to assemble as many delegates as possible at the Democratic Convention, where we will be able to exert significant influence over the party platform."[33] Critiquing a woman for behavior deemed acceptable when a man does it is clearly sexist. In all of these ways, then, there is a strand of sexism in the use of the snake emoji even as many who used it ostensibly oppose sexism.

Socialists Who Love Billionaires: Incoherent Politics

As with engaging in sexist actions while agreeing that sexism is bad, the politics of snake emoji users are often incoherent more broadly. On one hand, they position themselves as progressive or left. While they do not often directly self-identify as such in tweets, these terms do appear in several of the bios for the prominent accounts in the data set. There are also a few direct tweets proclaiming this identity, as in "All of Us on the REAL LEFT have always known about LYING SNAKE ELIZABETH WARREN 🐍🐍🐍🐍," thus positioning the tweeter as a real leftist as opposed to Warren's alleged fakeness. More frequently, investment in progressiveness as a position is clear from the fact that people responded to Khanna identifying Warren as "a champion for progressive values" with vehement claims to the contrary.[34] The idea that snake emoji users are progressive is thus reinforced by their repeated insistence that Warren is *not*; they call her "pseudo-progressive" or "fauxgressive," and say she is "cosplaying" or "LARPing" as a progressive.[35] In one typical example, a tweeter asks, "Wtf will Warren do except cosplay as a progressive while f*cking over workers? 🐍🐍🐍" Fundamentally, the upshot of all such comments is that Warren is faking her progressiveness for political gain.

Posters do frequently advocate progressive political positions on some topics. On economic issues, for example, prominent tweeters' bios include phrases like "class solidarity." Many such tweeters are critical of Warren for not more aggressively working to limit the power of banks and the rich. As one commenter alleges, "🐍Warren does the bidding of central banks. Her 'grilling' of CEOs is an act." Similar to the notion of Warren as fauxgressive discussed above, the idea is that she is insincere and only outwardly opposes corporate power without taking meaningful action as a senator. Some commenters even accuse her of being an oligarch. While, with a net worth "reported on her annual Senate financial disclosure form [. . .] somewhere between about $5.4 million and $15 million,"[36] Warren is likely in the infamous 1 percent critiqued by Occupy Wall Street and other left movements, she is nowhere near a billionaire and definitely not on the Forbes 400 list of richest Americans.[37] As an indication of the importance of such issues to emoji users, the hashtag "#classwar" recurs frequently, as with the person who responded to Khanna's critique of the emoji as sexist with a non sequitur: "No sexism, just a #classwar by you people against US people." There is thus a clear center of gravity in the corpus that is critical of concentrated wealth.

Emoji users also support a few other progressive issues. "Medicare for All" and the abbreviation "M4A" appear repeatedly, and healthcare is listed in multiple bios of prominent tweeters. "Medicare for All" also comes up in laundry lists of important issues for tweeters. Some of these issues are things Warren is alleged to have undermined, such as "Elizabeth Warren is a backstabbing 🐍 who single-handedly destroyed Bernie's campaign—and with it any hope for Medicare For All, $15 min wage, free college + student debt cancellation, legalized cannabis, green new deal, etc." In other cases, tweeters are simply stating what they think matters: "We're not going to get very far if we're more concerned with 🐍 emojis than we are the people we bomb, or the people we starve, or the people we deny healthcare." On one hand, war and hunger and healthcare are indeed important issues. On the other hand, noting the problems with the snake emoji is collapsed into caring *more* about the emoji than these problems, delegitimating critique of the emoji.

This move to assert some progressive value(s) in order to legitimate criticisms leveled at Warren is a broader pattern. For example, as discussed above, emoji users often signal that they agree that sexism is bad, but dispute that attacks on Warren are a real instance, in a move familiar from attempts to deny structural inequality and microaggressions. One tweeter says, "Throwing around baseless accusations of sexism, and racism for that matter, to deflect from the real issues is such a cynical move—and liberals seem [to] do it as much as the zionists cry antisemitism." This comment does several things. First, it slips from sexism to racism to antisemitism as prejudices people make up and not "real issues"—in a blatantly antisemitic move to drag Jewish people in as a category of manipulators. It also implies that such allegedly "baseless accusations" are "cynical" ploys for distraction rather than considering that these forms of discrimination may have subtle workings the poster has missed. Similarly, one tweeter flatly says, "This isn't sexist. Don't use women's oppression to justify Warren's shitty policies thanks 🖕♀." This user does agree that women face oppression, that is, but does not think that this situation qualifies, suggesting a sense of sexism as a false claim, similarly to the previous commenter.

Another key feature of the political stance of emoji users is a hard-line demand for political purity in which no deviation from approved stances is permitted.[38] The fact that Warren was formerly a Republican is often seen as disqualifying, with comments such as, "You dont go from being a Republican to progressive." The idea that Warren might have genuinely come to understand the world differently over time is not considered. Notably, some snake emoji users are also quite willing to turn on Sanders when his choices stray from their desires. One tweeter writes off multiple politicians, saying, "Everyone in the Squad, plus Bernie, has become like 🐍 Warren." "Squad" here references the nickname for four women of color elected to Congress in 2018, Alexandria Ocasio-Cortez (D–NY), Ilhan Omar (D–MN), Ayanna Pressley (D–MA), and Rashida Tlaib (D–MI), who, along with Sanders, are widely considered very progressive. However, these representatives are now apparently not lining up to the poster's expectations and, as a result, termed snakelike. More pointedly, a commenter accuses, "Bernie became Biden's bag boy after he turned his back on the movement." This identifies Sanders as subservient to Biden or helping him, and connects this to "turning his back on the movement"—abandoning his commitments. Any cooperation with other political positions, that is, is figured as a betrayal of progressiveness.

However, on the other hand, these posters promote right-wing buzzwords, figures, and beliefs. For example, they are often critical of "identity politics" or "idpol," terms that arise repeatedly, as in one tweet claiming that "Elizabeth 🐍 Warren accusing Bernie of sexism and then backing Biden is a perfect example of how liberal identity politics has all but killed the American left." The argument here seems to be that Warren chose to value her identity as a woman, which led her to reject Sanders due to sexism, over her economic beliefs, which would have led her to prefer Sanders over Biden. While the statement is a bit incoherent, as Biden is not particularly known for being a feminist either, the rejection of identity-based political values as detrimental to the Left is clear. This presents a contradiction, as being opposed to sexism is in theory a progressive position, and criticism of politically valuing identity has traditionally been a feature of right-wing politics. Tweeters also refer repeatedly to the idea of a "sexism card," invoking the notion that sexism is cynically deployed to win arguments, as in, "Oh come on @RoKhanna that is absolutely complete grotesque nonsense to use sexism card." Similarly, commenters use "woke" as a pejorative as well as terms like "fee fees," a feminized and pejorative name for "feelings" used to suggest that political opponents are weak and emotional, and "virtue signaling," a claim that someone is insincerely pretending to hold an ideological stance for political gain—all of which are tightly connected to right-wing positions.

Emoji users' approach to public figures is also at odds with their stated politics. Some argued in favor of removing California governor Gavin Newsom from office in the 2021 recall election, despite the fact that this would have guaranteed a Republican would take over the state. One typical comment from this group argued, "The fact that Biden, Harris, and the snake 🐍 WARren are campaigning on behalf of Gavin newsom and his losing recall election should tell you to vote his ass OUT!" However, the most notable figure to receive a positive response from snake emoji users is billionaire Elon Musk. One commenter compares Musk favorably to Warren, citing her false claim to being Indigenous (which I will discuss further in the next section): "Elon Musk is much more authentic than Native American Warren." Most incoherent of all is the poster who has apparently moved from supporting Sanders to supporting Musk: "Aren't you enjoying Elon dunking on Bernie, who broke our trust by sheepdogging his supporters over to Biden?" That is, this commenter was so incensed by notoriously antibillionaire politician Sanders's decision to band together with Biden to defeat Donald Trump that the commentator now prefers billionaire Musk, notorious for committing securities fraud,[39] being an abusive boss,[40] and becoming vicious in response to criticism.[41]

Snake emoji users also directly promote right-wing beliefs. While, as I will discuss in the next section, it is reasonable to criticize Warren's illegitimate claims of Indigenous ancestry, calling her "LieAwatha" and "Fauxcahontas" is not; two racisms do not actually make an antiracism. Most notable is tweeters' consistent support for Bitcoin and other cryptocurrency, which is fundamentally an antiregulation, pro–free market position, not a progressive one. One tweeter contends, "Elizabeth Warren don't like bitcoin? This is why she is a snake. She wags her fingers at the Banksters for votes and theater while pushing Federal Reserve talking points. 🐖" This tweet was posted the day after Warren, in a hearing, critiqued the ways "cryptocurrency has created opportunities to scam investors, assist criminals, and worsen the climate crisis," arguing that "the threats posted [sic] by crypto show that Congress and federal regulators can't continue to hide out" but rather need to take regulatory action to mitigate dangers, including taking steps like creating an official Federal Reserve cryptocurrency product.[42] Warren was not proposing to outlaw cryptocurrency, merely to make it safer through regulation such as is in place for other financial instruments. While this person does not give off any signals of being progressive, another Bitcoin fan does suggest that "Elizabeth Warren sabotaged Bernie's campaign now she's trying to sabotage Bitcoin." The equation of Sanders, a socialist, with the hypercapitalist Bitcoin suggests that the terrain they have in common is populism or antiestablishment beliefs.

This commonality points to the ways in which a politics organized around wanting to disrupt the world is not necessarily progressive. As shown by the roughly 12 percent of Sanders primary voters who later supported Trump in the 2016 election,[43] what holds such disparate ideas together is a common thread of supporting the ingroup against an outgroup who must be punished for their alleged threat. The qualitative description of the Other changes between the two instances, but the Othering remains the same. The combination of Sanders support and attacks on Warren thus shows political supporters "emulating patterns of effusive hero worship (and ridicule of perceived enemies) that are familiar in online fan communities."[44] Fundamentally, what these tweets demonstrate is that "contemporary political leaders are often represented and read in ways not dissimilar to celebrities drawn from the world of show business."[45] Taking seriously how politicians function like celebrities with fan bases helps explain why "fandom proves to be a more useful framework through which to understand political engagement [. . .] through its focus on how objects of interest can serve as a means of engaging in politics rather than through a fully formed political identity or ideology."[46] That is, people can support Sanders as well as Musk because they are attached to Sanders as a figure, not necessarily to progressive politics in general or socialism in particular. This is why the politics of Warren antifans are all over the place, from those alleging she is not progressive enough to those ready to support a particularly nasty billionaire. These affective attachments arise "through the selective reading of highly polysemic objects,"[47] taking what serves the fan's needs and jettisoning the rest.

Waffling Warren: Substantive Critiques

This is not to say that snake emoji users do not on occasion raise substantive critiques of Warren's politics and actions. As one tweet points out, her shifts in stance, pragmatic though they may have been, were seen as breaking the trust of those who supported her: "Bernie Bros: Elizabeth Warren cost Bernie the election 🐍 Mature Leftists: Elizabeth Warren betrayed her base, abandoned her own Plans™, and placed her ego & career before the country she pretended to want to serve." That is, this poster rejects as "immature" the Bernie Bro position that constructs critique of Warren solely in relation to Sanders, but does critique Warren for changing her position (though here again we see the specter of excessive ambition in the critique of putting her "ego and career" first). Substantive critiques of Warren arise in three areas: campaign funding, Medicare for All, and her claims to Indigenous heritage.

Complaints about Warren's campaign funding center on her taking money from, variously, a "PAC," a "super PAC," and corporations. Those critical of such funding use multiple terms, including "PAC money," "dark money," and "corporate cash." This represents some slippage. While there is overlap between these terms, PACs are explicitly political, they have to disclose their donors, and corporations (and unions) cannot donate to them. Corporations and unions *can* donate to super PACs. Dark money comes from groups that do not have to disclose donors. These are important distinctions, but the overall point that Warren took money from the powerful—in an apparent contradiction of her stated values—stands. On one hand, some critiqued taking such money at all. One tweeter declared, "Elizabeth Warren is garbage. She took Super PAC dark money." More specifically, many pointed out that she had broken a campaign promise not to use such funds. One was critical of Warren "deciding to go against her own campaign promises to not take PAC money." Another put a finer point on it, saying, "🐍 Elizabeth Warren swore she would never take dark money only to willingly receive bucketfuls months later when her campaign was floundering." It is entirely fair to critique a politician who breaks her campaign promises, and for progressives to be unhappy with any candidate who is cozying up to the wealthy.

A second area of substantive critique was Medicare for All. Over the course of the 2020 primary, Warren shifted from supporting Medicare for All to advocating a more gradual transition plan: "In the great debate between Sanders' big leap to a single government-run health plan and Biden's incremental steps toward broader coverage, Warren declared herself in favor of both. She's still in favor of Sanders' plan. But she acknowledged that it would take a while to get through Congress."[48] Tweeters describe Warren's shifting stance as a "flip flop," "backtrack," "backpedal," and "walk back"; others say she "abandoned" or "dropped" Medicare for All or "rescinded support." Some claim she "didn't support" it at all. Some of the critique was about her support of the public option, i.e., letting people choose to participate in Medicare without getting rid of the existing private insurance market. One tweeter complained, "Warren cosponsored M4A then flipped and supported public option. Her biggest problem, she's untrustworthy." Shifting her approach to healthcare toward more gradual change is thus seen as a betrayal of those who supported her more aggressive earlier stance. As another poster pointed out, correctly, "It's also not sexist when people criticize Warren for abandoning #M4A during her campaign." Another contended, "I LIKED Warren at first until she backtracked on M4A, and had a plan that takes 10YEARS." Though many of these posts demonstrate the kind of magical thinking discussed earlier that ignores the pragmatic realities of politics, dissatisfaction with Warren's policy positions is legitimate terrain for criticism.

The third source of substantive critique is Warren's false claim to be Indigenous. While she took a DNA test in late 2018 that showed she does likely have Indigenous ancestors, proving that she was not lying in a simple sense, her claims were nevertheless false because Indigenous peoples themselves define their communities far differently—and theirs is the definition that matters. As the spokesperson for the Cherokee Nation said, "Being a Cherokee Nation tribal citizen is rooted in centuries of culture and laws not through DNA tests."[49] Critics linked Warren's ancestry claim to her hire at Harvard, suggesting it was unfairly earned.

One tweeter argued that "she appropriated 'American Indian' identity to steal a diversity hire spot at Harvard."[50] Warren was also called "a Dolezal," referencing a white woman who created a false identity as a Black woman and became a media sensation when this was exposed in 2015.[51]

Some posters framed the issue as Warren misrepresenting herself, as when one contended that she "repeatedly misrepresented her heritage." Others took a firmer stance and said that she lied: "What do you call a white woman who lied and faked being an indigenous woman from the age of 25–70?" What is important in this critique is that, even if her claim was an honest mistake based on family lore (my white family from Oklahoma has much the same story), Warren certainly knew she was not an enrolled citizen of the Cherokee Nation. She certainly knew she did not participate in any Indigenous community. She therefore can reasonably be expected to know that she was benefiting from opportunities that were not really designed for her. This is not actually a victimless crime. As one tweet said, "Warren ain't shit She stole opportunity from Indigenous people." Any opportunities Warren got that she did not have a legitimate claim to were then not available to actual Indigenous people or people of color generally (depending on the particular opportunity). Moreover, assuming that her belief in her own Cherokee heritage was sincere, critics asked, Why did she not use her position of power to help the community she believed she was part of? As one commenter noted, "Lizzz 🐍🐍 Warren 'persisted' in gaining professional/political advantages from claiming to be Cherokee (and did nothing to help the actual Cherokee people)." In such ways, then, while most of the critique of Warren is somewhere between overblown and nonsensical, some critics do raise substantive points.

Conclusion

Antifandom of Senator Elizabeth Warren, as represented by those tweeting about her using the snake emoji, has some consistent features. It is sexist, but it is not only sexist. It is politically incoherent, including those who position themselves as progressive or left, critique concentrated wealth, support Medicare for All, and agree that sexism is bad—as well as those who promote right-wing buzzwords and unbridled capitalism, who are sometimes but not always the same specific people rather than groups who share the use of an emoji. And it is, at every turn, inextricable from fandom of Bernie Sanders. These links to Sanders, as shown in my opening narrative, suggest how "these 'unofficial' groups pose risks along with opportunities when ceding control to individual users who may or may not follow desired social and behavioral norms in their social media activities."[52] That is, nasty fans or antifans have the potential to shape views of candidates. In such ways, "they intervene in the mainstream media narratives that shape the political imaginary."[53] This (anti) fandom has impacts. This sense that politics breaks down into "us" and "the enemy" shows how "fan studies can help understand populist supporters' self-perception of being part of the pure people"[54]—and while Sanders is certainly populist, this is also a broader insight. Researchers have identified that sports often operate on fandom/antifandom antinomies,[55] and US electoral politics often resolve into Team Red versus Team Blue, but there has not been recognition of this sort of us/them within the same political party. Seeing another politician in one's own party as a mortal enemy is of course irrational. But what this case shows us is that *politics* is irrational. Yet fan studies takes both intense connections and intense antipathy seriously. If we do not understand how politics is not just ugly but fannish, we do not understand politics.

3

On the Homonormativity of Slash,
from Curtain Fic to Canonicity

If the overall purpose of this book is to explore when and how fandom is not progressive or inclusive, this chapter takes a somewhat different angle, considering when and how fandom is claimed to be *transgressive*, and whether this claim holds up to scrutiny. As noted earlier in the book, fandom has frequently been hailed as progressive, particularly with respect to gender and sexuality. This conceptualization of gender and sexual progressiveness often leads to assuming gender and sexual transgressiveness, seeing fandom as not just a space where women and queer people are welcome and included but a space that contests contemporary formations of gender and sexuality—a space that is queer. Authors have described fan fiction in particular as subversion,[1] transgression,[2] or rebellion.[3] While some of the bold language has gone out of fashion, the idea that fandom is a queer space or space that is inclusive of queer people continues.[4] This is particularly acute with respect to slash fiction, which romantically pairs men who are not gay in the source texts and which derives its name from the practice of labeling stories with character names separated by the slash punctuation mark.

But what does it mean to say that fans and/or fandom are queer? When people argue that fandom is queer, they tend to mean one of three things: that it is a site of erotics between women as fan fiction writers and readers, that it is a community that includes many nonheterosexual and/or noncisgender people (with "queer" used as an umbrella term akin to "LGBT"), and/or that it is a site of (particularly sexual) norm breaking and transgression. The great emphasis in fan studies has been on the first two of these; I argue that "queer" in the sense of norm breaking and transgression has not been sufficiently interrogated so far in the field. To put emphasis on norm breaking and transgression, I draw a distinction between "nonnormative"—merely outside the norm, a category that is often used to shore up the power of the norm—and "queer"—that which disrupts norms, and particularly that which does so deliberately. This conceptualization draws from queer and disability scholar Robert McRuer's distinction between virtually and critically queer: "By contrast to a virtually queer identity, which would be experienced by anyone who failed to perform heterosexuality without contradiction and incoherence (i.e., everyone), a critically queer perspective could presumably mobilize the inevitable failure to approximate the norm."[5] Taking this approach allows me to consider how and when fandom is queer and how and when it is merely nonnormative. Fandom surely breaks norms, but which norms are disrupted—and which are upheld?

In focusing on norms rather than people, I do not seek to evacuate the question of queer identity entirely. Julie Levin Russo is rightly critical of constructing "not necessarily queer-identified women writing about not necessarily queer-identified men as more queer than people who are queer."[6] That is, when fan studies lauds fiction about men who are typically heterosexual in the source text, written by women who themselves may or may not be queer, it focuses on risk-free fictional play and transgression at the expense of those who hold marginalized identities. Indeed, identity matters in multiple ways, as Rukmini Pande notes: fandom might be thought of as progressive, but it is still shaped by systems of power like race and class. Pande asks an essential question: "What happens when fan repurposing is subversive in one context (interrupting heteronormative canons) but coercive in another (reinforcing racial power structures)?"[7] While thoroughly endorsing the second half of the sentence—and I will return to the reinforcement of racial structures later in the chapter—I want to double back and trouble the first part: What happens when fan activity interrupts some aspects of heteronormativity and leaves other aspects untouched?

Yes, fans are queering texts by reading them against the grain, turning them slantwise and exploring same-sex desire. Yet as Christine Scodari reminds us, "Many of their motivations and outcomes are adaptive rather than opposed to the status quo"[8]—writing and/or reading same-sex love and sex, in and of themselves, do not necessarily disrupt norms, particularly when that love and sex involve cisgender, white, and middle-class gay men pursuing property ownership, marriage, and children.[9] As Russo quips, "If the defining fantasy of slash is that characters of the same gender are in love, I would propose that the defining fantasy of research on slash is that it is a form of grassroots resistance."[10] This chapter seeks to break out of this fantasy and interrogate this conceptualization of resistance, parsing out situations of existing outside norms (nonnormativity) as opposed to disrupting them (queerness).

In this primarily theoretical chapter, I interrogate these questions around norms. Through looking slantwise at claims about fandom as queer and working their weaknesses, I call on fan studies to pay more attention to multiple and intersecting systems of power. My focus here is primarily on thinking through and highlighting limits and contradictions of claims about fandom's progressiveness, rather than an empirical analysis, though I do analyze trends in metadata on fan fiction platform AO3 to support the argument. The chapter thus picks up the thread from chapter 2 that is central to these next three chapters: things that seem progressive (to scholars and to participants) often have serious limitations as to what kinds of inequality they challenge. On some levels, fan fiction is indisputably transgressive of heteronormativity: refusing the positioning of heterosexuality as default and normative, imagining otherwise than hegemonic masculinity, and positioning women as agential rather than passive in sex. At the same time, I argue, slash also very often upholds homonormativity through a drive to construct the men in slash as "normal" and reproducing the white supremacy of hegemonic culture through unwillingness to write stories about or have investments in characters of color. Finally, I contend that the contemporary tendency in femslash communities (those organized around romances between women) to value only overt representation is deeply conservative—in fact, itself a form of homonormativity letting straight norms dictate queer lives and desires. In this way, this chapter looks less at fandom as ugly and more at how and why fandom is less beautiful than is often claimed.

The Queer Erotics of Women's Desire?

There is no doubt that the explicit eroticism in fan fiction is transgressive of the norm that women are supposed to be passive with regard to sex: "As a mainstay of heteronormativity, women are taught to be responsive to men's sexual initiation but not to be agentic about starting sex."[11] Kristina Busse notes that "sexualizing celebrities, for example, is

accepted and expected among men but gets quickly read as inappropriate when done by women." She adds that "these women's fannishness is
inappropriate and clearly threatening in its acknowledgement of female
sexuality and desire, in its clear focus on excessive affect."[12] The ways the
erotic desires of fan fiction writers and readers are central to the practice
have been noted generally in the field.[13] There is a broad understanding that fandom lets (mostly) women "explore and negotiate issues of
sexuality by reading and writing their desires, by acknowledging and
sharing sexual preferences."[14] Importantly, this negotiation of desire is
often sexually explicit. This openness about—and even celebration of—
women's desire is clearly transgressive of gendered norms of sexuality.

Moreover, multiple scholars have pointed out that producing sexually explicit content for other fans can itself be seen as a sexual act. Eden
Lackner, Barbara Lynn Lucas, and Robin Anne Reid contend that "even
the 'straight' women are doing something that can arguably be seen as
pretty 'queer' (producing writing designed to give sexual pleasure to
other women, whether the texts are called erotica, pornography, slash,
or smut, whether the texts are defined as het or queer or bi)."[15] Abigail
De Kosnik similarly argues that "female fans *engage in queer relations* by
writing sexual or romantic fiction specifically for fellow female fans, for
the purpose of intentionally turning other women on."[16] This does in
fact compound the nonnormativity of women desiring by having them
give pleasure to one another. As an example to contextualize this argument in general terms, Marvel is the most popular fandom on fan fiction
site Archive of Our Own (AO3), and Bucky Barnes/Steve Rogers (often
referred to with the portmanteau "Stucky") is the most popular relationship within that, at nearly sixty thousand stories as of this writing.
Nearly fourteen thousand of these are sexually explicit, which is clearly
an erotic practice in which a writer, most likely a cisgender woman,
produces erotic content for readers who are most likely also cisgender
women.[17] This is sexual pleasure, and it happens both for the writer—
transgressing norms of women's passive sexuality—and between writer
and readers—and so is same-sex eroticism in that sense.

However, if women's erotic agency is transgressive, the power of this
transgression is blunted by slash's object choice. That is, for women to
desire men—even extravagantly, pornographically, and semipublicly—
presses *right* up against the edge of the norm. It is valuable, and opens up

important space, for slash to "reverse, or at least complicate, traditional scopophilia of the kind Mulvey describes, casting men as objects of visual desire."[18] It is valuable, and opens up important space, that these women "liked porn, sex, men and television and [. . .] wanted to have their delicious way with them."[19] It is valuable, and opens up important space, to treat love between men as positive and worth pursuing, particularly in the face of society's homophobia. These things are undoubtedly true.

But it is also the case that these formations have some pretty significant limitations. The object of this desire is often two (conventionally attractive, white) cisgender men, complying with norms that value such people over others. Scodari identifies slash as having "roots in heterosexual desire"[20]—for what else to call women desiring men (though the individual participants may hold other identities)? She also notes that slash might be understood as "having a motivation comparable to that associated with male-targeted pornography featuring lesbian encounters—namely, removal of the competition and the desire to frame both attractive characters of the opposite sex as performing for and serving only the individual indulging in the fantasy."[21] That is, to write Steve and Bucky as loving and desiring each other requires removing the women with whom they have relationships in the source text, producing a structure in which the slash writer or reader gets to be the only woman involved in the erotic exchange, making the heterosexual dynamic of the character with the writer or reader the important one. This is women desiring men, and getting rid of other women who stand in the way. In such ways, the transgression of women's desire is partially recuperated by pointing it in a quite normative direction.

Breaking Norms by Contesting Heteronormativity?

Slash fan fiction, because it centers same-sex desire, is in some ways indisputably transgressive of heteronormativity, meaning the cultural structure that identifies heterosexuality as default and normal.[22] First, although, as Sara Gwenllian Jones notes, "Cultural logic dictates that heterosexuality can be assumed while homosexuality must be proved,"[23] slash instead takes homosexuality for granted. In this way, it refuses—implicitly or at times explicitly—the positioning of heterosexuality as normative.[24] Second, slash can rewrite sexuality beyond norms. The idea that especially slash between men is potentially egalitarian—in a way gender norms and sexual scripts make difficult in a heterosexual context—was established early on in the study of this practice.[25] Slash can thus potentially escape the norms of heterosexuality—in a story with no women, gendered assumptions about penetrator/penetrated, active/passive, stoic/emotional, etc., no longer have an immediate mapping onto bodies. Part of the equity in the slash formula came from the fact that in the early days slash tended to center on "male-male buddy series" or close friendships between men in general, such as when "writers began to suggest, however timidly, that Kirk and Spock cared more deeply for each other than for any of the many female secondary characters who brush past them in the original episodes."[26] To return to the Stucky example from the last section, a huge part of what gives that pairing its interest and emotional weight is the bond between the two characters, exemplified by Steve's devastation when Bucky seemingly falls to his death (*Captain America: The First Avenger*, Joe Johnston, 2011). The relatively egalitarian power relationship can be seen from the fact that, within stories tagged "explicit," there is not a stark, essentialist opposition where one partner is always in the active role and the other always receiving; as an example, on AO3 the frequencies of the categories "Bottom Bucky Barnes" (1,990 instances) and "Bottom Steve Rogers" (1,455) are within 30 percent of each other.

Stories are now shaped by a wide variety of dynamics other than egalitarian buddyhood, but they similarly do not have an automatic mapping of bodies onto roles. In BDSM (bondage/discipline, dominance/submission, sadism/masochism) stories, power is (in theory) negotiated rather than assumed, and here too we do not see a clear sense of fixed, essentialized roles, with "Dom Steve Rogers" (523) and "Dom Bucky Barnes" (533) relatively equally frequent on AO3. In Alpha/Beta/Omega or A/B/O, a type of fiction characterized by animal-like heat cycles and a strict biologized hierarchy with alphas at the top and omegas at the bottom, power is an arbitrary assignment that (in theory) is not gendered. While there are clear disparities between the instance of "Alpha Steve Rogers" (667) and "Alpha Bucky Barnes" (426), and "Omega Bucky Barnes" (550) and "Omega Steve Rogers" (328) on AO3, similar to the gap between the incidence of "Sub Bucky Barnes" (521) and "Sub Steve

Rogers" (410), it is nevertheless still true that there is not a fixed power relation where one character is always in the more powerful and controlling role and the other is always weaker and controlled.[27] All of these cases are very different from the normative model of men's allegedly innate dominance over women.

Moreover, slash often contests heteronormativity through imagining otherwise than hegemonic masculinity. This includes writing "(straight) men the way (straight) women want them or want them to behave."[28] In particular, slash writers are known for constructing men as nurturing and "placing emotional responsibility on men for sustaining relationships while men in reality frequently dodge such responsibility."[29] These stories, that is, are often much less in lockstep with toxic masculinity than the norm is (though of course exceptions to every one of these patterns exist in nontrivial numbers). Such contestations of heteronormativity should be taken seriously—and have been by scholars in the field. I certainly do not dispute any of this transgression of the norm, and I am also a strong advocate of the value of pleasure—both its political value and its value in its own right.

However, alongside transgressing in some respects, slash also very often upholds homonormativity. As Lisa Duggan describes, homonormativity is "a politics that does not contest dominant heteronormative assumptions and institutions, but upholds and sustains them, while promising the possibility of a demobilized gay constituency and a privatized, depoliticized gay culture anchored in domesticity and consumption."[30] The critique of homonormativity shows that heteronormativity is not merely heterosexuality but a constellation of norms that replicates white, middle- and upper-class life: marriage, children, property ownership, and normative gender. That is, analysis of homonormativity calls us to take into account intersectionality, a concept introduced by Kimberlé Williams Crenshaw to describe the need for analysis to consider how "women of color are situated within overlapping structures of subordination. Any particular disadvantage or disability is sometimes compounded by yet another advantage emanating from or reflecting the dynamics of a separate system for subordination. An analysis sensitive to structural intersections explores the lives of those at the bottom of multiple hierarchies to determine how the dynamics of each hierarchy exacerbates and compounds the consequences of another."[31] This is to say that the ways in which systems of inequality intersect with each other shape how they play out in people's lives. Cathy Cohen extended this concept to think about the role of sexuality in addition to race and gender, insisting on the importance of understanding "the varying degrees and multiple sites of power distributed within all categories of sexuality, including the normative category of heterosexuality," meaning that heterosexual people of color do not have the same privilege as their white counterparts and typically do not hold power over white queer people.[32] As Roderick A. Ferguson argues, "As they [. . .] access racial and class privileges by conforming to gender and sexual norms, white gay formations in particular become homonormative locations that comply with heteronormative protocols."[33] This emphasizes the power held by gay people with race and class privilege. Jasbir Puar adds that "the homonormative aids the project of heteronormativity through the fractioning away of queer alliances in favor of adherence to the reproduction of class, gender, and racial norms."[34] These are positions from which those who can closely replicate the norm—because, though gay, they are white, middle-class, and cisgender—access power, reinforcing the norm by doing so through supporting its claims to universality, as well as reinforcing the marginalization of those who cannot approximate the norm. Thus, the fact that someone is queer does not shape that person's life chances in a vacuum, but rather that marginalization can be sharpened or muted by race, gender, class, and other systems. With these critiques of homonormativity in mind, some aspects of slash raise concerns because norms of domesticity and consumption, misogyny, racism, and homophobia are all often upheld.

Domesticity and Consumption in Slash

Domesticity has often been noted as a common trait of slash, and is at times quite literal, with in-text focus on homemaking—stories often referred to as "curtain fic" because of their focus on things like interior decorating.[35] Slash stories also often feature a trajectory toward marriage as the teleological endpoint of a successful relationship.[36] Multiple scholars note the prevalence of childbearing and childrearing in slash fiction as the goal toward which successful relationships strive.[37] The male pregnancy trope (mpreg), in which a cisgender man becomes pregnant through magical, technological, or simply unexplained means, is a decidedly transgressive concept in itself, and significantly so given that it features in more than seventy thousand works on AO3 overall. However, it is also the case that "when pregnancy is brought into the equation, it brings concomitant narrative and social conventions, resulting in conventional stories set in a very unconventional universe."[38] This is to say that such a story that focuses on baby names, paint colors, onesies, and the joy of procreation for middle-class, white, home-owning, cisgender gay men reproduces a much longer list of norms than it violates.

These tendencies toward the homonormative are visible at scale. Unpublished research by Jingyi Li scraped fan fiction metadata from the Archive of Our Own and found slash stories to be 2.38 times more likely to use the tag "domestic" than heterosexual ones. For a broader set of domesticity-related tags ("Domestic," "Curtain Fic," "Sharing," "Bathing/Washing," "Marriage," "Children," "Adoption," "Kid Fic," "Pregnancy," "Mpreg"), Li found more than fifteen times the prevalence in slash as in heterosexual stories. As another facet of homonormativity, there is often a drive to construct the men in slash as "normal"—both rejecting stereotypes of gay men as feminine and even, as I will discuss in more depth below, denying they are gay at all.[39] Other scholars also note the heteronormative aspects of slash,[40] though longitudinal research by April S. Callis shows that between the 1980s and the mid-2000s, such elements decreased by between half and two-thirds.[41]

In such ways, slash shores up various norms. As Busse notes, "The romance plot has often been criticized as a patriarchal structure," and "when slash fans take it up, it can be difficult to see where texts criticize patriarchal structures and where they reinscribe them."[42] Ultimately, Catherine Tosenberger identifies the patterns in slash as "containment within Western romantic tropes that are relentlessly heterosexist"— though I would call it "homonormative"—which often "rewrite romantic comedies, Harlequin romances, and Disney movies."[43] Let us imagine an archetypical story: a tale of two conventionally attractive cisgender white men as competing business owners who fall in love despite themselves— perhaps exchanging messages with each other online without realizing who one another is, à la *You've Got Mail* (Nora Ephron, 1998)—is cute and sweet and perfectly lovely to write and read and enjoy, but it is not particularly challenging to norms, and this type of story abounds across fandoms. This example demonstrates how "directly dealing with issues of homosexuality does not necessarily signal a break from heteronormative narratives of romance and partnership."[44] There is nothing inherently wrong with narratives of romance and partnership, of course, but they provide quite a normative—and narrow—construction of what same-sex desire can be. That is not *bad*, but it is not particularly threatening to norms, either. This pattern of persistent homonormativity tracks with the depoliticization that Busse finds to be common in fan fiction; as she notes, "Many fans prefer not to see political concerns foregrounded in fan work: 'issue fic' can be a derogatory description."[45] In such ways, the transgressions of heterosexual norms that are so lauded by some strands of fan studies may be virtually queer, as in homosexual, but not critically queer, as in transgressive.

The Misogyny of Slash

In addition, slash fans often uphold norms of misogyny. At a basic level, as Henry Jenkins points out, the focus on men's bodies in slash frequently also involves "an often thinly veiled distaste for female sexuality and feminine bodies."[46] As we can see from the ways heterosexual desire gets recentered that I discussed earlier, slash is very much bound up in finding some bodies attractive and others decidedly not. Misogyny also plays out at the level of narrative. As Busse describes, slash shippers often resent women characters when they are perceived as a threat to the men of the slash couple being together, "an uncomfortable fannish reminder that a group of women who'd consider themselves feminist could nevertheless be vitriolically misogynist."[47] Scodari points out that "if canonical homosociality between men is a catalyst for traditional slash, it is not threatened merely by male/female romance but by a female character's centrality in the narrative."[48] Thus, there is often a sense that substantive women (as opposed to the girlfriend of the week who will disappear on her own) have to be removed in fan fiction because they represent obstacles to slashing.[49] While this sometimes-violent disappearing is often a continuation of the way women are treated in source texts,[50] it does not for that reason cease to be concerning.

While there are times when women are not removed in slash, this is not always a significant improvement. In such cases, women in slash stories are often plot devices, such as in stories where women are the matchmaker between the two men, or one or both of the men are in a relationship with a woman at the beginning of the story (establishing bi- or pansexuality), but realizes that the other man is The One for him. Treating women as plot devices is not particularly feminist.[51] Writing slash rather than stories that involve women (whether heterosexual or lesbian ones) is often explained away as resulting from the fact that most media texts do not center women, and when they do appear, they are often not complex, interesting characters.[52] This is, on one level, a fair point—fan fiction may reproduce the misogyny of mainstream media, but it certainly did not invent it. However, Scodari points out that "if fanfic authors can concoct all manner of the fantastic, they can also create transcendent, patriarchy-busting female heroes."[53] That these authors *can* imagine gayness out of faint textual traces but *cannot* imagine complex women out of such traces is telling. In all of these ways, then, slash fiction often reproduces, rather than challenges, the devaluation of women prevalent in hegemonic culture, calling attention to the need to consider more norms than heterosexuality.

The Racism of Slash

Slash fandom also frequently reproduces the white supremacy of hegemonic culture, in line with homonormativity. On one hand, this takes the form of unwillingness to write stories about or have investments in characters of color. The arguments commonly made in these communities were rehearsed in a lengthy meta (fannish essay) that caused an uproar in online fandom during May 2016.[54] The essay is a defense of slash fiction against arguments that it is sexist and, especially, racist in its arguably disproportionate focus on white men.[55] In response, the author of this quite representative essay seeks to explain away the absence of men of color in slash rather than confront the fact that race inevitably plays a role in fans choosing not to advocate such pairings. One of the piece's arguments is that men of color are simply absent in the source texts from which fan fiction writers work. Here again, we see that people who *can* infinitely expand traces of desire among men apparently *cannot* conceive of expanding an underdeveloped character of color.

However, as Pande points out, "Media fandom remains an inhospitable space for non-white characters, who inevitably get sidelined and erased even in the rare occasions that they have significant roles in canonical texts."[56] That is, more significant characters still do not tend to feature in slash. Indeed, there is a tendency to ignore men of color as valid love interests even if writers have to invent a white character more or less out of whole cloth to do so. In *Star Wars* fandom, for example, there are two to three times as many stories on AO3 with white characters Kylo Ren and Armitage Hux (Armitage Hux/Kylo Ren is tagged 11,301 times and Armitage Hux/Ben Solo | Kylo Ren 8,195 times; depending on the frequency with which both tags are used at the same time, this could be as many as 19,496 stories) as there are of the most popular pairing that includes characters of color, Poe Dameron/Finn (6,628), despite the white characters' "lack of screentime and lines, and the fact that they were actual space Nazis," while the men of color were significant characters with much more screen time.[57] In a particularly interesting instance of this pattern, white men can even take the place of men of color, as when Penley argues that slash stories rework the traditional literary narrative of interracial bonding (e.g., Huck and Jim, Ishmael and Queequeg) as erotic, which has "eliminated its racism by celebrating miscegenation."[58] Characteristically of slash's relationship to race, the miscegenation celebrated in the Kirk/Spock case lauded by Penley was a phenotypically white mixed-species alien and/or his romance with another white man.

In addition to arguments about the absence of men of color in source texts, there are common arguments that including them in stories is difficult. The 2016 meta argues that people write fan fiction out of pleasure, and men of color (who apparently do not bring pleasure) would have to be artificially added to stories out of antiracist duty. Additionally, the author argues, men of color cannot be written in raunchy or violent ways or in any other kind of negative situation because of the risk of reproducing racist stereotypes, and this takes the fun out of fan fiction. (This raises questions of why not being able to brutalize somebody is a deal breaker.) In all of these ways, the arguments for continuing to focus on white men are quite flimsy. However, as Poe Johnson argues, "When we call for greater inclusion within fan spaces, we must be careful what we are asking for, and from whom we are asking it."[59] That is, given these—at best dismissive and at worst actively negative—attitudes toward characters of color, we should be careful what we wish for, as their inclusion could do as much harm as good (or more). A story where the Black character is a drug-dealing, jive-talking sex machine is not progress.

The other aspect of the way fandom upholds white supremacy is its tendency to refuse to discuss race or racism, thereby leaving existing power dynamics intact. Discussing gender and/or sexuality is understood as vital fannish work, but discussing race is seen as "drama" or not appropriate for the space.[60] Fan fiction communities also participate in broader patterns that act to shore up whiteness, such as tone policing, which is well known in many spaces for the tendency to demand that people of color never be angry about their own marginalization. This is compounded in fandom due to what I have elsewhere called the "coercive positivity" endemic to contemporary fan culture.[61] These factors produce a doubly intense experience of tone policing for fans of color discussing racism.[62] For such reasons, "Fans who would like better representation, or pushback against the dominant view that media fandom spaces are subversive and liberatory by default because of their willingness to explore queer sexualities[,] also inevitably face a backlash."[63] This is the case because there is a tendency to center white feelings of hurt about being called to account or about the perceived injustice of being falsely accused.[64] Indeed, fans of color have asserted that such hurt white feelings are frequently held up as the reasons white fans are not willing to write about characters of color.[65] In all of these ways, then, slash fandom shores up the normativity of whiteness rather than contesting it, showing the necessity of an intersectional analysis that considers race and not just sexuality.

The Homophobia of Slash

Slash fandom is also, despite its centering of same-sex eroticism, often homophobic. As mentioned above, there is a frequent idea that the men in slash are not gay, meaning that they desire only this particular man and not men in general. While certainly not universal, this is frequent enough to have a name as a trope: "we're not gay, we just love each other," or WNGWJLEO.[66] Much like including women in the story to demonstrate the character's attraction to women, this trope insists that they are still available to the slasher's gaze as an object. This construction recenters heterosexuality in a narrative ostensibly about same-sex desire. On one level, this decentering displaces gay men from stories about themselves. However, at a more fundamental level, it is shot through with, and inextricable from, the broader homophobic insistence that "gay" is a bad thing to be. How else to explain the almost-panicked insistence on This Man and No Other often seen in slash?

However, much like Johnson's warning about the risks of simply adding characters of color, just giving the characters an identity as gay men does not necessarily resolve any or all concerns. As Busse argues, "Many gay, lesbian, and bisexual writers indicate that they perceive homophobia within slash writing and its surrounding discourses, most importantly in the fetishization of gay sex and the lack of a clear sociocultural and historicopolitical context."[67] This question of fetishization or exploitation ultimately rests on treating eroticism between men as entirely separable from the lived experience of queer men—a pleasurable plaything for the slasher's erotic enjoyment unmoored from social and political realities. This idea of extracting same-sex desire without grappling with the lived experiences involved explains why James Joshua Coleman calls slash "cultural appropriation."[68] There is a power dynamic when straight women use gay men as their playthings. As I have argued elsewhere, who is doing what to whom is important in understanding how power dynamics affect our sense of right and wrong in creative work.[69] The identity of the author matters to understanding what is happening in these spaces, and is another place where attention to multiple systems of power is vital—a heterosexual woman slash writer might be privileged by sexuality and marginalized by gender, and which one of those attributes is most salient is not always clear.

Moreover, there is frequently outright homophobia from slashers toward femslashers, fans who advocate for and write fiction about same-sex desire between women. While this has not yet been empirically studied (though research by Victoria M. Gonzalez considers it in passing),[70] anecdotally, femslashers believe it to be common. Femslashers are told they are mentally ill, invoking the homophobic trope of queer

desire as a sickness. They are told their interest in same-sex love is por-
nographic, invoking the homophobic trope of queerness as inherently
sexually explicit. They are seen as threatening for desiring their preferred couple, invoking the homophobic trope of the predatory lesbian.
And—again anecdotally—a nontrivial percent of the time the response
to this homophobia being pointed out is to argue that participating in
slash shipping of men means the person attacking femslashers cannot
be homophobic. This compounds the troubling instrumentalization of
same-sex desire between men by leveraging it to shield people from consequences for homophobia enacted against actual queer people.

On Femslash and the Homonormativity of Canonicity

As this mention of femslashers begins to suggest, it is important to consider how they occupy a distinctive position. First, it is necessary to
recognize that "femslashers and those passionate about fictional female-
female couples" have often "felt that their identities and practices are
marginalized."[71] According to statistics about AO3, slash is the majority
of fic, 56 percent in 2022; femslash is just 6 percent.[72] Femslash is also
fundamentally different from slash because of the closer correspondence of writer and/or audience identity with the content of the stories,
as "an overwhelming majority of active participants in femslash fandom
identify as lesbian, bisexual, and/or queer women."[73] As Sneha Kumar
argues, in femslash, "authors are given the opportunity to explore the
potentialities not only of a fictional universe but also of their own bodies and identities."[74] Writing about your own group is not inherently
superior—though it does avoid the "gay boys as playthings" model discussed above as well as "straight savior" models of "I'm just so devoted
to those poor gay people's representation and/or gawking at their pain
as long as it requires nothing from me." This correspondence of author
and content also relates to Busse's argument that in the contemporary
moment "authors have returned to the forefront of interpreting texts
not via interpretive privilege or singular access to the meaning of their
writing but via their identity and how that identity affects reading and
writing practices."[75] Holding the identity they write about helps legitimize these works in the contemporary fannish value system.

Undoubtedly, femslash's insistence on the right for queer women to take up space in public, and in the media, is transgressive, "a deeply political project of resistance and *in*-sistence that people have the right to make and circulate meanings outside the circuit of ideologically or institutionally guaranteed" ones.[76] Specifically, as Russo argues, "It is the fusion that femslash presumes between fans and characters in terms of sexual and gender identities—its primary difference from the ways male slash has been defined—that affords it this powerful platform for literal campaigns of resistance to heteronormative structures."[77] It is, however, important to note that, much like slash, femslash fandom both contests some aspects of heteronormativity and upholds other systems of power. In particular, it reproduces whiteness by centering white characters and white fans' feelings at the expense of characters and fans of color.[78]

Femslash's resistance to norms is also bound up in the desire of femslashers to see queer women like themselves represented in media. As Russo notes, "If we're interested in resistance and what it means to fans, the politics of visibility is a popular phenomenon that we should not discount."[79] This desire for visibility has led to accusations that media makers are queerbaiting, which occurs when "those officially associated with a media text court viewers interested in LGBT narratives—or become aware of such viewers—and encourage their interest in the media text without the text ever definitively confirming the nonheterosexuality of the relevant characters."[80] Queerbaiting (or the perception thereof) has become a source of producer/fan conflict.[81] Eve Ng's model of queerbaiting emphasizes the importance of context; the expectations in a particular place and time and industry that actual representation is feasible profoundly shape fan expectations as to whether suggesting a queer love story without following through on it is perceived as manipulative. As Ng's comparison of *Xena: Warrior Princess* (syndication, 1995–2001) to contemporary TV demonstrates, expectations have shifted over time. This sense that queer people have a right to exist in mainstream media is undoubtedly transgressive—and contested.

However, as Russo points out, "Queer theory has a stake in troubling these assumptions [about visibility] because of the hierarchies and ideologies they leave undisturbed—the unified subject, the monogamous couple, binary gender, whiteness, capitalist aspirations, to name a few."[82]

That is, treating the presence of a married, cisgender, white, same-sex couple on a television show—such as Sara Lance and Ava Sharpe from *Legends of Tomorrow* (The CW, 2016–2022)—as a victory for all queer women everywhere shores up a lot of norms. In a similar way, I would like to argue that the contemporary drive for visibility in media, and the concomitant tendency in femslash communities to value only relationships officially present in the text (generally called "canon"), is deeply conservative—in fact, is itself a form of homonormativity in the sense that it allows straight norms to dictate queer lives and desires. Daniel Allington, in his discussion of subtext in the *Lord of the Rings* films, argues that, "given the ideological emphasis our society places on authorship, perhaps the strongest legitimation slash consumption could receive would be an endorsement from the creators of the texts being slashed."[83] This presumes that such readings are not in themselves legitimate and need permission. I do not want to downplay that the demand to be unambiguously present is significant—it does important work to be visible—but it comes at a cost. Gonzalez describes the ways one such fandom's centering of canonicity "insinuates that abiding by canon is the primary way in which normal or sane shippers function within fandom." She adds that the further implication is that "canon and TPTB [The Powers That Be] are infallible, inflexible, and not something that fans control."[84] This is a contention that it is not sane to have readings not explicitly in the text and fans must subordinate their interpretations to textual relationships, and it is one that in this context is specifically weaponized against same-sex love.

Ultimately, beliefs about the superiority of visibility, representation, and canonicity rest on an "underlying assumption that presumes authors (or multibillion-dollar media corporations) have a say in how their stories are read and interpreted."[85] This gives away the power to determine queer presence to heteronormative structures of TV production. The following of television's lead is at times quite literal. There is a GIF that goes around Tumblr showing a flock of flamingos changing direction in sync, captioned as showing how femslashers or lesbians (the slippage between which is routine but problematic) migrate from show to show following canon lesbians. And it is funny, except that it is true. More troublingly, this trend goes hand in hand with browbeating other fans into supporting any show that includes a lesbian couple.

Such browbeating is particularly concerning in light of the tendency to support any show that includes a lesbian couple regardless of what else is happening in the show, such as racism. As Pande notes, fans of *The 100* (The CW, 2014–2020) reacted strongly when a lesbian character was killed off, but as "some non-white fans of the show pointed out, the same fanbase had been ignoring the hugely racialized violence that was a staple of its narrative from its inception"; she argues that "it is therefore necessary to pay attention to patterns of fan prioritization so as to identify which characters are consistently valued over others within fandom spaces, even when issues of social justice are highlighted."[86] Here, too, femslash fandom reproduces white supremacy *at the very moment that it is contesting homophobia*, showing the necessity of intersectional analysis. In much the same way, the repeated and uncritical return to a Nazi-esque parallel universe in the Arrowverse (The CW, 2012–2022) and *Arrow* (The CW, 2012–2020) star Stephen Amell's intermittent racist tweeting were disregarded because the shows had canonically queer characters like Sara Lance and Alex Danvers (*Supergirl*, The CW, 2015–2021). In such ways, femslash has a history of using the fact of white queer representation as a shield against criticism of the shows with such canonical queer women.

These examples show that canon exaltation runs a very real risk of straightening out the (real, albeit limited) ways that fandom is queer. As one fan put it, "Canon is canon. However crappy it may be, it counts for something huge. It's representation, recognition and validation [. . .], but fan works are the raw scraps we've been tossed . . . while canon is being cooked and served a fresh, homemade, full course meal."[87] Such marginalization of the power of fans to make texts queer is common from outsiders, but the diminution of fan works by otherwise transformative fans has developed since the 2010s and is cause for concern for those who value fandom's transformative and transgressive traditions. Despite resistance from scholars to the idea that the text is straight, the tendency—particularly prominent among those who read and write stories about love between women—to chase canon demonstrates a sense that texts *are* exactly straight unless there are overtly LGBTQ+-identified characters. As Ng points out, "The fact that in such critiques a text is deemed queer enough only when two characters are in a canonically romantic relationship tends to obscure other nonnormative modes of being and relating."[88] These moves to exalt canon and never question showrunners or writers and abstain from criticism may be related to a sense that if fans behave well enough, media makers might treat them well this time, a response to what at this point is a repeated cycle over more than two decades of fans getting their hopes up about a character or pairing, only to be disappointed—often as the result of direct manipulation. But they are nevertheless ways of capitulating to norms that are fundamentally of a kind with the broader formation of homonormativity.

Conclusion

In the end, slash fan fiction is in some ways indisputably transgressive of heteronormativity. The explicit eroticism in fandom is transgressive of the norm that women are supposed to be passive rather than agential in sex, and producing sexually explicit content for other fans can itself be seen as a sexual act between women. Slash refuses—implicitly or at times explicitly—the positioning of heterosexuality as default and normative. It can rewrite sexuality beyond norms. It often contests heteronormativity through imagining otherwise than hegemonic masculinity. It is true that femslash's insistence on the right for queer women to take up space in public, and in the media, is transgressive.

At the same time, slash also very often upholds homonormativity. This occurs through a focus on domesticity and a drive to construct the men in slash as "normal." Moreover, for women to desire men—even extravagantly, pornographically, and semipublicly—presses *right* up against the edge of the norm. Slash fans also often uphold norms of misogyny. Further, slash fandom frequently reproduces the white supremacy of hegemonic culture through unwillingness to write stories about or have investments in characters of color and its tendency to refuse to discuss race or racism, thereby leaving existing power dynamics intact. Slash fandom is also, despite its centering of same-sex eroticism, often homophobic. And the contemporary tendency in femslash communities to value only canonical ships and textual inclusion is deeply conservative—in fact, itself a form of homonormativity letting straight norms dictate queer lives and desires.

This is not to say that we cannot just have fan fiction for pleasure. We can. This is a valuable tradition that should not be abandoned. My point here is not (particularly) a critique of slash writers and readers themselves. But it *is* a critique of how we make sense of them. Claims about political progressiveness and transgressiveness need to be much more specific, as slash often upholds norms. Fundamentally, if we are going to talk about transgression, we have to grapple with the ways in which any given subversive move with respect to one system of power may well be—and often is—a normative one on another axis. Slash may be nonnormative, but it often does not succeed at being queer. By returning to queer theory as well as Black feminism's concept of intersectionality, we can think much more clearly about the multiple systems of power at play. Slash fandom has a whole lot of ongoing and new attachments to normativity that we have to take seriously in order to understand it as a social phenomenon.

4

Hell Hath No Fury like a Fan Queerbaited

The Death of Lexa and Fan Vitriol

It has become an all-too-familiar occurrence. The makers of a media text choose to change the content in some way and fans descend in fury. There are hashtag campaigns. There are attempts to defund the media object such as by getting advertisers to withdraw support. There are calls for those responsible for the decision to be fired. Those industry workers are vilified, and at times fans cook up fantasies about violent retribution or even directly make threats. This is #Comicsgate;[1] #ReleaseTheSnyderCut, a campaign for the release of director Zack Snyder's intended version of the film *Justice League*;[2] and #GetWokeGoBroke, a campaign against inclusion in media.[3] But it is also #LexaDeservedBetter, the response to the death of lesbian character Lexa on *The 100* (The CW, 2014–2020). This is what this chapter investigates, considering what it means that a campaign against exclusion, run by marginalized people, has substantially the same contours as other vitriolic campaigns.

On March 3, 2016, *The 100* aired the episode "Thirteen," which engaged in a common television practice: killing off a character because the actor who played her (Alycia Debnam-Carey) had taken other work, which was both dramatic and closed out the storyline. This narrative turn followed "the *queerbaiting* the executive producer Jason Rothenberg shamelessly performed for the promotion of the show's third season. Rothenberg interacted with his lesbian fan base," including "stating multiple times on Twitter that Lexa is a defining representation and very important to people creating the show."[4] That is, these lesbian fans were specifically sought out and engaged in a way many came to describe as queerbaiting, in which, as Mélanie Bourdaa describes, the show "offered the suggestion that queer characters will be prominent in the narrative only to negate that promise." As Kelsey Cameron recounts, the production staff had a history of engaging with fans on social media, and particularly cultivated interest in Lexa, "promoting articles that praised the show's queer representation and encouraging speculation about her future storylines."[5] Through this practice of routine response to fans in fan spaces, and especially by encouraging attachment to Lexa specifically as a queer character, the show's creative team cultivated the commitment that later turned sour.

There was, particularly, engagement with fans about the romantic relationship between characters Clarke and Lexa. "When Clarke and Lexa kissed for the first time, Rothenberg and [writer] Shumway tweeted extensively about the scene as it was airing, discussing the characters' connection with each other and general understandings of sexuality in *The 100*'s universe."[6] Moreover, the term "Clexa," the portmanteau name of Clarke and Lexa used as the name of their relationship, "was also used by the show's official Twitter account, @CWThe100, and the official Tumblr of the show's writer's room posted and reposted content focused on the couple."[7] Additionally, Rothenberg tweeted in support of the relationship ("ship" for short in fandom terminology), saying, "You guys know I don't ship. But I gotta admit, #Clexa is seaworthy. #justsaying #The100 @miselizajane @debnamcarey."[8] However, these industry workers did not just promote the character and the ship but actively sought to suppress discussion of the potential for Lexa's death: "When a rumor of her demise leaked, Rothenberg tweeted pictures from set in which she appeared to be alive and well and invited fans to come watch filming in downtown Vancouver."[9] This courting of fans included infiltrating fan spaces and lying to them about upcoming plot points to keep them watching.[10] Overall, it was quite an involved process of cultivation of fans.

In this chapter, I look at what came after the courting and baiting: Lexa's death produced an intense backlash, substantially because she was a lesbian and killed off in a way widely discussed as traumatic and socially harmful, following what Rothenberg later admitted was "aggressive promotion of the episode, and of this relationship."[11] Rothenberg "lost thousands of Twitter followers [. . .], and the March 10 episode got the series' worst-ever ratings [. . .], demonstrating that [fans] can use their collective might to very different uses than a network might like."[12] *The 100* undoubtedly mistreated these fans. As Myles McNutt describes, they broke the contract of social TV: "The reaction of the show's

LGBT fan base—feeling manipulated and betrayed—points to the stakes of violating the social contract in situations where social media engagement moves beyond inane on-screen hashtags and cast live tweets, and intersects with the identity politics of the series, its viewers, or its producers."[13] That is, as engagement moved past just superficial Twitter hype practices to be substantive and connected to broader social systems, "this came with a certain responsibility on the part of the writers and the network,"[14] a responsibility they ultimately failed to fulfill. This queerbaiting and/or broken social TV contract produced an explosive response—hundreds of thousands of tweets, activist campaigns, and organizations. And there were also threats. This case is interesting because these fans were so clearly wronged, so clearly marginalized, and in that sense sympathetic—at the same time that a significant number of them were also clearly awful in the way they responded. Like Comicsgate, this case tests the sympathies we may have for fans in conflict with media industries, particularly a conflict that many (including me) have lauded as an impressive moment of fan activism for its successes in leveraging social media, raising money for charity, and securing an apology.

To examine how the backlash played out, I use as my primary objects of analysis two data sets of tweets, one for #LexaDeservedBetter (containing 10,000 tweets from 2,941 unique users posted March 8–April 2, 2016) and one for #LGBTFansDeserveBetter (containing 1,650 tweets from 745 unique users posted March 9–April 2, 2016), collected using the Twitter Data Scraping Jupyter Notebook created for the NEH Understanding Digital Culture Summer Institute.[15] In my initial investigation of this incident in October 2016, I found there to be significant prevalence of what Mar Guerrero-Pico, María-José Establés, and Rafael Ventura conceptualize as "toxic fan practices," meaning "fannish discourses and actions that constitute harassment and ad hominem attacks on media producers or that promote racism, sexism, homophobia, and other reactionary currents by exploiting fan discontent,"[16] and that this toxicity particularly focused on Rothenberg.[17] Therefore, I searched within both bodies of tweets for "Rothenberg" and "Jason" as well as terms "JRot" and "JRat" that I had observed being used. To look for other terms I might have missed, I examined a random sample of one hundred tweets from each hashtag; this surfaced the in-universe phrase

"Jus drein jus daun" and its English equivalent, "blood must have blood." All tweets using any of the terms were collated and analyzed as a single corpus. Twitter was key here because it is both a significant platform for television production staff engagement with fans and a key site for various forms of collective action and activism.[18] This data was supplemented with Tumblr posts collected in October 2016 in the tags "JRot" and "JRotInHell." Tumblr's greater length of posts and poorer content moderation mean that these posts describe more graphic violence.

For analysis, I removed duplicates where there were identical tweets that were posted purely to leverage the Trending Topics affordance on Twitter; for example, there were approximately one hundred tweets that were slight variations on "ALYCIA IS OUR COMMANDER #AlyciaIsOurCommander #WatchAlyciaOnFTWD #JasonBringLexaBack #LexaDeservedBetter," with a number appended at the end to get around Twitter's prohibition on tweeting an identical tweet; one of these tagged Rothenberg directly. I also excluded tweets from users that seem to have been taking advantage of the trend to try to raise their own visibility, such as multiple tweets where the text was "Link in Bio" and a series of hashtags (and, visiting those user profiles now, one finds that the links are gone).

In this chapter, I will first examine how fans address Rothenberg through media industry value systems. Tweets discuss canceling the show, refusing to watch, and unfollowing Rothenberg. Fans also call on the CW network to intervene in the situation. Further, they frequently tag Rothenberg and address him directly as at fault for the negative outcome. Next, I consider how fans frame him as the villain and even include threats. Third, I examine how this behavior is consistent with the fan base's history of emphasizing only its own marginalization as queer without thinking intersectionally. Ultimately, I argue that it is important to understand this backlash in relation to other moments of intense social media anger from fans directed at a single figure or particular group. In this, I somewhat follow Matt Hills, who contends that "in each of these otherwise diverse cases—Gamergate and toxic geek masculinity, Puppiegate and the Hugos, and #BuryYourGays—a form of consciously and spectacularly abusive, disrespectful behaviour is directed as [sic] specific Others such as feminist/female gamers, feminist/left-leaning SF fans, and TV producers."[19]

However, I do think it is important not to completely collapse these different moments, as Hills does. Rather, my point is that these cases can illuminate one another. As Guerrero-Pico et al. argue, the Lexa incident shows that "fan-tagonism may lead to anti-fandom and thus anti-fandom to toxicity."[20] By "fan-tagonism," they reference Derek Johnson's term for the "ongoing, competitive struggles between both internal factions and external institutions to discursively codify the fan-text-producer relationship according to their respective interests," meaning that fans struggle with each other and producers over preferred interpretations and story outcomes, as well as the way fans and industry relate.[21] This fan-tagonism carries the potential to escalate from routine forms of dissatisfaction and contestation to something far more harmful. Moreover, as Hills notes, "Toxic fan practices can be seen as 'good' by those carrying them out,"[22] which becomes clearer when we place a case where fans have legitimately been wronged alongside more imaginary grievances like the existence of feminist games (the complaint in Gamergate). In the end, what the Lexa case shows is how the combination of fans' belief in their own powerlessness in the face of industry and the amplification power of social media facilitates extreme responses, such that the structures of social media reaction make one group of people who are angry on the Internet look much like another.

Ratings and Twitter Mentions: Using Industry Metrics against Rothenberg

The social media response to Lexa's death was constructed by its participants as an activist campaign, but continually slid toward being just an outpouring of anger. First, fans directly discussed taking action against Rothenberg, the show at large, and the network, and did so using the very measures industry valued. At a basic level, this discussion consisted of declaring that they would not watch. Some fans addressed this threat to Rothenberg: "@JRothenbergTV Still not watching." Others told the CW network, "@theCW Since I don't want to talk to him, could you tell Jason that I'm not watching the show." This refusal to watch was not purely individual, but came in the context of wanting to lower overall viewership or ratings in particular. As Guerrero-Pico et al. note, this was one of the "objectives" of the campaign that developed in response to Lexa's death: "to lower the audience ratings of *The 100* and its presence in social media to force its cancellation."[23] Fans thus often framed the issue in terms of lower audience at scale: ".@JRothenbergTV I think you may have lost at least 30 percent of your #the100 audience after last week's #Lexa death." There was in fact a substantial decline in viewership as "fans boycotted the live broadcast and managed to make the audience drop from 1.47 million viewers for 3x07 [the seventh episode] to 1.25 for 3x08 [the eighth episode]"[24]—though this is more like 15 percent lower than 30 percent lower. This number was nevertheless "the show's lowest ratings ever to date, including the pilot episode."[25]

In addition to the campaigns around ratings, fans lobbied advertisers to cease supporting the show. As Erin B. Waggoner describes, this campaign "was so effective that advertisers for the show publicly announced their pull from the series. In response to a post regarding the social movement, Maybelline announced via social media that it would be pulling its advertisements from *The 100*."[26] Fans expressed excitement about this announcement, with one tweeting "Holy. Shit. That's a big win. kudos to the movement and @Maybelline for taking a stand. #lgbtfansdeservebetter" in response to a now-deleted tweet announcing the makeup brand's departure as a sponsor. Other fans thanked the company: "Thank you @Maybelline for not advertising on the 100 anymore #lgbtfansdeservebetter." Fans also lobbied multiple other advertisers, as seen in tweets tagging and appealing to Revlon, Pantene, Target, Tide, and MetroPCS. As Waggoner notes, "If major companies like Maybelline, who fit within the targeted audience of the CW Network, are pulling their backing, then this will resonate more in a cost-benefit analysis" than the campaign's other tactics.[27]

However, when Maybelline clarified its position and appeared to backtrack, the company was subjected to backlash in turn: "@Maybelline We trusted you. You know what happens to people who stab us in the back? #The1OO #LGBTFANSDESERVEBETTER." This tweet is an implicit threat that the company's action is seen as betrayal and that it might be the next target of a campaign. This hint of a threat and immediate willingness to expand the campaign to a new enemy when anyone seems to cross these fans is a point of contact with Gamergaters, who also succeeded in lobbying for advertisers to withdraw from supporting *their* targets: "At the end of September 2014, Intel pulled its ads from game development news site Gamasutra, in response to Gamergaters' campaign to have Leigh Alexander's '"Gamers" are over' opinion piece read as bullying."[28] There is of course a difference here, as saying that the demographics of gaming have diversified is neither bullying nor the same as manipulating fans into watching one's show under false pretenses, but the similar breakdown of a campaign with a goal into a sheer mass of rage speaks to emergent formations of fan social media collective action.

Fans also "sought to capitalise on Twitter metrics' affordances to 'blackout' #The100 or related hashtags in trending topic lists."[29] One key tactic of this blackout was taking advantage of the fact that humans have greater interpretive powers than automated processes, using the letter "O" in place of the number "0" in "The 100," which was between three and ten times more frequent across the two data sets than the correct spelling. This was perfectly legible to a person, but—in light of the fact that "audience social media activity is both directly measured by Nielsen's Social Content Ratings and collected and analyzed as feedback within industry organizations"[30]—ensured that any social media engagement data aggregated using the show's title would not count these tweets as support. In this way, this incident demonstrates that "many fans are aware of industrial discourses about the value of social media, the affordances of the platforms they employ, and current best practices in social media marketing"[31]—and were able to leverage them in the opposite direction.

The point of intersection between savvy and rage was the focus on decreasing Rothenberg's number of Twitter followers, which was both action taken to leverage industry metrics and very targeted and personal. As Guerrero-Pico et al. note, "The boycott protocol included a widespread 'unfollowing' campaign centred on Jason Rothenberg."[32] This goal showed up repeatedly in the tweets, such as "UNFOLLOW @JRothenbergTV !!!!" Accounts of the number of followers he lost in the wake of Lexa's death vary, but some scholars cite a number as high as forty-seven thousand.[33] Fans commented on the unfollowing campaign several times in the tweets, as in "@JRothenbergTV You deserve it (105K)," which referenced his number of followers and identified its decrease as retribution. Fans also expressed excitement about the success of this tactic, as when one Tumblr post said, "Jason Rotinhell just went under 105k followers I am laughing hysterically right now."

On the other hand, while of course I specifically sought out tweets that named or engaged with Rothenberg, the particular means of that engagement are important to examine, as they often abandon the framework of activism altogether. First, Rothenberg's Twitter handle was frequently tagged in protest tweets (1,052 instances, not counting any misspellings, of which there were a handful). This tagging could have several purposes. Some tweets were directly addressing Rothenberg. Others could have been intended to increase the chances that he would see the protest by putting it into his notifications. Fans also may have used the tag to try to increase the visibility of the tweet in general rather than to Rothenberg in particular. Importantly, like Gamergate before it, this was an Internet-organized anger campaign.[34] As Michael Trice and Liza Potts put it in discussing Gamergate, "Suddenly the functionality that allowed some to speak truth to power in the Arab Spring, and later #BlackLivesMatter" brought "the prolific anger of thousands of aggrieved and loosely organized user accounts."[35] While one might want to see a campaign against violence done to queer people as more like Black Lives Matter than Gamergate, the prolific anger and vitriol that characterize the Lexa campaign trouble such analogies. These were "organized brigades," a tactic developed by Gamergate that later spread to the alt-right[36]—and also spread to other fan backlash. Much like being targeted by Gamergate brought "a barrage of largely negative attention,"[37] so too was Rothenberg's Twitter bombarded, by some accounts driving him from the platform.[38] Effectively, what happened to Rothenberg was what Gamergate and similar reactionary campaigns inflicted: "punishment [. . .] carried out in public by a seemingly undifferentiated, amorphous body."[39]

However, one key difference in the Lexa campaign is that unlike most of Gamergate's targets, Rothenberg was powerful in the traditional media industry and already had a Verified Twitter account. Importantly, the fan tactic of mass tagging Rothenberg did not demonstrate awareness of the affordances provided to Verified accounts on Twitter, which beginning in 2013 had the option to "toggle between mentions in three categories: all, filtered and verified. Selecting 'Filtered' will show mentions based on an algorithm we use to filter out spam, and choosing 'Verified' means they'll only see mentions from other verified accounts."[40] Thus, it was quite possible for Rothenberg to use this setting and entirely avoid the thousands of messages directed at him by regular people. That said, it matters that this was technologically enabled, large-scale angry engagement, whether Rothenberg saw all of the tweets directed to him or not, as #LGBTFansDeserveBetter "trended for over 24 hours worldwide and reached over 212,000 posts."[41]

Many of these tweets addressed Rothenberg. Sometimes, such tweets used his handle in place of his name, as in "To @JRothenbergTV : Thanks for absolutely nothing good." These moments of direct address were often aggressive. After Rothenberg retweeted a comment referring to the campaign as bullying,[42] one fan asked confrontationally, "If fans who raise 30k for charity in response to homophobia are bullies, what does that make you?" This comment emphasized both the good aspects of fans' actions and the fact that they were responding to harm caused by Rothenberg's actions. At other times, he was addressed by name, as in "Float you Jason!!"—using the in-universe expletive referencing the practice of expelling criminals from airlocks. Using Rothenberg's first name in this way also helps flatten the power imbalance between him and fans; as Judith Butler describes of people calling them "Judy" in critiques of their work, "there was a certain exasperation in the delivery [. . .], a certain patronizing quality which (re)constituted me as an unruly child, one who needed to be brought to task,"[43] and this dynamic echoes in these "Jasons" as well. Use of "Jason" was often precisely dismissive, as in, "pfff yeah sure Jason sure."

At other times, addressing Rothenberg took the form of a direct, almost intimate appeal. One fan asked, "Did you really have to kill her Jason?" Another took an interesting and similarly intimate approach to framing the question of mistreatment by appealing to Rothenberg's own marginalized identity as Jewish to help him understand what the problem was, saying, "@JRothenbergTV As Jews, we know minority representation in art affects life. You should be ashamed. #shylock #fagin #lgbtfansdeservebetter." The hashtags here somewhat confuse the issue, as they might out of context be perceived as *calling* Rothenberg "Shylock," but in context they are references to harmful representations that had negative consequences for Jewish people, used in an attempt to make the issue clearer for him. In these ways, then, speaking directly *to* Rothenberg was a common tactic of the protest tweets.

It was also common to insist that fans had been mistreated. Some framed this complaint with awareness of media industry practices such as ratings, saying, "@JRothenbergTV @The100writers shame on you for using a vulnerable audience to get higher ratings." As Bourdaa notes, fans collected evidence of how they had been used and "wrote a statement in which they archived all the tweets from the writers' room, the showrunner, the network, showing how misled they were and reinforcing their decision to take actions."[44] Others were more simply angry: "Yeah, and then you screwed those fans over . . ." Fans at times brought fandom concepts into play, mentioning Clexa and the concept of a relationship as "endgame"—the couple who will be together at the end of the narrative—"Shame on you for manipulating fans into believing Clexa is endgame!" The idea of being "endgame" is often understood in fandom as signaling the relationship's importance in the narrative, even to the point of seeing the entire narrative as leading up to this relationship, despite the fact that the trajectory of a TV show or film almost never centers on getting two characters together (with the exception of the romantic comedy genre). Nevertheless, endgame is a powerful concept in fandom that is often perceived in contentious fandoms in terms of winning or losing compared to factions supporting other relationships. When Rothenberg and others were publicly supportive of Clexa, then, fans drew such conclusions about it, and later felt that they had been manipulated into drawing them, even though industry and fans operate with different value systems and "endgame" is generally uninteresting to media makers.

As part of calling on and calling out Rothenberg, the CW network was often also addressed, and these communications constituted another site where strategy and the use of industry metrics did not hold. The network was directly tagged in many tweets either as the primary account @TheCW (more than three thousand mentions across the two data sets) or as the specific public relations account @TheCW_PR (more than twenty-three hundred mentions). At times this tagging was an appeal to the network to remedy the situation, as when fans trended the statement "CW STOP JASON ROTHENBERG" or used the hashtag

"#CWCancelThe1OO." Notably, this hashtag replaced the zeroes in "100" with the letter "O," which, as noted above, separated it from support of the show. Similarly to Twitter calls to take action, one user also created a petition that appealed to CW CEO Mark Pedowitz to replace Rothenberg as the showrunner, using Change.org the way many activists do, to try to gain enough traction to secure the desired result. This pattern emphasizes that many of the responses were oriented toward collective action, particularly against Rothenberg.[45] Some tweets did show awareness that going after Rothenberg might do collateral damage to the show itself, and so were careful to distinguish him from the larger show, particularly the actors. One directly insisted, "@TheCW We love the cast but #LGBTFansDeserveBetter #LexaDeservedBetter #AlyciaDeservedBetter and #JasonNeedsToGo." Another tweet framed Rothenberg's removal as beneficial to the cast: "#LGBTFansDeserveBetter & the cast deserve a better showrunner! Fire @JRothenbergTV or #CWCancelThe1OO." This user apparently did not perceive the irony in claiming to support the cast while trying to put them out of work by including "Cancel The 100" in the tweet.[46]

However, sometimes the tweets consisted of pure emotion rather than strategy. One genre of tweets is essentially tattling on Rothenberg to his boss, as in, "@TheCW_PR @TheCW #ReplaceJRothenberg. He's a Narcissist. His latest interview proves He's learned nothing and frankly #LGBTFansDeserveBetter." Reporting Rothenberg's alleged bad behavior is here constructed as sufficient to result in replacing him, demonstrating that the savvy about industry structures that fans demonstrate at other times is uneven. Sometimes these appeals were very directly to The CW (or just the universe) to fire Rothenberg, some of which explicitly named queerbaiting as the issue: "@TheCW_PR @TheCW Fire @JRothenbergTV for queerbaiting!" Similarly, here there seems to be no awareness that fan values decrying queerbaiting are simply not shared by media industries.[47] However, fans also at times considered the CW network complicit in what had happened. As one tweet said, "CW Used LGBT Fans and refuse to take responsibility and are siding with showrunner @JRothenbergTV @TheCW @TheCW_PR #lgbtfansdeservebetter." In all of these ways, then, protest about Lexa's death was often couched in terms of media industry figures and values, seeking to gain redress by doing so, which shows fan awareness of industry systems, but this was uneven, interspersed with tweets thoroughly within fan value systems.

Threats and Villainy: Targeting Rothenberg for Violence

However, one reason why action against Rothenberg was part of fans' strategy—and why I focused on fan responses to him in particular in my data collection—is that the fandom constructed him as the villain. As Cameron notes, when queer characters are killed off, "Fans often respond with anger, and #BuryYourGays protests spill over into ad hominem attacks against the writers and showrunners behind queer deaths."[48] Responses to Rothenberg exemplify this pattern. Fans very clearly blame him for Lexa's death, using hashtags like "#badJason" and "#fuckjason." One fan on Tumblr quipped, "I got 99 problems and jrot is responsible for one hundred of them." Related to tattling on him and trying to inflict consequences on him such as being fired, discussed above, there was a desire to see him get his comeuppance. This led to cheering on a fan who told him off at the WonderCon fan convention a few weeks after Lexa's death—where, according to Bourdaa, "all Lexa-related questions were banned at the demand of the showrunner."[49] Waggoner adds that during the panel "Rothenberg repeatedly avoids using Lexa's name. During the question session, one fan asked questions regarding the queerbaiting, and fans responded to this by praising the fan and further denouncing Rothenberg."[50] In one such tweet, a fan said, "Jason Rothenburg was just drag[g]ed by a fan. Bless you whoever you are." There is a strong, almost Manichean moral stance here. Fans have been wronged. It was Rothenberg's fault. He must pay. There was, just as in Gamergate, a very clear "us" and "them."[51]

One frequent aspect of treating Rothenberg as a villain was accusing him of lying, which was rooted in a belief that he had deliberately misled fans about Lexa's importance to the narrative, suggested that she was safe from harm, and generally manipulated fans for his own benefit. This set of accusations included creating the Twitter trending topic "JROTH IS STILL LYING." The trend featured such tweets as "JROTH IS STILL LYING What else in [is] new under the Sun?" which emphasized a sense of Rothenberg as a serial or unrepentant liar. As Waggoner describes, "A few fans even speculated that, because of the creator interaction with the fans online, this character was safe because of the promises and assurances made that she was. The particular fan criticism was that engaging in this behavior was a form of queerbaiting, or promising positive representation to increase viewer ratings."[52] The lying was central for many. One tweeter responded to an entertainment news outlet to say, "@Zap2it it isn't just #Lexa's death that has us upset with JRot. It was the lies, false hopes & queer baiting." There was a very real sense of betrayal on the part of fans, specifically with regard to the promises they perceived Rothenberg to have made. "Remember when jrot said HE would treat us better? With respect? Bullshit at its finest." The implication in many of these tweets is that if there had not been such manipulation, the reaction to Lexa's death would not have been as intense.

As part of constructing Rothenberg as a villain, he was provided with a variety of colorful nicknames. As Cameron notes, "Previously called 'jroth' in fan spaces, Rothenberg earned a slate of new, less affectionate nicknames on Tumblr: 'jrot,' 'jrotinhell,' 'jflop,' 'jrat.'"[53] In addition to the terms "JRot" and "JRat" that were part of my data selection strategy and showed up in tweets like "#fuckyoujrat," there were also variants like "Jrotten" used on both Twitter and Tumblr. On Tumblr, Rothenberg was also frequently called "Jatan" or other variants on calling him Satan. One key pattern in these nicknames is to create names that sound somewhat like "Rothenberg" or "JRoth" but that combine with something disparaging. "Rothenberg" thus becomes "rotinhell," and "JRoth" becomes "jflop," referencing the slang term for failure, or "jtwat." These terms served both to express distaste for him and to obscure the posts from searches for his name.

Fans also quite directly say that they hate Rothenberg. Some such declarations were made directly to him: "@JRothenbergTV I hate you so much :(." Others, particularly on Tumblr, where fans could both post longer comments and elude content moderation, were more extravagant: "I would stop talking about how much I hate JRat when that little shit stop giving me more reason to hate him. HE'S A FUCKING RAT AND I WANT HIM FIRED." Several posters insisted that everyone hated Rothenberg. One fan had enough anger to fuel photoshopping his face and the faces of the characters onto a promotional photo for the show "Everybody Hates Chris" (UPN 2005–2006, The CW 2006–2009), changed to read "Everybody hates JRot." Another fan, in response to a video of the hostile fan at WonderCon discussed above, said, "Just watched #The100 @WonderCon well Jrat well and truly knows he fucked up nd is hated by all." In such ways, as Guerrero-Pico et al. describe, "Fan-tagonists or anti-fans use social media to denounce unfair and stereotypical representation or what they view as poor narrative development although unethical toxic fan practices (e.g., cyberbullying the producers) can pose a threat to the ultimate social mission of fan activism as a whole."[54] Framing the situation this way—saying that these campaigns were fundamentally fan activism with a social mission but threatened by fan toxicity—echoes tendencies in Gamergate to disavow those who engaged in the most harmful practices.[55] However, as Cameron notes, "We should neither dismiss fan anger nor reduce it to a symptom of present-day audience entitlement."[56] While it might seem impossible to bully someone with more power than you—though the incredible scale of the response does change this estimation, as I will discuss later in the chapter—that this behavior was harmful is clear.

As part of seeing Rothenberg as a villain came a belief that anything done to him was therefore justified, and accordingly fan responses included threats. Bourdaa notes that Lexa's "death provoked passionate, violent, and activist reactions from the fans,"[57] and it is important to emphasize "violent" here. As Guerrero-Pico et al. point out, "Reasoned debates and campaigning efforts by fan-tagonists and newly converted anti-fans coexisted with examples of toxic fan practices, such as defamatory and vexatious messages, as well as death threats against Jason Rothenberg, forcing him to abandon his interaction on social media."[58] I want to go beyond these scholars just mentioning the violence aspect and look at it much more closely, as understanding it is in fact essential to making sense of this incident. It is important to note here that actual threats of violence would violate Twitter's terms of service (TOS), and when the subject of such threats is a powerful white man like Rothenberg, threats are more likely to be taken seriously by content moderators. Thus, by the time the Twitter data was collected in August 2020, the worst threats had likely been removed. However, there remains a spectrum of threatening posts in my data set that evidently did not rise to the level of a TOS violation and/or were not noticed—and surely there were many more posts that users made just speaking to their own followers without putting them into this campaign hashtag designed to be seen, which were likely worse. On the mild end, one fan said, "@JRothenbergTV You think WE'RE cowards? LOL. we haven't lost. Just getting started. STAY MAD #LGBTfansDeserveBetter." This is a promise of more of the campaign, and even if what is "just getting started" is simply Twitter bombardment and an attempt to get him fired, it is still somewhat threatening. Others more directly declared, "We're coming for you @JRothenbergTV , because we deserve better! #CWcancelThe100 #LGBTfansdeservebetter." While this tweet does not indicate what "we're coming" to do, it *is* a promise of direct action against Rothenberg.

Other fans directly use violent language. One tweet declared, "#LGBTFansDeserveBetter Jus drein jus daun! (Blood must have blood) Revenge for Lexa!!" Calling for revenge and blood for blood is much more threatening, though it does not directly state that harm will come to Rothenberg or that it will be this particular user who will do it, which is typically the threshold for a social media post to be considered a genuine threat. However, other tweets do directly discuss harm to him: "@JRothenbergTV be careful Jason because #the100 's fans gonna hunt you down p.s. blood must have blood #lexadeservedbetter." This is quite direct, saying that Rothenberg will be hunted down and that the hunt will involve blood. The tweet likely avoided removal by not saying that the user who sent the tweet would secure the blood demanded. In the most graphic threat in my Twitter data set, one user mixed in-universe violence and real-life violence, saying, "I hope Octavia kills pike slowly and painfully maybe she will do us a favour and kill Jason #ClexaForever #BringLexaBack #LexaDeservedBetter." This tweet obliquely wishes on Rothenberg a slow, painful death.

Threats were more graphic on Tumblr, where content moderation is far laxer. There were multiple posts wanting Rothenberg to "choke," as in "girls don't want boys. Girls want Jason Rothenberg to choke." In itself, this is not all that terrible, but it *is* wishing bodily harm on him and gains additional meaning as part of the broader pattern of violent comments. Other posts were more oblique, wishing harm on Rothenberg by pretending to be worried about harm coming to him: "I am just as mad as the next Clexa shipper, infuriated in fact, but I am actually concerned for Jason's well being. It may be best that he just doesn't go to Wondercon. Or if he shows up, he better be wearing a bulletproof vest." At a plain text level, this is saying that there is a risk Rothenberg will be shot by a fan. Though the post does reference a popular fandom meme at the time about lesbians needing bulletproof vests—sparked in part by Lexa being killed by a bullet intended for another character—the underlying idea of Rothenberg being shot persists. Other posts just hope something bad might happen: "I'm not a violent person, but I hope JRoth'll trip and fall headfirst into the water (pool, lake, sea, bathtub, I'm not picky) with his phone in his pocket!" Prefacing that the poster is "not a violent person" makes it clear that this is a desire for Rothenberg to be electrocuted, not just for his phone to be destroyed.[59] In such ways, we see how fan response included "ad hominem attacks on media producers that go beyond potentially justifiable anger at misleading producer actions, the kinds of fan-producer interactions that many in fandom would like to disavow. These practices include, for example, responding to death of a queer character by wishing death on the people who wrote or directed the episode of their demise."[60]

The Tumblr corpus also included a looping animated GIF showing characters Clarke and Octavia repeatedly punching another character, on whose face Rothenberg's had been superimposed, thus producing images of two of the show's protagonists punching him over and over again. Some fans even directly said that they themselves wanted to commit violence to Rothenberg. One spoke of the show's airing as reinvigorating "my desire to hit a certain Jason in the face with a brick," which was in bold text. In the most graphic threat of all those I found, one fan announced, "It is Saturday March 26, I'm still bitter and angry about Lexa's death, I want to, now more than ever, literally just slam JRotinhell's head in car door repeatedly while the car is in full motion :))))." This is not only something that would cause grievous bodily injury, but really quite specific and detailed, suggesting more than a fleeting thought. While discussions of violence are of course not themselves violence, and were clearly intended as cathartic expressions of frustration, and generally were said in fan spaces and not something Rothenberg himself was subjected to, it is nevertheless the case that fans were discursively violent toward him, sometimes viciously so.

These posts seem to demonstrate a sense that anything and everything is permitted, because Rothenberg is out of fans' reach as a powerful media industry figure, because they are punching upward at him, but also because they are members of a marginalized group that he had

harmed. Seeing their own powerlessness as justifying any and all response is precisely the same logic by which "Gamergate participants
adhered to a normatively white masculine subject position that viewed
itself as being under attack from SJWs and feminists, and thus justified
harassing behavior through a mantle of victimhood."[61] That is, because
Lexa fans and Gamergaters saw themselves as marginalized, harassing
behavior became much easier to justify, diminishing or removing constraints they might (or might not) otherwise have felt. While from an
etic perspective, this perception of powerlessness is far more justified in
the Lexa case than in Gamergate, recognizing the similarity of the emic
perspective provides insight into Gamergaters. Similarly, the tweets focused on hatred or harm for Rothenberg cannot reasonably be described
as activism toward better outcomes for other queer characters. Instead,
just as Gamergate's "purpose is not some set policy outcome or achiev-
able condition, but rather the unconditional defeat and apology" of their
enemies,[62] the Lexa campaign sought to defeat Rothenberg.

The Intersectional Limitations of The 100 Fan Activism

These moments when this activist campaign tipped over into violence
might seem to be the result of hurt feelings gotten out of hand—and to
some extent they are. But the tendency of the Lexa and Clexa fandom
to think only about their own marginalization at the expense of others
actually had a much longer history. Particularly, these same fans were
studiously not intersectional in their approach to marginality, ignoring the show's flagrant racism in the way it depicted characters of color.
Rukmini Pande notes that "as some non-white fans of [The 100] pointed
out, the same fanbase had been ignoring the hugely racialized violence
that was a staple of its narrative from its inception."[63] Given that part
of the complaint was that the show had not been thoughtful about the
impact of violence on an already marginalized group such as lesbians,
that is, it is notable that violence against characters of color had been
ongoing throughout the show's run without producing backlash. As one
fan of color put it on Tumblr, "The 100 has been serving its audience a
giant bowl of tropios [a portmanteau of 'trope' and Cheerios cereal] and
sour milk since its very beginning but because these tropes are mostly

centered around race, those of us who can see them have just swallowed the plot whole."

As an example of this lack of interest in resisting racist tropes, across the two Twitter data sets, there were around 350 posts mentioning Lincoln, a Black man character killed March 10, 2016, in the episode following Lexa's death, but the vast majority of these posts either simply appended him or subordinated him to Lexa by emphasizing her more. Only around twenty-five tweets, or 7 percent of the Lincoln tweets (0.21 percent of all tweets), were substantive mentions of Lincoln and the issues with killing him off. Granted, this data is drawn from tweets about Lexa and LGBT fans, but as an investigation of how these particular people paid attention (or didn't) to this character's death, the differential concern does seem to be at least somewhat representative. One fan tweeted that "I follow a few Clexa people who raged for weeks about Lexa's death . . . And all I see for Lincoln's is 1 post about how 'he deserved better . . .'" This observation about the disproportionate concern is borne out by the corpus.

Some tweets mentioning Lincoln grouped him together with Lexa as "minorities," as in "Lexa deserved better. Lincoln deserved better. Minorities are not disposable. #cancelthe100 #cancelthe1OO @cwthe100 @TheCW." Notably, many of the tweets in the "minorities are not disposable" trend (383 instances overall in my data set), which was ostensibly about coalition in relation to killing two characters from marginalized groups so close together, did not mention Lincoln at all. Lexa and Lincoln were also lumped together as "diverse," as with one tweet that decried "when #The100 keeps killing off important, beautiful, diverse characters. #lincolndeservedbetter #lexadeservedbetter." It was most frequent for tweets to use the generic term "POC," which, while it is much like the generic "LGBT" that the same group used, did flatten out some important differences in racialized experiences. Some fans did directly name that Lincoln was Black, and that he was not the first Black man killed: "So now the 100 killed off the lesbian and another black man. #LincolnDeservedBetter #lexadeservedbetter." However, such specificity was rare. Ultimately, as Rukmini Pande notes, it is "necessary to pay attention to patterns of fan prioritization so as to identify *which* characters are consistently valued over others within fandom spaces, even when issues of social justice are highlighted."[64] The (lack of) response to Lincoln shows this well.

Conclusion

In the end, the social media response to Lexa's death showed a duality of fan savvy and intense emotional reaction. Tweets were often couched in terms of media industry figures and values, seeking to gain redress by doing so, showing fan awareness of industry systems. Tweets discuss canceling the show, refusing to watch, and unfollowing Rothenberg. However, posts also frequently tag Rothenberg and address him directly as at fault for the negative outcome and call on the CW network to intervene in the situation. In these ways, fans demonstrate far more affect than strategy. As part of seeing Rothenberg as a villain, there seems to be a belief that anything done to him is justified, and fan responses included threats. Moreover, the tendency of the Lexa and Clexa fandom to think only about their own marginalization at the expense of others was not unique to the backlash after Lexa's death, but actually had a much longer history rooted in ignoring the show's racism. Ultimately, I argue that it is important to understand the Lexa incident in relation to other moments of intense social media anger directed at a single figure or particular group. As in this case, such campaigns carry the potential to escalate from routine forms of dissatisfaction and contestation to something far more harmful. In the end, what this case shows is how the structures of social media reaction make one group of people who are angry on the Internet look much like another.

In some ways, the excesses of the response to Lexa's death have everything to do with fan powerlessness. As an organized group, or even a diffuse, angry mob, they had incredible capacity to do harm, but this group/mob was comprised of individuals who themselves did not have power. From the perspective of any given fan, they were David and Rothenberg was Goliath, with the odds against them and their ability to have any success something like a miracle. The sense of Rothenberg as powerful and distant, someone fans could not hurt, who would perhaps not even see their posts, was true for any given fan in isolation. It is also true of Gamergaters—though they were not really victims at all—who as individuals did not in fact have the power to do any of the things they did as a group. The Lexa case, and connecting it to Gamergate, shows that the belief in powerlessness is itself powerful.

That belief matters because it led to feeling that there was no need to pull punches, but thousands of fans all convinced of their inability to do any harm are harmful indeed. This is how network effects matter to incidents like Gamergate or the post-Lexa backlash. That is, this is also a story about the amplification and aggregation potential of the Internet. Fan complaints about media production choices, even vitriolic ones, have always existed, but they never used to be visible, and certainly not at scale the way they are now. A single person making a one-off comment to a friend can now be given a megaphone (whether that person wants one or not). Andrea Braithwaite argues that "in many ways, #Gamergate is simply Internet business as usual; much of the vitriol chronicled here is routinely found in other virtual places."[65] Plenty of people say mean things on the Internet, but it is when the meanness is aggregated—and particularly when it is deliberately collectivized—that it begins to look like Gamergate or the Lexa incident. As Michael Salter argues, "Gamergate's abuse campaign became endemic because its underlying rationalities were evident in the design, governance and communicative culture of a range of online platforms."[66] That is, the ability to group people together such as through hashtags, the optimization of platforms for the most controversial content,[67] and platform usage norms of large-scale collective reaction are the foundation of social media, and also of these campaigns. When media makers such as Rothenberg and the rest of the creative team of *The 100* tried to use fans for their own benefit and it backfired, they did not understand the power of this amplification and aggregation. *But neither did the people engaged in the backlash campaign.* They cannot imagine (or, in what is a crucial question about empathy, perhaps cannot be bothered to imagine) being the recipient of what they dish out. It is this particular combination of circumstances that produces outcomes like Gamergate and the post-Lexa backlash. By looking at the Lexa case—where the underlying feelings are sympathetic, but the actual response was nevertheless to bombard the Twitter accounts of those considered enemies with mass quantities of messages, many of which contained threats of varying intensity—we gain insight into the important role played by the underlying feelings of reactionaries as well.

5

The Anti Wars

Sex Crimes, Free Speech, and Papering Over Racism

In 2003, scholar Jonathan Gray coined the term "antifan" for "those who strongly dislike a given text or genre, considering it inane, stupid, morally bankrupt and/or aesthetic drivel."[1] Since that early-2000s moment, "antifan" has become widespread in academic analysis of fandom, including a dedicated anthology.[2] However, the term "anti" has also become prominent in transformative-works fandom in recent years, and it is used in a way that is apparently disconnected from the scholarly version, as "the fannish anti identity seems to be directed toward other fans, rather than toward a fannish object."[3] Antis are fans who oppose particular categories of fan fiction and fan art, such as works that include rape, or particular preferences for relationships between characters, such as works that feature underage sex or incest. The pro-shipper or anti-anti, by contrast, sees this opposition as censorship impinging on freedom of speech.[4] If the anti in Gray's sense is a taste argument, the anti of the Anti Wars is a moral position—held by those who, as Lauren Rouse notes, "dislike a certain relationship or pairing because of moral or personal reasons"[5]—and so is the anti-anti. However, as I will show, this morality is narrowly fixated on the question of sexuality in fan fiction in a way that elbows out other concerns about the ways pleasure is not harmless, particularly the ways fan works can be racist.

The fandom construction of the anti and the anti-anti as types of people seems to have arisen out of the use of "anti-" as a prefix appended to the names of media objects, ships, and characters in Twitter and Tumblr tagging to signal opposition—as one user on Twitter notes, "the emphasis on 'anti' originates from their own tagging of their tumblr posts." As Louisa Ellen Stein describes, "Although tags are intended to help with categorizing, archiving, and retrieval, Tumblr users often include tags to capture their momentary response to an image, to theorize or extrapolate, or to inscribe the imagined audience into the post."[6] "Anti" may thus have arisen out of this sort of position taking or audience inscription, though as a noun it refers specifically to people who oppose certain categories of fan work, and in particular "an anti is someone who hates something so much that their fandom activity revolves exclusively around fighting it or mocking it"; whatever the target, "the focus of the anti's fannish energy is about tearing down the thing."[7]

Such opposition becomes more than a matter of personal taste because of the vitriolic forms it often takes. In the corpus of tweets I collected, tweeters identify cases where fans were "spammed [with] gore, attempted doxxed, actually doxxed," including "doxxing undocumented people,"[8] harassment "even to the point of sending people to the hospital," such as instances of fans being "suicide baited," and not infrequent rape threats and death threats. Similarly, the Organization for Transformative Works (OTW) reported that one such fan who had gained access to the email addresses for the OTW's volunteers began "sending our volunteers threatening emails with illegal child sexual abuse material"; volunteers were also informed by an internal communication that the messages included complaints about the fact that the OTW's fan fiction site Archive of Our Own allows works that include underage sexuality.[9] Fan commentator Stitch noted that they "have a lengthy list of people who've [. . .] even had their jobs threatened or damaged as a result" of the Anti Wars.[10] What makes this an important phenomenon to study is that it is so hotly contested and has such clear material harms. Much of the conversation around such campaigns is focused on the targets—and given the real harms such campaigns can bring, that is an important area of inquiry. However, what I want to do here is focus on the perpetrators, considering both how people justify their actions through appeals to moral imperatives and the internal contradictions that arise, using a case where both sides of the argument think of themselves as progressive. As in the situations described in chapters 1 and 4, in which there might be an impulse to root for the fans versus industry, arguments that representation matters or that sexual minorities should not have their speech suppressed because somebody does not like it seem reasonable on their face. This therefore calls for deeper attention to the dynamics of the dispute. The case also ties in to the theme in chapters 3–5 that emphasizes how transformative-works fandom has frequently had troubling practices around race. Ultimately, I consider how the ends are used to justify the means, to elide questions of collateral damage, and to suppress attention to other forms of harm.

To examine the circulation and functioning of the anti in contemporary transformative-works fandom, I turned to Twitter as a platform that is searchable, popular among fans, and, with its trending hashtags, television live tweeting, and political engagement, tends to be used in at least a semipublic way. I collected a set of tweets for the search term "anti" using the Twitter Data Scraping Jupyter Notebook and the Twitter API widget in data analysis software Orange.[11] After initial analysis revealed many false positives, I used Microsoft Excel to filter for only those tweets that contained "antis" with a space in an attempt to use the plural to differentiate "anti" the noun from the prefix "anti" or "anti-" or as instances of the term "antisemit*," unless "antis" as a stand-alone term also appeared. I then refiltered this data set in Excel to select tweets with "fiction," "ships," or "shipper" from the main "antis" corpus in order to focus on the kinds of antifandom I wanted to address, moving iteratively between scraping and filtering to attempt to reach one thousand relevant tweets. Ultimately, I collected 909 relevant tweets from a total of 435,000 scraped that were posted between May 31 and August 30, 2020 (Twitter Data Scraping Jupyter Notebook, 420,000; Orange, 15,000).[12] The corpus includes comments from 751 unique users. By collecting discussion of these terms in this distanced, systematic way, I am able to see how they appear in everyday social media conversation as well as capture a broad swath of users. This allows general patterns to emerge.

To interpret the broad themes and currents in this body of tweets, I began by taking two samples, one a random sample of one hundred tweets, and the other a combined set of the top one hundred most-retweeted and top one hundred most-liked tweets in order to explore sentiments that appear to be widely shared (given that many highly liked tweets are also highly retweeted, and vice versa, the total was 121 tweets after duplicates were removed). When the two samples were cross-referenced and duplicates were removed, there were 201 unique tweets in total. These tweets were grouped according to emergent themes such as the role different groups ascribe to fiction, emphasis on sexuality, etc. Subsequently, keywords related to the themes, such as "harass" and "race," were searched in the full tweet corpus to collect all relevant text, which was then examined holistically within each of the identified themes to interpret how the anti is understood and contested. In what follows, I will first explain the anti position, including a critique of how it produces an essentialist model of sexuality. Next, I will explain how anti-antis articulate their opposition to antis through an individualist language of free speech. Finally, I explore the limits of how both sides of the debate leverage a language of progressiveness, arguing that defining the problem of fan fiction as about sexuality forecloses taking a hard look at the costs of stereotyped and dehumanizing representations of people of color.

The Fandom Sex Wars: Shipping as Identity and Essence

The anti side of the argument contends, first, that writing or reading fan fiction is advocacy for whatever sex appears in the story. Moreover, antis argue that reading or writing something in fan fiction is a statement of identity. Antis posit that production or consumption of stories with troubling sexuality, whether treated erotically or not, endorses its harms. This is a belief system in which "representation is being perceived to cause harm, because the depiction of something in fiction is being perceived as advocacy for its perpetuation in the real world."[13]

While I filtered for "fiction" to capture both "fan fiction" and "fanfiction" spellings, doing so revealed a lively debate about how fiction relates to reality that demonstrates anti beliefs. Antis' first premise is that writing or reading about a romantic relationship or a kind of sex is advocacy for it (shipping it). Antis see a strong relationship between fiction and the real beliefs and desires of readers and writers. As one anti describes, "'Antis' as a general fandom term means ppl [people] who do not support incest/underage/abusiv[e] ships being normalized (and are often very combative ab[ou]t this and can harass ppl ab[ou]t it). an anti anti does support that content basically & often fights for it to exist." This defines antis as against incest, underage sex, and abusive relationships, which they perceive their opposition to support (and indeed to fight for those things in fan fiction).

At root, antis contend that engaging with such topics is advocating for them. This contention arises in part from what Alexis Lothian describes as "a concern that if you don't denounce something as harmful, then you become part of the harm yourself. This is certainly not only a fandom issue—far from it—but it plays out intensely in fandom discussions."[14] I argue that this collapse of discussion or representation of a topic into advocacy for the behavior is a consequence of the framing of reading and writing fan fiction as shipping that is currently dominant in fandom. Shipping is thus constructed as advocacy for the relationship. While outside this debate, fan fiction is typically understood as a way to imagine otherwise, this understanding is not central to the antis' position. One is therefore not just depicting X, but shipping it. Thus, one anti defines anti-antis/pro-shippers as "into shipping 'problematic' things"— not writing or reading them, but shipping them.

Contending that all fan fiction is shipping raises questions about shipping "in canon," meaning that the relationship appears—or is desired to appear—in the official text, as opposed to "in fanon" (fan interpretations).[15] Thus, one tweeter notes, "i only ship fanon and idk [I don't know] anyone who ships them canon yet all of antis' hate on us is based on the assumption that we ship them canon." The tweeter does not want the characters as officially written to date or have sex, but despite this, backlash from antis assumes both advocacy for the ship to be canon and that shipping is an endorsement of the ship and any faults it or its characters have.

Shipping as advocacy for canon is a subset of the broader notion of shipping as advocacy, but particularly consequential. Fan activity like shipping and writing fan fiction has traditionally been associated with transformational fandom—fandom that reworks the text to better suit fan desires[16]—and for fan fiction to center or even exalt canon is a remarkable abandonment of those traditions of contestation.[17] But it is remarkable only within these fandom traditions; as I have argued elsewhere, the rapid growth of fandom has meant increasing numbers of new fans who are not socialized into previous generations' norms.[18] Without the countervailing force of fannish norms, culturally inculcated reverence for the author and/or text constructs what is in the text as superior to what is not. As Victoria M. Gonzalez notes of the fandom she studies, the dominant position "insinuates that abiding by canon is the primary way in which normal or sane shippers function within fandom." She adds, "The conception of normal fans established here suggests that they must pay deference to the creators of the program."[19]

However, norms of deference to canon are unevenly distributed. In her discussion of *The Flash* (CW, 2014–present), Kristen J. Warner calls attention to "the strain of racism present in the fandom not fond of an interracial couple," although the relationship between white character Barry Allen and Black character Iris West is canonical.[20] Differential respect and enforcement of canon is also frequently used to justify homophobia, as in one comment about "antis who loveeeee hating on gay ships if it's not official," suggesting that only officially sanctioned same-sex desire is permitted. As Gonzalez describes, some fans consider "portraying a character in a queer relationship more of a violation than portraying them in a heterosexual relationship that is not canon."[21] Canon is seen as less binding when the relationship in question is an interracial relationship and as more violated by queer desire.

If contemporary fannish culture assumes the superiority of canon, then it makes sense that fans might advocate for anointing things they enjoy *as* canon. This is particularly common where shipping touches on marginalized groups who are routinely either excluded from media or treated as peripheral compared to straight, white, and men characters. Historically, one of the arguments for the value of fan fiction was that it permitted reworking media texts to include groups that are otherwise excluded.[22] In particular, fan works have often been framed as making media texts serve women's needs.[23] However, as Warner, among others, has pointed out, there has been inordinate focus on these practices as done by white women. Fans of color engage in much the same practices, "consciously moving mediated women of color, who often occupy supporting roles, to the center, transforming them into leads in fan-produced discourse."[24] The combination of seeing fan fiction as a practice of inclusion for marginalized people and contemporary intensified desires to secure canon status invites advocacy for canonical inclusion of more such representations—and as important, rather than background, characters. The stakes are (or feel) higher for fan practices when they are intertwined with broader struggles over representation and inclusion.

In particular, as the counterpart to the rejection of noncanon same-sex relationships discussed earlier, there has been an upsurge in advocacy for same-sex ships to appear in canon. Eve Ng notes that fans' sense that representation of same-sex relationships is possible has increased over time, increasing expectations that queer people will appear in canon (and frustration when they do not).[25] I argue that believing that it is reasonable to expect queer relationships in media has strengthened the marginalization of transforming the text. That is, rather than same-sex desire being impossible in media and necessarily relegated to fan fiction (as was the case historically), there is a belief that such relationships could be equally represented, so if media makers do not do so it is because they do not want to. A lack of representation is understood as an active rejection rather than simply making other narrative choices—because discrimination is over and if the characters were queer, we would know it already in canon. This vastly overstates the social acceptability of queer characters, especially as central rather than supporting, but the fact that fans believe queer pairings are textually possible is what matters. The false sense that every ship is equally possible in canon elides the fact that heterosexism makes some outcomes far more likely than others.[26]

Putting it all together, if fan fiction is shipping is advocacy, especially when the relationship in question departs from canon, and if advocacy is particularly acute around sexualities outside of heteronormativity, then we have the ingredients of the anti argument that fan fiction is advocacy for whatever sex appears in the story.

The second branch of the overdetermined relationship that antis posit between fiction and the real desires of readers and writers runs through the construction that people who ship are "shippers." Under this framework, to read or write something is not only advocacy but an identity. Enjoying stories about a particular kind of sex is not only what you do but who you are: "Antis, in my understanding of the position that they profess, would argue that if we do happen to have fucked up fantasies, then we should keep them out of the public view, and we're probably also fucked up people for having them in the first place."[27] Seeing sexuality as a fundamental, immutable truth of the self has some unintended consequences. As Shannon Weber notes, this is "an always already defensive position that argues not for sexual agency and freedom, but an acceptance of same-sex desire only inasmuch as it cannot be cured away into reformed heterosexuality."[28] That is, while seeing sexuality as innate and fixed has undoubtedly provided grounding for lesbian and gay civil rights advocacy that leverages the Equal Protection Clause of the Fourteenth Amendment,[29] it also has reinforced the notion that if homosexuality were a choice it would be wrong (because it is only *not* wrong because it is not a choice) and/or that no one would ever choose to be gay (because homosexuality is an awful thing). This is the implication of arguing that people should not be discriminated against because they cannot help it (if they could help it, discrimination would be legitimate). These are the logical entailments of constructing sexuality as an immutable essence, rather than arguing that sexual acts should not be grounds for discrimination.

It might seem hyperbolic to equate fan fiction preferences to sexual orientation, but only under such a framework does it makes sense to connect unsavory fiction to accusations of offline crime. Kristina Busse argues that in the contemporary moment, "authors have returned to the forefront of interpreting texts not via interpretive privilege or singular access to the meaning of their writing but via their identity and how that identity affects reading and writing practices."[30] That is, the author matters to interpreting a story not because a text is "a line of words releasing a single 'theological' meaning (the 'message' of the Author-God)," the model Roland Barthes famously declared to be over in "The Death of the Author,"[31] but because authors are understood to write from their personal identity. We see such arguments explicitly from fans who contend that "'problematic' fiction is a normal way [to] cope or grow" for "people with sexual trauma and rape/abuse survivors." This is an argument that otherwise unacceptable stories become acceptable when they reflect the truth of their writer.

I want to also run this argument the other direction: unacceptable stories, too, are seen to reflect the truth of their writer. As one anti argues, "Anyway, to reiterate: the terms anti and anti-anti were literally coined by pedophiles seeking to create a smokescreen by getting y'all to fight about 'problematic ships' and it worked." This reductio ad pedophilium is an incredibly consistent move among antis. If troubling, controversial, or even just personally distasteful subject matter is raised, the conversation always seems to slide to children having sex—among specific reasons given for being opposed to a ship or work of fiction in my sample, 54 percent are about sex involving minors. Among mentions of sex as a reason for opposition, a full two-thirds mention sex involving minors. In part, this is the case because, as Gayle S. Rubin notes, "For a century, no tactic for stirring up erotic hysteria has been as reliable as the appeal to protect children."[32] This could be an instance in which the concern about children is what gets an anti fired up enough to take action against distasteful stories. Alternatively, antis may (as is sometimes claimed) cynically exploit the near-universal drive to protect children as a cultural lever.

Moreover, the anti perspective on sexuality in fan fiction also relies on what Rubin calls "sex negativity"; as she notes, "Western cultures generally consider sex to be a dangerous, destructive, negative force." In particular, there is a sense that sex is incredibly more dangerous than other things (like violence or racism), which she calls "the fallacy of misplaced scale." Rubin further notes that American culture "always treats sex with suspicion. It construes and judges almost any sexual practice in terms of its worst possible expression." It is under this logic that stories that freely engage sexuality must always and inevitably end in pedophilia or rape, representing what Rubin calls "a domino theory of sexual peril. The line appears between sexual order and chaos. It expresses the fear that if anything is permitted to cross this erotic DMZ, the barrier against scary sex will crumble and something unspeakable will skitter across."[33]

If writing is advocacy, and being a shipper is a (sexual) identity, we arrive at the model that troubling sexual content is endorsed by its readers and writers. There is no notion that difficult topics can be handled either carelessly or carefully. One tweeter defines antis as "short for 'anti-shipper' and it basically means they're against pedophiliac, toxic, and incestous ships that sexualize minors or unhealthy relationships." This is one of the longer aggregations of impermissible types of fiction, and the slippage from more standard and specific targets like pedophilia and incest to nebulous ones like "toxic" and "unhealthy" is revealing. Even if we bracket the question of who decides what is toxic and/or unhealthy, these categories are fundamentally unlike pedophilia and incest. Instead, the way this comment treats toxicity and unhealthiness as interchangeable with sex crimes reveals the organizing principle to be "bad sex" or a "bad relationship," and particularly these are interchangeably bad. Moreover, the fact that the base format is "a toxic ship," as an essence, ties back to identitarian models of sexuality. In this framework, what is depicted in the story is not an action, but a fundamental characteristic of the ship. That is, this is "a rape ship" and not "a story in which there is rape."

This is the logic under which another commenter announces in the context of the *Avatar: The Last Airbender* (Nickelodeon, 2005–2008) fandom that "i'm no longer supporting ships that are fire nation person/anyone they colonized bc[because] it's anti-indigenous."[34] Plenty of relationships between colonizer and colonized have existed—most of them coercive—but the decision to flatly refuse to engage rather than call for the power dynamic to be addressed disregards the *how* (an action) in favor of the *what* (an essence). The way that this critique of relationships between Fire Nation characters and colonized people is tied into not "supporting ships" again shows slippage from enjoyment to advocacy. The framework for sexuality within anti culture tends to default to identitarian models as the determinant of morality rather than considering how power dynamics are or are not addressed in the story.

In these arguments, reading or writing a romantic or sexual relationship that raises questions of unequal power is seen as inevitably supporting the abuse of that power. This view of sex as inevitably dangerous is quite conservative, and so it may seem strange to find it couched in social-justice language. However, there is a precedent: the Feminist Sex Wars of the 1980s that the heading of this section riffs on. This period of contestation within feminism had factions both for and against pornography.[35] Similarly, BDSM enthusiasts opposed those who contended that it is always abuse.[36] Perhaps most importantly for the Fandom Anti Wars, there were some participants in the Feminist Sex Wars who argued that heterosexuality is always and inevitably rape because gender inequality makes it impossible for women to meaningfully consent: Catharine A. MacKinnon contended that "if sexuality is relational, specifically if it is a power relation of gender, consent is a communication under conditions of inequality,"[37] such that there was a real question "whether consent is a meaningful concept."[38]

These decades-old arguments may have been incorporated in fandom because they have become prominent in the contemporary culture wars. In particular, similar positions are taken in anti-trans rhetoric that argues that trans women are inherently violent, and particularly sexually violent, because they were born with penises. This similarity is not lost on at least some fans. One contended that "they actually use the term 'terflings' because there's links between terf rhetoric and anti rhetoric," referencing so-called trans-exclusionary radical feminists

(TERFs). Another said, "Every time some antishipper/anti fujo person gets exposed as a radfem/terf/massive hypocrite, it feels like unmasking a fucking Scooby Doo villain. Predictable and disappointing after about the 5th one."[39] There is continuity between other absolutist approaches to sexuality and that of antis.

Because of this absolutism, rather than calling for authors to be thoughtful in how they engage with underage characters, sexual assault, or other potentially troubling content, we get a complete rejection of any engagement. This is the case because troublesome sex is not seen as something a story does, but something a ship, in its essence, *is*. Ultimately, only "good" sex is allowed, and broadly, antis seem to identify permissible sexuality in ways reminiscent of Rubin's "charmed circle": "Good, Normal, Natural, Blessed Sexuality" is "heterosexual, married, monogamous, procreative, noncommercial, in pairs, in a relationship, same generation, in private, no pornography, bodies only, vanilla."[40] Under this belief system, "bad" sex should not be in fan fiction at all.

Antis' arguments thus rest on two (not entirely conscious) premises: shipping as advocacy and shipping as identity. Both flatten stories' content into deeply held positions of readers and writers. If sexuality is something you are and not something you do—and particularly, something you do in a context where there are no pure choices—then the author of a story that includes sexual assault must think rape is okay. For antis, this is true whether that story luxuriates erotically in the crime or is a tale of survivorship. At a fundamental level, the argument goes, the nature of the fan fiction is the nature of the author—if you write it, you endorse it and maybe (want to) do it offline. Ultimately, what antis show is what happens when people with a moral investment correctly identify a troubling power dynamic, but draw an absolutist conclusion about it.

Fan Fiction Wants to Be Free: Free Speech Absolutism Strikes Back

The anti-antis' or pro-shippers' argument, on the other hand, emphasizes, first, that the content of stories is fictional, and no one is hurt by it existing. Moreover, they argue, impeding enjoyment of fan fiction harms them as writers and/or readers. This construction valorizes individual pleasure in stories and emphasizes individual responsibility for one's own harm over any responsibility to others who may be harmed by a story.

Fundamentally, anti-antis reject drawing direct relationships between fan fiction and reality. This body of discourse is characterized by variations of "it's not real," as in one tweet contending, "Its fiction and not real. Go try to report Game of Thrones for existing!" While certainly *Game of Thrones* (HBO, 2011–2019) faced backlash for what many saw as gratuitous sexual violence, this commenter is correct that people did not respond by trying to remove it from existence, unlike works of fan fiction opposed by antis. This position tracks with the perspectives of reactionary movements like #Comicsgate (chapter 1) and #VoxAdpocalypse (chapter 6) that, when a media text is critiqued as exclusionary, describe critics as overly sensitive, confused about the distinction between fantasy and reality, or both. Anti-antis emphasize the difference between fiction and reality; often, this distinction is premised on the idea that the depiction of a crime is not itself a crime. Notably, as Lothian points out, "It seems to be a given within some of the most vociferous anti arguments that we can make universalizing claims about morality, desire, and harm in which context is irrelevant—which then elicits equally broad counterarguments that risk dismissing the question of harm altogether."[41] As one commenter notes, "i think the stupidest thing about antis is we literally need to tell them 'fiction isn't reality' as if that's not the literal fuckin definition of fiction." Related to the argument that fiction is not reality, anti-antis point out that characters are not people and therefore no one is harmed by *any* event depicted: "It would be if they were real people. But they're fictional characters. They are fake." Importantly, this argument implicitly agrees that, were the depicted acts actually happening, they would be bad.

The anti-anti position contends that anything appearing in stories is just ideas, as in one tweeter's comment that "fiction is an entirely safe environment to explore & deal with difficult topics." Moreover, anti-antis reject the simplistic media-effects arguments they ascribe to their opponents, as when one said, "You know I just realized ive never once seen any anti post actual evidence that enjoying fiction a certain way leads to crimes against children or any of that." Another tweeter contends that the existence of the anti argument disproves its premise: "If fiction could force you to believe something you don't already believe, we'd have a whole lot of people who are actively trying to censor fandom taking sweeping anti-censorship stances because their freshman english teacher made them read Fahrenheit 451." If *Fahrenheit 451* cannot automatically cause anticensorship beliefs, this argument goes, stories about sexual violence won't cause *that* either. As Rubin notes, "Anti-porn propaganda often imagines that sexism originates within the commercial sex industry and subsequently infects the rest of society. This is sociologically nonsensical."[42] That is, social attitudes and beliefs are ontologically prior to and shape both the people who take action and what makes sense to those people to do. Identifying fan works as the cause of sexual violence is equally sociologically nonsensical.

Moreover, anti-antis argue, while no one is hurt by controversial fiction, contesting such fiction *can* hurt people. At its most basic, this is an argument that harassment in the name of stopping harmful fiction harms real people. First, such comments draw a distinction between critique and harassment. One anti-anti argues, "Having dissenting opinions is fine, not liking tropes/ships/content is FINE. Those have never been bad to voice, to have lengthy thinkpieces about the negatives IS FINE. But the Antis/Fanpol[ice] have twisted that into meaning dogpiling/bullying/doxxing creators/staff/fellow fans." The opinion is FINE, but the behavior undertaken as a result of it is not. In particular, antis are seen as engaging in harassment illegitimately. As one commenter ventriloquizes, "Antis be like 'I bully and abuse people because i care so very deeply about the fictional rights and fictional feelings of these fictional characters, who are fictional.'" The repetition of "fictional" here emphasizes how misplaced the defense of the characters is, and particularly when it comes at the expense of "bullying and abusing" real people. Similarly, another commenter asks, "Hmm, and which side of the argument was it that staged a mass harassment campaign at a 17 year old cuz they said not to harass ppl over ships again . . . oh yeah, the anti-problematic fiction crowd!" This stresses the disproportionate reaction compared to the reasonable suggestion that precipitated it. The second version of the argument is a contention that fictional people are not helped, but a real person is hurt. This tends to involve explicit comparison, as in "as always antis care more ab[ou]t fictional characters['] rights than. real people" or "harassing people over a fucking FICTIONAL NOT REAL ship but hey, bullying irl [in real life] is okay actually uh."

While this behavior may be the inevitable result of the anti tendency to see fiction as an expression of inner criminality discussed above, it is certainly contested by anti-antis.

Another facet of the argument that disputing controversial fiction hurts real people is less straightforward, ultimately arguing that by critiquing the fic, the anti impedes the enjoyment of fan fiction readers or writers, which harms them. One anti-anti reassures another, "You go ahead and enjoy whatever makes you happy and never mind what the antis or snooty little crybabies think. they're dumb and a waste of energy, trust me. your fav[orite] characters are yours, don't waste your feelings on moral purity. fiction is meant to be enjoyed, it's a gift." This is a focus on the joy of fiction and an explicit rejection of consideration of the antis' perspective; it is also conveyed in terms reminiscent of advice to deal with schoolyard bullies in a way that delegitimizes the opponent. Much like the argument that the reaction to troubling fiction is illegitimate because it is disproportionate, one sarcastic post points out that the concerns are often so hyperbolic that they are easily parodied: "How dare people sexualize fictional characters! Even worse since they were once teens! Doesn't matter that they're cannonically adults it's still a crime! *insert a series of the dramatic emojis antis like to use here* Seriously are we just not allowed to enjoy anything 'impure.'" The critique here is partially about rejecting antis' allegedly overblown sense of what is troubling, but it is also substantially about rejecting the denial of enjoyment and asserting a right to enjoy the "impure." Another tweeter is direct, announcing that following them means accepting that "I don't have to justify my kinks and ships to anyone. No, not even you."

A key position among anti-antis is that tagging stories enables readers to consent to what is in them. This has been a traditional view in transformative-works-making fandom in general, where, as Busse argues, "warnings and content notes enable consent negotiations between readers and writers. Through these frameworks, writers offer readers the ability to affirmatively consent to read their stories and to expose themselves to the ideas and emotions the fan fiction may engender." This constructs a shared responsibility—of writers to label stories and ask for consent, and of readers to take heed of those warnings and make decisions accordingly. Particularly important for the Anti Wars is the aspect of taking responsibility for one's own experiences, in which, as Busse describes, "clicking through or scrolling down to the story is, in fact, an act of affirmative consent."[43]

This framework of tagging as enabling consent allows anti-antis to argue that their practices around troubling content are actually superior. As one tweeter argued, "Antis claim to care ab[ou]t 'abuse' in fiction yet never use trigger warnings when discussing because r[ea]lly they don't care ab[ou]t the real life implications that may have so they use it as a defense 4 their ship instead." That is, if antis cared about harm as they claim to, they would warn about these topics, and the fact that they don't proves that their concern is a smokescreen for ship preferences. Similarly, another anti-anti argues that "if anything, pro-shippers are the only ones actually out here trying to advocate for the fandom safety by encouraging tagging and wanting to have difficult discussions." Thus, the willingness to work through challenging topics, enabled by responsible tagging, is what is valued by anti-antis. It is precisely *through* tagging that troubling content becomes possible in such communities: "Mandating that potentially harmful fic be appropriately labeled (or explicitly marked as unlabeled) allows AO3 to offer readers a way to avoid the harm such fic can cause while maintaining its commitment to full freedom of sexual and other expression."[44] However, as Busse notes, even within the model of tags and warnings as consent, "Fans debate not only when and how to apply these warnings but also whether some of these stories should even exist. Rape/noncon [nonconsensual], dubcon (dubious sexual consent, including drug use, external forces, and retroactive consent), underage sex, and extreme violence tend to be the warnings that many communities agree on and require."[45] Importantly, these are the exact issues that antis say should never appear in fan fiction, indicating a shared set of norms on some level even as there is dispute over whether a model of consenting to read these topics is legitimate.

However, valorizing individual pleasure in stories and highlighting individual responsibility for one's own harm demonstrates that this is a model that emphasizes the individual right to pleasure in a story over responsibility to others who may be harmed by that story. The emphasis on the right of fan fiction writers and readers to take pleasure in stories becomes clearer still from the fact that it implicitly includes a right to avoid unpleasantness. That is, anti-antis assert not only a right to enjoy the thing but a right to enjoy enjoying it—to not have to feel bad about their enjoyment. Thus, one anti-anti chides, "Antis, especially those who go out of their way to make ppl feel bad: if you really, TRULY cared about other people and not just your fictional favorites, you wouldn't be acting the way you are." This carries shades of "you are hurting real people in the name of fiction," as discussed above, but the formation constructing the problem as "making people feel bad" is telling. It is not doxing, threats, or dogpiling that are at issue: it is unpleasantness and possibly guilt (tripping).[46] Framing anti practices as a drive to make people feel bad—as opposed to seeing antis as disputing the premise that sexual violence should generate pleasure in the first place, which is how they would describe their position—is a negative-freedom argument. It seeks freedom from being acted upon. This is consistent with what Mary Anne Franks describes as "the civil liberties approach to constitutional rights," which "emphasizes individual rights and the need to protect them"; by contrast, "the civil rights approach emphasizes group rights and the need to ensure their equal protection."[47] Seeing the anti-anti position as in the orbit of civil libertarianism (transposed outside the realm of government) explains much about the tendency to center the individual's wants and pleasure over any other consideration. From the anti perspective, of course, their actions are not about making anyone feel bad, but the presence or absence of pleasure drives the anti-anti conversation.

It is from this civil liberties perspective that criticizing particular types of fan fiction is seen as about freedom of speech or expression. Anti-antis sometimes describe themselves as "PEAR (Pro Expression, Anti Repression)." From this position, anti-antis frame disallowing (or even contesting) such stories as repression of expression—censorship. As one tweeter complains, antis insist that "if you dare question someone's bullying anti-shipper behavior and their *actual statements rooting for fics to be deleted and censored* yoU aRe a bUlLy." In addition to accusations of bad behavior, which are ultimately more or less reciprocal between the camps, this comment describes a key point of contention: it is not just that antis are critical of stories they disagree with (even aggressively so) but that they think such stories should be forbidden and those that already exist should be deleted. Anti-antis perceive this prohibition and deletion as censorship, and reject it, instead proposing a distinction between having or expressing personal distaste for a given story and forbidding it from being posted: "i'm all for blocking content that squicks you, but 'it upsets me/triggers me' and 'i don't think it should even exist in FICTION' are vastly different takes lol."[48] Thus, this post (and many like it) does not say antis cannot personally object, but does argue that it is illegitimate to impose that personal objection as a universal rule.

To frame restrictions on fan fiction as censorship rather than something like social media content moderation is akin to the understanding of censorship often seen from (right-wing) free speech absolutists. In such ways, anti-antis participate in what Franks calls First Amendment fundamentalism, an approach to freedom of speech—championed by organizations like the American Civil Liberties Union—that disregards structural inequality in favor of positing a marketplace of ideas where all speech must be equally protected and allowed to compete—even, she points out, speech that chills other speech. As Lothian and I note, this has some real limitations, as "'maximal inclusivity' already operates to implicitly exclude when it is not accompanied by a commitment to minimal harm."[49] Anti-antis tend to take an absolutist position against any constraint. As one tweeter argues, "Being proship means /zero/ ship policing. I'm not a fan of underage/adult or incest, but I'm gonna defend others' right to ship it without being harassed for it. If you're only pro-ships you personally find acceptable, then congrats you're an anti." This is an argument that there is only a binary—either anything goes or nothing is safe.

One anti is scathing about "people who argue [. . .] that trying to regulate what ppl post is censorship," and they are not wrong that regulation and censorship are distinct things anti-antis tend to conflate. This is the slippery slope argument that drives First Amendment fundamentalism, which "warns that even the most modest regulation of any speech rights will lead to mass censorship and that the devastating effects of abusive speech must be tolerated to protect freedom of speech for all."[50] Thus, while (as I will discuss in the next section) anti-antis have a sense of themselves as progressive, just as antis do, the free speech fundamentalism gives them some bedfellows they would likely find troubling: "Ever-expanding definitions of what counts as 'free speech' give constitutional cover to practices that disproportionately harm women and minorities, while attempts to ensure women [sic] and minorities' equal exercise of freedom of expression is labeled 'censorship.'"[51] Taking this overlap of anti-anti absolutism and free speech fundamentalism seriously demonstrates the concerning implications of refusing to consider the harms that one's pleasure in fiction might do. It also encourages us to consider how the right to speech is often understood as a right to speaking without discomfort, or even a right to pleasure in speech, a position that deserves reflection and interrogation.

Acceptability's Politics: Sexuality over Race

Ultimately, both the moral absolutist approach (which treats all fiction as reflecting its writers' and readers' real desires) and free speech fundamentalism (which refuses any concern for the harms that fiction might do) are troubling if subjected to scrutiny. Additionally, they share some fundamental premises. The two camps have a common vocabulary of progressivism that identifies bigotry such as racism as unacceptable, yet overall it is uncommon for racism to even be mentioned. When racism does appear, it tends to be glossed over rather than considered in a sustained way. The framing of the Anti Wars as about sexuality thus acts to foreclose serious conversation about the harms of stereotyped and dehumanizing representations of people of color. As Sneha Kumar argues, much of the problem "comes from fandom thinking that it's this inherently liberatory and utopian space that cannot possibly be embedded in systems of power even as it replicates those very systems."[52]

First, both sides use interrelated vocabulary of progressivism. One manifestation of these shared values is remarkably similar lists of villains that show up in both sides' Do Not Interact (DNI) labels; the DNI is an increasingly common social media practice, often found in a user profile or pinned post, as in "please DNI if you are a pro shipper/anti anti." One anti proclaims distaste for "a problematic shipper (i.e, g//m//ly, incest, forced ship or ANY pedo[phile] ship) MAP Ally, or MAP [Minor Attracted Person], pedosexual, PEAR (Pro-expression anti-repression, or, a cover up for MAPS) TERFs Racist Or just a hater," while an anti-anti announces, "I've new followers so a few things: I highly dislike anti shippers, antis in general, terfs, racists." This aggregation of disapproved categories is part of identifying those who are opposed to the poster's position in the Anti Wars with more widely condemned groups. One

anti-anti argues that there is "overlap of fantis [fan-antis] and purity police and christian right programming." Another is critical of an anti's
attempt "to change the meaning of anti shipper to mean 'anti bigo[t]ry.'"
In such ways, categories that progressives disapprove of, from the Christian Right to bigots such as TERFS and racists, are mapped onto the opposition, arguing for its bad status by analogy.

Perhaps the most important thing these two arguments have in common is that they are—if not precisely worried about the wrong things—
worried about a suspiciously narrow subset of things. Both antis and
anti-antis frequently use the term "problematic" about one another,
but what, specifically, do they find to be a problem? If the Anti Wars
are a fight about what kind of fiction is acceptable, we should interrogate the politics of that acceptability. What are the issues the combatants foreground (or don't)? I contend that the argument's fixation on
the most extreme kinds of sex functions to secure the unproblematic
status of one set of things by locating trouble elsewhere. That is, focusing
on appropriate sexuality as the only terrain for argument has the effect
of marginalizing concerns about racism in fandom. But the absence of
"problematic" sex does not mean a story cannot still participate in domination and discursive violence.

On some level, constructing sexuality as the most central issue in fan
fiction—which antis and anti-antis alike agree on—might seem unsurprising given the widespread sense that fan fiction is an inherently or
even primarily sexual practice. However, as anti-antis note, it takes some
"mental gymnastics" to focus so narrowly on sex. Multiple posters point
out that nonsexual violence is not subject to the same scrutiny, critiquing the contradictory assumption that "watching graphic depictions of
cannibalism doesn't make anyone a cannibal but reading incest fanfiction will make people think incest is okay." Another contends that the
selective outrage is due to the fact that "most antis are US centric where
violence and war is extremely normalized, meanwhile sex is icky and
taboo," and it is likely that that is indeed a factor.

One particularly important issue that is rarely factored into fiction's
acceptability is racism, as "it is quite possible to be progressive in some
ways and nevertheless racist."[53] While it is uncommon for racism to even
be mentioned, at just 6 percent of tweets that listed a particular topic
or behavior antis take issue with, it is not for that reason unimportant.

Indeed, the near invisibility of race, given that the Anglophone world, at least, is structured by it, points to how the anti conversation is conditioned by unacknowledged whiteness. As I have argued elsewhere, "Whiteness is the unmarked category (marking others), the unexamined category (subjecting others to examination), and the norm (making others abnormal), and the cumulative effect is privilege (and disadvantage for others)." In addition to the effects of whiteness as the norm, "Because whiteness is unmarked, 'race' is often taken as a synonym for 'people of color,' and if people of color are who 'have' race, whiteness becomes race free, or, crucially, race neutral."[54] Moreover, to ignore race is to support the "racial status quo," which is also an implicitly white position that relies on benefiting from current racial systems.[55]

One sign of this tendency to deemphasize race is that when racism does appear in the anti conversation, it is treated as incidental rather than central. In such ways, "Media fandom's claims to feminist and queer politics share the limitations of other feminist and queer communities and movements dominated by white participants—they fail to incorporate an analysis of race."[56] Thus, anti-antis contend that arguments about racism are a false accusation, and particularly a smokescreen for an anti's true concerns about sex. As one anti-anti complains, "TW [trigger warning] anti-Black racism I think my biggest pet peeve is ppl who use the existence of racist tropes in fanworks as a vehicle to get to their REAL point: disliking the existence of incest & adult/minor ships. You're a lot more transparent than you think you are." This is a claim that these critics are not actually acting on the basis of opposition to racism in fan works, but rather disingenuously use the mention of racism to further an unrelated agenda about sexuality. Another commenter imagines a dialogue of a fan and an anti in which racism is mentioned in a similarly irrelevant way: "Fan: I don't mind them, but don't really ship them Anti: *cry yelling* You *bleep* racist and pedo Fan: *thinking* what?" This is an argument that simply by not liking a particular pairing, people will be illegitimately called pedophiles and racists, which are constructed as borderline interchangeable in antis' discussions. Such conversations demonstrate how "anti," when used by anti-antis, has a kinship to the term "social justice warrior" (SJW), typically used as "a pejorative within [reactionary] communities to describe individuals who they claim are overly invested in identity politics and political correctness."[57] That is, there is often an implication that antis' concern is insincere and trying to score points.

In the other camp, the same slippage between race and sexuality runs the opposite direction as an argument that troubling sexuality in stories is incompatible with antiracism. One anti claimed to be having "*war flashbacks to the mfer [motherfucker] who said antis can't be in support of BLM or say ACAB [All Cops Are Bastards] as if punks or black ppl are cool and supportive of their weird pedo[phile]/incest/abuse ships.*" The poster is implicitly making the (strange) assumption that all Black people and antipolice activists share their position on what kinds of sex happen in fan fiction. Ultimately, both sides are projecting their own morality onto a group with which they share some (but not all) beliefs. This is as true of the anti-anti arguing that hostile responses to fan fiction are incompatible with valuing Black lives and/or criticism of police as it is of the anti arguing that it is obvious neither group would support troubling sex. This argument is, "Black Lives Matter and All Cops Are Bastards are good views, so those who hold them must agree with me." It is also exactly the kind of instrumental or maybe even cynical use of these movements that the anti-anti discussed earlier was complaining about and that SJWs are often accused of. Sometimes even when there is direct engagement with racism, it is still strangely conflated with unrelated issues, as when one Black fan argues, "'Anti-antis' and 'pro shipper' fandom freaks who now wanna try to feign support for BLM when they were just calling black people speaking out against racism and pedophilia 'antis' and fandom polices [police] ARE COMPLETE JOKES your support means nothing to us." This poster demonstrates the tendency of all anti discourse to land on sexuality, because the poster drags pedophilia back in for no apparent reason. The only behavior that is relevant to whether anti-antis sincerely or legitimately support BLM is that they dismiss racism in fandom (and it is indeed a real problem, as I will discuss below).

Similarly to racism being unable to stand alone as a harm in its own right in many of these conversations, it is often used as just one example in a list of prejudices and negative behaviors, which is a tendency seen from both sides. One anti-anti argues that "most of us pro shippers are pro extensive trigger tagging systems, [. . .] and that includes racial bias, ableism, etc . . ." This evokes what Judith Butler calls "an embarrassed

'etc.' at the end of the list"; these are uses of "etc." that "strive to encompass a situation, but invariably fail to be complete."[58] Racism is thus apparently something people feel it is necessary to mention, but it is often
not engaged more deeply than a mention. Antis do the same thing, as in
one argument that "all fiction has effects on the reader so actually when
people include harmful racist, anti-trans or ableist stereotypes in their
fanfiction bc [because] they couldn't be bothered to do a google search
or talk to one person, they do harm." In these ways, many of the (already
few) moments when racism is discussed are not particularly about race
at all.

The way in which talking about race is treated as peripheral reflects the fact that the "normative" or "universal" or unmarked identity
in transformative-works fandom is implicitly a white one.[59] Both fandom itself and fan studies have begun to have serious and widespread
conversations about this, and in particular an upsurge was sparked by
what came to be known as RaceFail '09, which, Rukmini Pande notes,
"refers to a series of blog posts written by SF/F [science fiction/fantasy]
fans" in 2009 both in response to a particular author with a poor "record
of portraying people of color" who decided to give advice about "writing
the other" and about "the failings of the SF/F genre as a whole on the
issue of race."[60] There have been several subsequent upsurges in such
discussion; in particular, the data set for this chapter captures the one
that came in the wake of George Floyd's murder in 2020, which led to
widespread reckoning with racism, including in fandom.[61] However, despite this important and growing awareness, there is clearly still a great
deal of work to do.

Fans are also at times actively racist. As Stitch notes, "There are anti-
fans/shippers who do harass people of color, out and harass queer people, and mistreat survivors, and there are also proshippers or anti-antis
who do the same thing in defense of fandom," and at times the same
people will "support accounts defending white supremacist violence
like that committed by Kyle Rittenhouse."[62] This is a repeated pattern in
which "fan critics of color have been particularly subjected to racist silencing and harassment when they have spoken up in both physical and
online spaces."[63] At times, this occurs because "people view criticism of
open racism in fandom—including purposeful racist stereotypes, slurs,
and hate symbols in fan works on top of harassing celebrities or fans of

color—as antifandom, as inappropriate."⁶⁴ In such ways, there is both direct racism from fans and often intense resistance to recognizing this racism.

The few moments when racism is fully centered look quite different from the main body of the anti conversation. There is resistance to collapsing "antiracist" into "fandom anti" as well as critique of anti-antis for refusing to address racism (or worse). As one fan argues, "There's a big diff[erence] between arguing over fictional ships and pointing out discomfort over fic being potentially racist and often it gets brushed aside as 'anti' behavior which is . . . hmm." This tweeter thus agrees with the anti-anti view that arguing over fictional ships is not very important, but resists the ways actually important conversations about racism get collapsed into that and brushed aside. While the argument above about whether you can like certain kinds of sex in your fan fiction and also support Black Lives Matter is nonsensical, the hard-line argument refusing any relationship between fiction and reality and any responsibility to be thoughtful about representation raises different questions when considered around racism. One fan described the argument that "people cannot be 'anti/antis' and also support BLM because they've [anti-antis have] done nothing but attack black/brown people for being uncomfortable as well as claim fiction doesn't affect reality despite racial stereotypes proving otherwise." This is a contention that racial stereotypes in fan fiction should not be so easily dismissed and that those who do so cannot legitimately turn around and say they value Black people.

Indeed, at times defending fan fiction is accomplished by attacking Black fans. Another tweeter is critical of "'proshippers' who are being anti-Black on main and lying about POC fandom critics and saying they're pro-harassment." This criticism ultimately comes from the same place—if all critique of fan fiction is flattened into illegitimate harassment about a fake problem, the actual problem of racism becomes impossible to confront. This, too, is a tactic of the culture wars, where perspectives that the political Right disagrees with are actively constructed as outlandish. This became particularly clear in the 2021 campaign against critical race theory (which I will discuss further in chapter 7), as the initiator of the campaign announced, "[We] are steadily driving up negative perceptions. We will eventually turn it [critical race theory] toxic, as we put all of the various cultural insanities under that brand category"; he continued, "the goal is to have the public read something crazy in the newspaper and immediately think 'critical race theory.'"[65] This conflation of legitimate concerns with illegitimate or even ridiculous complaints—either deliberately to discredit the legitimate ones (as with CRT) or carelessly—is often effective, and is another place the Anti Wars replicate broader patterns of cultural contestation. In the Anti Wars, a story that mixes sex and slavery—either explicitly race based or metaphorically so—is disputed or defended only with respect to the sex. Asking hard questions about the slavery part and what it means to eroticize or even deal casually with such deep violence and trauma is actually suppressed by the framing around sex. Other interrogations of the ways people of color get eroticized in stereotypical and dehumanizing ways, such as "why all of these fandoms, across decades, write Black characters as uber tops,"[66] invoking the myth of hypersexual Black men, are similarly foreclosed by the structuring absence of race from the conversation. The argument is so consistently defined in this narrow way that "what does it mean to represent people this way?" or "is it ethical to do so?" are not intelligible questions.[67]

This is part of why choosing the civil liberties model of individual rights over the civil rights model of group protections matters—the right of the individual to enjoy a story is seen as outweighing the right of the group not to be stereotyped and devalued. As legal scholar Mari Matsuda notes, there are "competing values of liberty and equality at stake in the case of hate speech."[68] While certainly stories that treat the suffering of Haitians after the 2010 earthquake as a backdrop for two white men to find love and the tendency to ignore men of color as valid love interests even if you have to invent a white character more or less out of whole cloth do not rise to the level of hate speech if we define it as "true threats, incitement, defamation, obscenity, fighting words, or certain kinds of discriminatory expression,"[69] they do operate from a place of devaluing people of color, such that hate speech scholarship usefully helps us make sense of them.

One key argument in hate speech research that is illuminating for fan fiction is that the costs of inaction are unevenly distributed, borne not by society at large but by the targets. Matsuda calls this "a psychic tax imposed on those least able to pay."[70] Charles Lawrence III notes that in framing hate speech through free speech, "we ask Blacks and other

126 | THE ANTI WARS

subordinate groups to bear a burden for the good of society—to pay the price for the societal benefit of creating more room for speech. And we assign this burden to them without seeking their advice or consent. This amounts to white domination, pure and simple."[71] That is, if we protect and defend the devaluation of Black people and other people of color because of freedom of speech, we are implicitly arguing that their suffering is a cost we, white people, are willing to pay. Positioning racism in fan fiction as part of the Anti Wars—as a debate about taste, appropriateness, or free speech, and not about discursive violence—produces a similar nonconsensual burden. This is what is obscured by focusing narrowly on free speech and troubling sex. The two camps talk past each other, to be sure, but by and large this conversation is not even on the table. The collapsing of the entire conversation into sexuality—which, as I have noted, absolutely comes from both sides—makes racism much harder to address.

Conclusion

On one level, the combatants in the Anti Wars are wildly different. Antis contend that the content of fan fiction constitutes advocacy, and being a shipper is a (sexual) identity, such that troubling sexual content is always and inevitably endorsed by its readers and writers. The existence of a romantic or sexual relationship that raises questions of unequal power is therefore seen as supporting the abuse of that power. Anti-antis, by contrast, emphasize individual pleasure in stories, individual responsibility for one's own harm, and an absolutist free speech model where any call to consider the harms of fiction is censorship. Ultimately, both camps, though rooted in an apparently shared sense of social justice, largely make the wrong argument. Fixation on the most extreme kinds of sex serves to construct the problem as related to sexuality, thereby defining other problems, like racism, as irrelevant. What the fandom Anti Wars demonstrate particularly clearly is how contemporary cultural battles tend to be insufficiently intersectional, even among self-identified progressives who might be expected to know better, revealing that "this presumption of progressiveness has suppressed attention to structural inequality within fandom, particularly racism."[72] Sexuality does not exist in a vacuum. Neither does (white, middle-class women's) speech. Taking too simplistic a view, ignoring the other systems of power that are involved, leads these groups—who on many points fundamentally agree—to talk past each other, but also to miss a very significant structure conditioning the practices they are fighting about.

6

"I Just Joined the #MugClub!"

Fan Consumer Activism meets the Culture Wars

In June 2019, journalist Carlos Maza posted a since-deleted Twitter thread detailing harassment he had received from YouTube commentator Steven Crowder, which had been going on for years by this point.[1] Crowder attacked Maza on the basis of his race—calling him a "gay Mexican" (Maza's parents immigrated from Cuba) and an "anchor baby"—as well as his sexuality—through calling him a "lispy queer" as well as making "an offensive pantomime of Maza's voice in which Crowder pretended to eat chips and exclaimed 'just can't eat one, like dicks.'"[2] As a result of Crowder's targeting, Maza said, he regularly received a "'wall of homophobic/racist abuse on Instagram and Twitter,' as well as waves of taunting texts to his cell phone number and on one occasion, a phone call."[3] Maza posted his thread not as a complaint to Crowder himself but directed toward YouTube,[4] arguing that "Crowder had broken YouTube's Terms of Service."[5]

Initially, YouTube determined that the videos were within its policies, saying in a blog post that "a thorough review over the weekend found that individually, the flagged videos did not violate our Community Guidelines."[6] However, the platform subsequently "made the decision to suspend monetization. In order to be considered for reinstatement, all relevant issues with the channel need to be addressed, including any videos that violate our policies, as well as things like offensive merchandise."[7] The "offensive merchandise" in question was a "Socialism is for F*gs" t-shirt for sale on Crowder's website, which was linked from his YouTube channel.[8] In their policy announcement, YouTube said that "in the case of hate speech, we are strengthening enforcement of our existing YouTube Partner Program policies. Channels that repeatedly brush up against our hate speech policies will be suspended from the YouTube Partner program, meaning they can't run ads on their channel or use other monetization features."[9] This policy defined hate speech as "videos alleging that a group is superior in order to justify discrimination, segregation or exclusion based on qualities like age, gender, race, caste, religion, sexual orientation or veteran status."[10] YouTube's extension of its response to Crowder's harassment to all channels with repeated near-violations of their hate speech policies meant that "several 'far-right influencers' have lost the ability to earn ad revenue on their videos."[11] However, in line with YouTube's history of what I have elsewhere called "governance-washing," meaning "producing the appearance of governance without substantive action,"[12] this was a blunt instrument and not a calibrated act of platform governance; the policy change "also impacted history-based channels that discuss white supremacy and nazism [*sic*] in an educational context."[13]

In response to the demonetization, Crowder tweeted a since-deleted call to action under the hashtag #VoxAdpocalypse, saying, "We have details in incoming video, but YouTube and Vox have launched an all out WAR on ALL independent creators. Thousands of channels under review! PLEASE TWEET us if you've been demonetized under the new #VoxAdpocalypse guidelines!" Crowder's tweet connected this tightened enforcement on accounts that just barely skirted hate speech to the "Adpocalypse," an incident from 2017. Stuart Cunningham and David Craig describe Adpocalypse as "a rolling series of crises," explaining that "investigating journalists revealed that multinational and national brand advertising was appearing programmatically alongside YouTube videos featuring terrorist organizations, antisemitic clips discussing a 'Jewish World Order,' and Swedish neo-Nazi groups." After this news broke, more than 250 large advertisers removed their YouTube ads, and the company took steps to "crack down immediately on this flagrant failure of programmatic advertising to maintain baseline community standards."[14] This resulted in tighter restrictions on what content was monetizable, and many content creators had videos demonetized for not meeting these criteria. Crowder's supporters took up the rallying cry, and #VoxAdpocalypse ultimately produced nearly 130,000 tweets between June 5 and June 30, 2019.

This incident is interesting for this book in part because it *does not* immediately seem like a fandom issue. However, both the history that led up to #VoxAdpocalypse and the hashtag itself were actually deeply bound up in fandom. First, as Maza pointed out, the people who had been harassing him were fans of Crowder's content: "Audiences don't need to be explicitly asked to harass a target to become abusive. [. . .] If they see a major YouTuber doing it, they get the message that that kind of abuse is acceptable. [. . .] My issue isn't that Crowder is asking his followers to harass me. It's that he's harassing me, with homophobic and racist language, in front of millions of loyal listeners, thanks to an audience that YouTube helped him find and build."[15]

Corresponding to Maza's identification of his harassers as Crowder fans, the #VoxAdpocalypse hashtag featured numerous instances of announcing that users were fans. Many such tweeters also announced that they intended to join Crowder's subscription Mug Club, which—according to the homepage for his *Louder with Crowder* show—allows them to "get exclusive content for Mug Club members ONLY!" as well as "exclusive access to the daily show." Mug Club bills itself as "the only place for all of Crowder uncensored and on demand." It also invites site visitors to "get conservatism's premium drinking vessel" (the Crowder mug), and at the time I looked, the site offered "Use code JAN6 to get $20 off!"—both of which make its political commitments clear.[16] #VoxAdpocalypse is clearly a moment in the culture wars, but the key move in this section of the book is bringing fandom to bear as an explanatory framework in places whose fannish valences might otherwise be overlooked. Taking this approach calls for thinking about political consumption not merely as instrumental but as deeply emotional and potentially fannish, putting it into conversation with things like "save our show" campaigns and the construction of belonging through public consumption.

This analysis begins from the complete set of all 129,455 tweets from this public outcry, collected in May 2020 via the Twitter API to study #VoxAdpocalypse in general.[17] From this data set, I extracted the tweets that mentioned the term "fan," then noticed the prevalence of mentions of "Mug Club" in this corpus and collected the tweets containing "mug" as well, combining the results from the two search terms in a single corpus. I then read through this body of tweets for common themes. I also conducted a word-frequency analysis in Orange data mining software for both the text of the tweets and the "Bio" field for the 454 unique tweeters in order to gain a broad overview of common terms in both user self-descriptions and tweets.[18]

In examining joining Mug Club as a fan response to Crowder's demonetization, I begin from the recognition that fandom is tightly interconnected with consumption. As Garry Crawford points out, "The activities of fans and fan cultures are principally constructed around consumer activities."[19] More intensively, both Matt Hills and Cornel Sandvoss define being a fan specifically *as* consistent, emotionally invested consumption of the object of fandom.[20] In particular, Mug Club membership is what I have elsewhere called "supraconsumption," which describes "licensed or franchised extensions of an object of fandom" that fans can consume "independently of whether or how they consume the 'main' or 'real' object of fandom."[21] That is, fans could join Mug Club or buy a Crowder t-shirt even if they did not regularly watch his show or had not done so previously. To make sense of this incident through the intersection of fandom and consumption, it is also important to recognize how Crowder can be understood as a brand. As Khadijah Costley White argues, "A brand functions as a personality for products and represents core values and a pleasurable emotional and familial connection that meets a consumer's social, psychological, and emotional needs, desires, and satisfaction."[22] Brands and fandoms serve many of the same affective purposes, and branding can be a particularly productive lens through which to focus on consumptive aspects of fandoms.

As a brand and as an object of fandom, then, Crowder is a site of connection and expression of values for his supporters. This connective role also explains why fandoms often feature specifically public consumption.[23] As Henry Jenkins notes, "No longer a matter of individual choices and preferences, consumption becomes a topic of public discussion and collective deliberation" in fandoms,[24] and this is indeed what we see in #VoxAdpocalypse. Moreover, beyond just publicly consuming, fans are known specifically for consumer activism. Jenkins identifies Internet interaction—like #VoxAdpocalypse as a collective outcry—as key to fandom becoming "much more effective as a platform for consumer activism."[25] Through such activism, "the consumption community may well hold the corporations accountable for what they do in the name of those brands and for their responsiveness (or lack thereof) to consumer demands."[26] Jenkins also runs the relationship the other way, from fandom to activism: "Our political struggles often take place through languages and contexts heavily shaped by commercial culture, making fan and consumer activism central to contemporary social movements."[27] That is, fandom can be a springboard toward broader issues, as we will see happens with Crowder's fans moving from supporting him to conservatism in general.

In thinking through the response to Crowder's demonetization as activist consumption, I turn to research on "political consumerism, which includes the related acts of boycotting (punishing businesses for unfavorable behavior) and buycotting (supporting businesses that exhibit desirable behavior)."[28] Specifically, the fan response of joining Mug Club can be understood as a buycott of Crowder (and to a limited extent there was also a boycott of YouTube). However, I also depart from the tendency of this research to assume that political consumerism is in the service of progressive causes like "social and environmental concerns" or "freedom, justice, and equality."[29] There is in fact nothing about consuming politically that carries a particular political ideology, as the case of right-wing supporters rallying around Crowder (and brands like Goya,[30] Black Rifle Coffee,[31] and more) shows. If political consumption is typically understood by its practitioners as a moral act,[32] these fans, too, think of what they are doing as deeply moral. Ultimately, #VoxAdpocalypse is characterized by public performances of financial support for a perceived like-minded community, at the same time that it is deeply enmeshed in contemporary culture-wars discourses and a concept of free speech as a right to get paid. At a fundamental level, the incident turns on questions of identity, in particular tweeters' sense of themselves as victims of marginalized groups they both mock and see as extraordinarily powerful, and in this way it helps us see one key feature of ugly fandom: it understands its in-group to be a target rather than a wielder of sociocultural power. The construction of group identity around a media object, consolidated through consumption, makes fandom a useful interpretive lens for #VoxAdpocalypse.

Voting with the Wallet: The Public Performance of Financial Support

The most common feature of tweets in the corpus is announcing the user's support of Crowder or of the campaign to resist YouTube's content-moderation decision more broadly. This support comes significantly through subscribing to Crowder's Mug Club, which was frequent enough in the "fan" tweets to catch my eye and become an additional search term. This approach to support is visible at scale, with "joined" appearing in 21 percent of all tweets in the corpus (fourth most common word), "join" in 13 percent (sixth most common), and "joining" in 5 percent (twenty-first); this is in addition to "member" in 8 percent of tweets (eleventh), for a total of 47 percent that discuss one's intention to join Mug Club or announce that one already did. As part of this emphasis on Mug Club, there were numerous tweets of screenshots of purchase confirmations or, for those whose mug had arrived, the mug itself. One tweeter colorfully referred to such images as "proof of purchase snitches." These public declarations function both as information about the self—which these tweeters clearly see as positive—and to build connections and community among those who have participated by creating networked awareness of other like-minded people, using support of Crowder as the point of connection.

That tweeters' behavior is closely tied to backing Crowder or his views or his right to say offensive things (distinctions that, as I will discuss, are slippery) can be seen from the fact that "support" appears in 11 percent of the tweets (eighth most common word). A similar goal of assisting Crowder was shown by a user who tagged him to ask how best to go about it: "@scrowder apart from joining #MugClub is there any other way we are able to help or contribute to defending you guys?" Mug Club is thus clearly understood as a form of patronage. A sense that Crowder was just one piece of a much larger story was also common, as I will discuss further in later sections. As part of connecting Crowder to that larger story, tweeters articulated other figures and organizations that they supported with subscriptions: "Just subscribed to #MugClub/@scrowder/@TheBlazeTV and @realDailyWire. I love their content and it's time to monetarily support them during #VoxAdpocalypse." This tweet combines not only Crowder but BlazeTV, a streaming service founded by former Fox News commentator Glenn Beck—which bills itself as "News & Entertainment for People who Love America" and as having "the biggest names in conservative media. All in one place,"[33] and which is the primary host of Crowder's content—and the *Daily Wire*, a news site that describes itself as "meant to be something unique in the right-of-center media landscape."[34] The buycott sparked by Crowder's demonetization thus expanded out to what users saw as allied entities.

Notably, many of the tweets in the corpus (68 percent) tag Crowder's handle. Some of these are Twitter replies, which by default tag and embed the username being replied to (e.g., "@scrowder Joining #MugClub due to #VoxAdpocalypse"). However, some tweets use Crowder's handle to name him (e.g., "What is happening to @scrowder is egregious") and some directly address him (e.g., "We're with you, @scrowder!"). At a basic level, there are many, many tagged tweets that are versions of this chapter's title, as in "@scrowder Just joined #MugClub." Much as we saw in chapter 4 with fans tagging *The 100* showrunner Jason Rothenberg, some of the tags directly address Crowder. In tweets that address him, there is at times almost a parasocial relationship with him. One such tweeter said, "@scrowder I finally joined #MugCLub. I'm sorry it took so long." This implies a sense that tagging Crowder is speaking to him, that the tweet will be read, that this tweeter would be noticeable to Crowder as an individual, and that an explanation/apology for the delay in joining was needed. Given the scale of #VoxAdpocalypse (nearly 130,000 tweets), Crowder's number of followers (1.9 million as of October 2022, and web metrics site Social Blade suggests that in 2019 it was well over 1.5 million),[35] and the fact that Crowder has a Verified account, a tweet from a regular user was unlikely to gain his attention. This is the case because beginning in 2013, Verified accounts could adjust the settings on their Twitter mentions to either use an algorithmic spam filter or see only other Verified accounts;[36] someone with Crowder's reach is likely to use such filters as his default mode of engagement with Twitter to manage the volume of interaction, and is especially likely to do so during a large-scale hashtag event such as this one. Thus, the odds are that Crowder did not see (m)any of these direct-engagement tweets.

Nevertheless, such personal address was common from tweeters. This included not just talking to Crowder with a tag of his username but writing out his name, a seemingly more intimate approach. This is particularly acute in a tweet calling him by the nickname "Steve": "I just joined the #MugClub of @scrowder btw Steve i want my mug soon 😂." This tweet, too, suggests an expectation that Crowder will see and potentially respond to a tweet from a regular user, despite this actually being un-likely. Other tweeters self-identify as fans, and sometimes longtime fans: "Steven, I've been a fan since long before #neverdaily and almost joined #MugClub about a year ago. With this latest BS stunt from @YouTube and @voxdotcom , I've had enough. I'm now a member." While on one hand, these tags and personal appeals may arise from the ways taking collective action creates a sense of empowerment—like fans tweet-ing at a TV showrunner or network who are convinced they will be heard—on the other, their content seems to signal an idea of Crowder as approachable.

That is, despite being a media personality with many Twitter follow-ers and a lucrative career making online content, Crowder is not re-ally understood as like a celebrity but more like a regular user. This is consistent with research on YouTube microcelebrities, who, as multiple scholars have shown, operate on intimacy and a sense that they can be accessed through social media platforms.[37] This sense of intimacy and parasocial relationship with Crowder are some of the hallmarks of con-temporary social media–enabled fandom. Importantly, this perception of the hierarchy of Crowder and his audience as largely flat has a con-comitant effect of making Crowder seem less powerful than he is, which is important to the construction of him as a victim that runs throughout the tweets about this incident.

One aspect of publicly announcing one's Mug Club membership is a tendency to something like one-upmanship. Some tweeters announce that they were already a member and that, in order to expand their sup-port of Crowder in the face of his demonetization, they will provide additional monetary support. Indeed, "already" is the twenty-fourth most common word, appearing in 4 percent of tweets. At times, tweet-ers frame their monetary contribution through the idea of a "donation," emphasizing the way supporting Crowder is seen as a worthy cause: "I was already a member [of] #MugClub but #VoxAdpocalypse makes me want to donate more." In much the same way, others announce that they are forgoing the discount: "I decline your discount code, Steven. Keep doing what you do." Through approaches such as these, supporters make public displays of spending additional money, reproducing patterns of fan hierarchy centered around collections and owning more stuff that have been described in other fandoms.[38]

When a particular item is mentioned in the context of such purchase intentions, it is most commonly the "Socialism is for F*gs" shirt. In part, the frequent mentions of this item were due to the shirt having been specifically identified by YouTube as beyond the pale, but it also participates in broader patterns in which "the most consistent kind of licensed-good consumption constructed as normative for fans is clothing."[39] For example, one tweeter says, "@scrowder I don't normally buy merch, but seeing as I'm already a #LWC #MugClub member, I thought the best way to help support Crowder during this #VoxAdpocalypse would be to buy myself a #SocialismIsForFigs t-shirt and some other cool stuff from https://louderwithcrowdershop.com." Notably here, the poster not only announces the poster's own purchase but includes the link to encourage or facilitate additional purchases from those who see the tweet. The shirt in question is no longer available from Crowder, but judging by knockoffs that are still available on various online t-shirt sales platforms and a contemporary news article, it read "SOCIALISM IS FOR F*GS" alongside the iconic Che Guevara image "raising his arm in a pose that has generally been interpreted as a 'limp wrist.'"[40] The obvious conclusion is that the asterisk replaces an "A," but "Crowder has repeatedly declared that the shirt actually says 'SOCIALISM IS FOR FIGS,' apparently due to the fact that the asterisk in the word 'F*GS' is a tiny image of a fig leaf"[41]—despite the fact that "fag" is a type of person and "fig" is not, and particularly is a type of person conservatives tend to be hostile toward in a way corresponding to their hostility toward socialism, and Crowder had been targeting gay Latino man Carlos Maza for mockery over a long period of time, and "figs" is nonsensical in context. Crowder's fans consistently maintain this fig fiction, perhaps because, as I will discuss further later in the chapter, it gives them license to say "fig" and mean "fag"—and they do, with abandon. Overall, throughout this group of tweets, there is a commitment to publicly supporting Crowder monetarily in a way that exceeds the minimum of becoming a paid subscriber. His supporters thus participate in the norm that public, substantial consumption is important in fandom.

In addition to discussing their own spending, many tweeters advocate for others to join Mug Club. A typical example of this pattern reads, "Everyone should join #mugclub right now!" Sometimes, such suggestions involve a sense that joining Mug Club has broader implications, as in,

"There has never been a more important time to join #MugClub. Now that YouTube's #VoxAdpocalypse is running rampant on independent creators, they need your support via various other platforms. Mug Club is $30 off with promos code FREE SPEECH. Go join up now. You won't regret it." This tweet does several things. It links joining Mug Club to supporting "independent creators," a term (which Crowder also used) referring to those who make online content individually, outside the auspices of the mainstream media and corporate sponsorship—which is, at best, partially true of Crowder given his employment by established web content service BlazeTV. However, shifting away from focusing solely on Crowder to encompass a category of creators recasts the situation as one in which a big corporation is doing harm to people who are powerless. This may have been a sincere belief for this tweeter (and others who used this framing), and certainly when YouTube tightened its rules about monetization, many other channels were affected. However, regardless of sincerity or intent, the effect here is to make Crowder the victim of corporate overreach, not someone facing consequences for his own actions.

Related to the buycott of Crowder, there was a boycott action toward YouTube. Thus, tweeters also announce that they are canceling their YouTube subscriptions to move to Mug Club. One such tweet said the tweeter was "already an @scrowder #MugClub sub[scriber]. Today I pulled the wallet out and voted with it! Cancelled my @youtube premium and tv subscriptions and signed up for the daily wire." It is notable here that this user employs the concept of "voting with the wallet," a common framing in political consumption such as boycotts and buycotts. Much like signing up for Mug Club, users also encourage others to boycott, as in, "If you stand with @scrowder then cancel your #YouTubePremium and sign up for #MugClub Don't let these assholes win." Tweeters also expressed a sense that these actions were widespread, as in, "I wonder how many new #mugclub members @scrowder gets because of #VoxAdpocalypse? On the flip side, I wonder how many #YouTubePremium members @YouTube gets/loses?" Much like announcing one's own intention to join Mug Club, discussed above, such tweets both assume a group of like-minded Twitter users and, in a feedback loop, help create the sense of this attitude as widespread.

Finally, it was common for tweets announcing buycott and boycott intentions to attribute their decision to Maza, to *Vox*, to YouTube, or to the #VoxAdpocalypse in particular. Commonly, the framework is to thank one or more of these for prompting the decision: "thanks" is the fifth most frequent word and appears in 14 percent of tweets and "thank" is in 6 percent (sixteenth most common), for a total of 20 percent of tweets. Within this group, the most focus is on Maza, who is thanked in 43 percent of thanks tweets (9 percent of all tweets); *Vox* is thanked 7 percent of the time and YouTube 5 percent (around 1 percent of total tweets each). Many such tweets thank Maza for the existence of a discount: "Thanks @gaywonk [Maza] for my discount with MugClub!" Other users offer more general thanks for the impetus to join up: "Will be joining #MugClub thanks for the push @voxdotcom @gaywonk." This idea that tweeters had been inclined to join before but had not done so for various reasons was recurring; "finally" appears in 9 percent of all tweets (tenth most common word). As part of the idea that Maza was driving sales of Crowder's content, several tweeters referred to him as employee of the month: "Congrats, @gaywonk, on being Employee of The Month and selling the most #MugClub memberships in the history of #LouderwithCrowder 🎉😄!! You rock!" In these various ways, then, the target of Crowder's harassment, and the target's employer, and the platform that took action to stop the harassment are all informed that these events have resulted in more, not less, support of Crowder. Whether or not it is true that increased Mug Club subscriptions or merchandise sales counterbalanced the loss of YouTube ad revenue, this was obviously part of the attempt. Ultimately, the public declarations of support, and the fannish community they functioned to cultivate, are the essential features of this campaign irrespective of its actual economic impacts.

A Skirmish in the Culture Wars: Battle Rhetoric and Political Framing

However, #VoxAdpocalypse was not simply an economic action but an outpost of the culture wars, and framing in these terms was central to the tweets. The construction of this incident as a battle is often quite literal, with discussions about the need to "fight," which is the sixteenth most common word, appearing in 6 percent of all tweets. In one particularly affectively charged tweet, a supporter says, "You inspire me to be brave, thank you. I just joined #MugClub, keep fighting the good fight! @scrowder." This comment has multiple valences. It claims that Crowder inspires bravery, suggesting that to harass someone weaker than you is brave, that joining Mug Club is brave, or both. It also links joining Mug Club to Crowder continuing to fight, echoing the financial-support logics discussed in the previous section. Variations of the phrase "the good fight" were particularly common. Encouragement of Crowder to continue was likewise frequent, with "keep" being the twelfth most common word, appearing in 7 percent of all tweets. Thus, one tweeter urged, "Keep fighting, Steven. We're behind you all the way." This idea that an unspecified "we" is supporting Crowder was repeatedly invoked, as was the concept of having his back, which originates in dangerous or violent situations such as the military or fistfights: "Got your back brother @scrowder." In these various ways, then, a dispute over YouTube monetization is framed in terms of (possibly violent) struggle.

The idea that this was a fight went hand in hand with seeing Carlos Maza, YouTube, and/or *Vox* as bullies, and Crowder or right-wingers in general as victims. This interpretation is deeply tied into the broader upsurge among members of the far Right of seeing themselves as victims as men,[42] white people,[43] and white men.[44] This sense that Crowder had been harmed (rather than experiencing consequences for his actions) was evident from the way some tweeters retold the events that led up to Crowder's demonetization: "Just so we are clear, the 'mug salesman' [Crowder] didn't command anyone to do anything. @gaywonk however asked his followers to go out of their way to try and get Crowder banned. It's not complicated to figure out who the bully is." In this way, Maza publicly asking YouTube to step in against Crowder after a long period of harassment is understood to make him a bully. This tracks with legal scholar Mary Anne Franks's argument that "victim-claiming is a reversal technique that puts the powerful in the space of the vulnerable, the abuser in the space of the abused."[45] This is precisely the intellectual contortion needed to construct Maza as the bully and Crowder as the victim.

Related to this contorted conceptualization of victimhood, there is, as Franks notes, structurally differential availability of free speech:

"Ever-expanding definitions of what counts as 'free speech' give constitutional cover to practices that disproportionately harm women and minorities, while attempts to ensure women and minorities' equal exercise of freedom of expression is labeled 'censorship.'"[46] This is the framework under which one can conclude that it is free speech for Crowder to mock Maza, but not for Maza to contest this treatment. Maza was both punching back at someone who hit him first and punching upward given his structural lack of power compared to a straight white man with an avid fan base, but in the estimation of that fan base, Crowder was somehow powerless. From this sentiment comes a tweet that constructs Crowder as a "little guy": "Tonight's #MugClub selection is brewed and packaged here in my own home town, in honor of the little guys"; the tweet goes on to tag Crowder and a series of similar Internet commentators. While it is reasonable to say that Crowder has less power relative to the huge social and economic heft of YouTube, it was entirely untrue relative to Maza. There is a tendency across the tweets to conflate YouTube's power with Maza's, which strategically furthers the notion of Crowder and others who share his politics as victims.

As a corollary of this idea of victimhood, and in alignment with Crowder having formulated the event as the "*Vox* Adpocalypse" in the first place, multiple tweeters positioned Crowder's demonetization as not a specific response to his behavior but apocalyptic for others—implicitly, those who share his politics. Multiple tweeters posted tweets that constructed the change as likely to spiral outward and encompass others: "Support free speech and join @scrowder's #MugClub today before the #VoxAdpocalypse comes for us all." This particular tweet was posted by conservative online personality Kaitlin Bennett who, as I have discussed elsewhere, has a history of provoking confrontations and then framing herself as the victim.[47] Bennett also might have cause to worry that the policy could be applied to her given her history of posting transphobic and antisemitic content on various platforms.[48] Nevertheless, it was not only similar content creators, who might be at risk of financial loss, who were sounding the alarm. Various tweeters who were not already right-wing influencers wrote tweets with hashtags like #JoinOrDie, both referencing the eighteenth-century cartoon that depicted the American colonies as a cut-up snake and called for unity and also invoking joining Mug Club, romanticization of the Founding Fathers often seen from the right wing, and the image's later morph into the Gadsden Flag, which has become widely understood as a far-right symbol.[49] The idea that the consequences Crowder faced were likely to spread was thus a repeated theme. Overall, then, there was an idea that this incident was part of a broader battle, and particularly one that Crowder and his fans saw themselves as losing.

In addition to general ideas that those who shared Crowder's views were at risk of demonetization, there were more specific moments of mapping this incident onto broader political positions and conflicts. Crowder's demonetization was frequently understood in terms of political philosophies, groups, and even candidates. As the "Socialism is for F*gs" shirt has already demonstrated, one belief system frequently constructed as an ideological enemy is socialism or communism. At times, the "fight" is understood in such terms: "@scrowder glad to be a part of #MugClub to fight against socialism." One tweeter was particularly emphatic: "JOIN @LouderWith CROWDER MUG CLUB. They need your support because the COMMUNIST LOVING LEFTISTS organizations want ABSOLUTELY NO OTHER VOICE BUT THEIRS. Fight back!" It is not at all clear how the economic system of communism relates to questions of Internet harassment, but the tweet certainly reflects the tendency on the contemporary Right to describe any person or policy they dislike as socialist.

In a related construction, the opposition is named as liberal or left. Thus, one tweeter declares that he has joined Mug Club "to support what is in my opinion exactly what we need more of in this world that you pc left wing liberal bastards have created." Supporting Crowder is thus directly opposed to "liberal" values. Similarly, another tweeter says of his mug, "Can't wait to catch liberal tears with it." This references a popular right-wing meme, "drinking liberal tears," that revels in harm done to ideological enemies in a way that is isomorphic with Internet trolls.[50] Trolls attempt "to disrupt and upset as many people as possible, using whatever linguistic or behavioral tools are available," usually understood as "for the lulz," meaning in order to obtain "amusement derived from another person's anger."[51] In these various ways, then, the political enemy of Crowder supporters is clear.

Additionally, and correspondingly, Crowder and his followers are associated with conservatism. One tweeter announced, "I been a fan for a while I was already leaning right but watching you made me go with them all the way I hope this gets better for you 🤜🇺🇸." That is, Crowder has recruited this tweeter to be fully on the political Right, which the user associates with both physical strength, perhaps suggesting hegemonic masculinity, and the US flag; as Crosset et al. note, "Flags are also a potent symbol for the far right, given their importance as a display of patriotism. Certain users display their country's flag, while others display the confederate flag, which has become a common white supremacist symbol."[52] Thus, while of course there are non–far right uses of the flag, this particular use is clearly part of that intensely nationalist far-right discourse. Indeed "American" is tied for the tenth most common word in the Bio field for tweeters in the corpus.

Other tweeters point to #VoxAdpocalypse itself as spurring on conservatism, as in one of the tweets thanking Maza: "Thank you @gaywonk for advancing sound conservative ideas. Now Louder with Crowder has more fans & more #MugClub memberships." By protesting his mistreatment, the argument goes, Maza has contributed not only to Crowder's popularity but to the advancement of conservatism itself. This idea that taking action against Crowder backfired and promoted him was described several times with the concept of the "Streisand Effect," named for an incident in which singer/actor Barbra Streisand sought to suppress a photo taken of her beachfront property as part of a survey to document coastal erosion, thus making people aware that her house was in the photo and driving interest in it.[53] This idea of resistance backfiring was also mapped specifically onto right-wing politics. For example, perhaps because one of Crowder's key sponsors is a gun company,[54] there were multiple mentions of firearms, a popular conservative issue. One tweeter announced, "@gaywonk @YouTube I joined Mug Club, as well. You're probably going to do for @scrowder what David Hogg did for the NRA." This references school shooting survivor and activist Hogg's campaign against politicians who take donations from the NRA,[55] which the tweeter is implying led to greater support for the organization. A similar tweet read, "@gaywonk is to mugs like @BarackObama is to firearms," gesturing toward the fact that "after Obama's 2008 election, gun sales skyrocketed and demand increased permanently in some states."[56] In such ways, there is a repeated sense that opposing Crowder makes him—and conservatism—stronger.

Finally, #VoxAdpocalypse was mapped directly onto electoral politics, most notably through tweets combining opposition to it with support for then president Donald Trump. Such tweets used hashtags like "#Trump2020Landslide" and "#VoxAdpocalypse #CivilWar #MAGA #MugClub #MugClubbers #DONTMESSWITHMYFREEDOM #MAGA," referencing Trump's 2016 campaign slogan "Make America Great Again." The use of these tags and the overall identification with right-wing politics is also consistent with the word frequency in the Bio sections, with "conservative" the most frequent word; "#MAGA" at sixth most frequent; "#KAG," referencing the 2020 Trump campaign slogan "Keep America Great," at ninth most frequent; and "#Trump2020" at tenth. In all of these ways, then, Crowder's fans map the consequences for harassing Maza onto contemporary political topics and issues.

Free Speech as the Right to (Get Paid to) Say Whatever You Want

"Free speech" was a frequent refrain both in the broader #VoxAdpocalypse hashtag—with 1,011 instances of "freespeech," 2,907 of "speech," and 4,537 of "censorship" overall—and in the corpus of tweets framed around fannish support of Crowder that I focus on here. Partially, this was the case because Crowder himself framed the incident that way, taking advantage of the moment to offer a discounted Mug Club membership using "FREESPEECH" as the promotional code. However, he was far from the only one to use this construction, and "freespeech" is the ninth most common term in the corpus, at 9 percent of tweets (encompassing both mentions of the discount code and instances of "#FreeSpeech"). In addition, "speech" was the fifteenth most frequent term (6 percent), for a total of 15 percent of tweets engaging this issue in some way. The incident shows the tendency to catastrophize about free speech described by Franks: "The mere *possibility* that white men's speech might be slightly curtailed is regarded as an unimaginable horror while the systematic silencing of women and minorities is dismissed as mere inconvenience."[57] Maza having been repeatedly targeted for his speech had sparked no such outcry, after all.

In one hyperbolic (but not therefore unrepresentative) tweet, the poster asked, "Where were you when #VoxAdpocalypse took over free speech? I was sipping my coffee out of #MugClub and standing fiercely behind EVERYONE's right to free speech. @scrowder." It is of course not reasonable to suggest that free speech has been "taken over," let alone by a single YouTube account being demonetized, but this tweet does demonstrate both posters' sense that the situation was dire and their tendency to platitudes about free speech for everyone or every perspective, which of course misses that free speech for bigots means silencing of bigotry's targets. Maza himself pointed this out, saying that if YouTube is "not willing to censor hateful and abusive content," then "hateful and abusive content flourishes. [. . .] But that isn't a free speech environment. [. . .] It's one in which marginalized people, who typically have the least access to speech platforms, get pushed out of the public square by powerful bullies."[58] As Franks points out, "While the chilling effects of free speech regulations are almost completely speculative, the chilling effect of unfettered harmful expression is not. It is undeniable that certain forms of speech can silence other speech."[59]

Tweets also constructed the incident specifically as a matter of the US First Amendment. In one such tweet, the poster said, "The #VoxAdpocalypse is here. Just joined #MugClub to support our First Amendment rights." However, in that there is no involvement of the government controlling speech, the First Amendment is not particularly relevant. As Franks notes, "Private citizens do not have First Amendment rights against each other, and private companies, with limited exceptions, have no First Amendment responsibilities"; therefore, "'censorship,' in the strict legal sense, refers only to actions taken by the government to restrict speech."[60] Nevertheless, popular perception tends to frame any adverse action against someone related to their speech—regardless of the involvement of government actors or whether the person is prevented from speaking, punished, or merely experiences a negative reaction—as censorship. This was certainly prevalent in the corpus. One tweet calls on others to "fight back against the liberal censors." Another tweeter declared, "#VoxAdpocalypse censorship never works must be time to join #MugClub." Notably, in addition to the First Amendment not applying to actions by private companies, Crowder's speech itself was not on particularly firm First Amendment ground. As Franks points out, "If what is meant by hate speech is merely unpleasant, unpopular, or crude expression, then it is true that the First Amendment protects hate speech. If what is meant by hate speech is true threats, incitement, defamation, obscenity, fighting words, or certain kinds of discriminatory expression, then it is not true that the First Amendment protects hate speech."[61] Crowder's campaign against Maza at least raises questions about discrimination, defamation, and incitement.

One key issue that arises within the discussion of speech and censorship is deplatforming, or the removal of access to media distribution, a consequence that is most typically applied to those using a platform to promote bigotry or disinformation. In one such tweet, the user said, "Just subscribed to Mug Club @scrowder Deplatforming is how fascists control the free flow of thoughts & information. It is NOT about stopping hate. I do NOT support harassment, doxxing, or political violence. I SUPPORT FREE SPEECH! 🏴 #VoxAdpocalypse @TeamYouTube #VoxAdpocolypse."[62] There is a lot going on here. First, subscribing to Mug Club is constructed as a response to deplatforming. Second, deplatforming is understood as fascist, despite (again) the fact that it is not a government action; in this case, deplatforming also resists rather than supports central fascist axioms of intense nationalism and belief that certain sorts of people are inherently inferior. Third, an action by YouTube could plausibly be seen to impact the flow of information, but certainly not to control it given the presence of large numbers of other media outlets that had not restricted Crowder at all. Interestingly, this user also takes some positions that are seemingly at odds, implicitly recognizing that stopping hate is a worthy cause by distinguishing the (allegedly) illegitimate demonetization of Crowder from it as well as criticizing tactics like harassment, doxing, and political violence that are associated with the Internet far Right, but ultimately they come down clearly on the side of arguing that Crowder's behavior toward Maza should not result in consequences.

Importantly, not being able to speak in one particular place is not necessarily a First Amendment problem either, and yet, as Franks explains, "Some users have even complained that being blocked or muted by other users is a form of censorship, implying that the right of free speech is not only a right to speak, but to demand a particular audience."[63] This is precisely what Crowder and his supporters assert: that he has a right to speak specifically *on YouTube*. This concept of deplatforming relies on what Tarleton Gillespie has described as an "architectural" definition of a platform as a raised place to stand.[64] In this model, deplatforming is declining to provide support to a speaker, or to allow the speaker to use one's platform for the speaker's own benefit, but doing so does not actually raise First Amendment issues.

This link of demonetization to deplatforming helps explain why conversations about deplatforming so often went hand in hand with statements about funding Crowder. This is the perspective from which one tweeter declared, "If you want to fight back against deplatforming then go put your money where your interest is, plus you get their awesome mugs ☺." Adding up these different aspects makes it clear that Crowder's supporters were asserting not just free speech as a right to speak without government interference, not just a right to use the private space of the YouTube platform to speak, but a right to get paid to do so. That is, it was not enough that Crowder's videos still appeared on YouTube without making him money (and indeed, in the process were subsidized by users who did not harass anybody), but because he was not being paid, his freedom of speech was still seen as harmed. Many tweets framed Crowder's demonetization as silencing him, and often themselves: "We will not be silenced!" This occurred despite the fact that not a single one of them was prevented from speaking. In light of the actual situation, claiming that removing Crowder's ability to make money is equivalent to "book burning"—as in "If you can't win with ideas, @gaywonk resort to book burning!"—is absurd, but it does clearly reflect this idea that if one loses the ability to be paid, it is identical to being unable to get one's ideas out at all.

It is in this framework that there is a concept of corporate censorship. As one tweet said, "The corporate bullying and censorship from @voxdotcom and @YouTube needs to stop." Notably, what is being described as bullying and censoring here is nothing more than YouTube changing its rules to (try to) stay advertiser friendly, and *Vox* supporting Maza as its employee who had been targeted in the course of doing work for them. Some tweeters tie this platform-governance decision back to what they believe are viewpoint-based reasons for Crowder's demonetization (rather than behavioral ones), as in, "There is blatant corporate censorship of public personalities on the right." In one particularly interesting tweet, the tone of grievance that is the baseline in the corpus is missing, but "takedowns," "free speech," and demonetization are all conflated, and the list of accounts the tweeter supports makes the tweeter's politics clear: "Dear @YouTube we're big fans but you've got to clarify your policies on what content deserves a takedown. Your platform is important for #FreeSpeech. Reinstate videos & monetization for @scrowder @BlazeTV @jordanbpeterson @benshapiro #VoxAdpocalypse." In addition to Crowder and BlazeTV, this tweet references self-identified "renowned conservative political pundit" Ben Shapiro,[65] as well as psychologist Jordan Peterson, whose Internet fame has been described as "emblematic of the way white male anxiety is producing new and powerful political movements across the West today."[66]

Throughout these tweets, the argument—though made by concatenation—is clear: free speech is harmed by demonetization; to be able to speak freely is to be able to use someone else's platform to get paid to say whatever one likes. It is important to note that there *is* actually a financial component to contemporary issues of Internet speech. However, rather than this being a question of monetization, the problem with the privately owned Internet we have ended up with is that there is no place where *anyone* has a right to speak. Instead, what is allowed is conditioned by what makes or costs platform providers the most money, meaning that advertisers—and their (often mistaken) sense of what the public accepts—are the deciding factor. But this is very different from saying that there is a right to cash in on speech, as Crowder's supporters seem to do. Through such examples, the truth of Franks's argument becomes clear: "The voice of white men dominates virtually every online and offline space, crying out ceaselessly of censorship."[67]

Of Figs and Fans: Identity and Victimhood in #VoxAdpocalypse

Ultimately, #VoxAdpocalypse is characterized by fannish public performances of financial support for a perceived like-minded community, at the same time that it is deeply enmeshed in contemporary culture-wars discourses and a concept of free speech as a right to get paid. Tweeters both see their fan community as powerful enough that boycotting YouTube and buycotting Crowder will matter, and as helpless victims of YouTube and Maza. This suggests that at a fundamental level, the incident turns on questions of identity, in particular an identity as victims of marginalized groups they both mock and see as extraordinarily powerful.

Similar to the sharp political divide between "us" and "them," ideas of identity are sharply polarized in the corpus. There are, first, repeated self-identifications as Crowder fans. Thus, one tweeter declared, "Keep up the great work @scrowder been a fan of your channel since the beginning will always be here to show support they will not get away with this #VoxAdpocalypse keep fighting it we'll win in the end." In addition to those announcing longtime fandom, some tweeted about being new fans: "Thank you @gaywonk and the #VoxAdpocalypse, without you I would have never heard of @scrowder. Now, I'm a fan of his." In much the same way, one tweeter declared, "#IHeartLWC #Crowderite." This hashtag constructing a group identity around supporting Crowder is an instance of what Emily Tarvin calls "fandom demonyms," which "denote those who make up a certain fandom and have communal ties to others in the fandom."[68] While Tarvin discusses tensions between the way creators might use demonyms top down and how fans use them bottom up, only the latter is visible in this data set. Mug Club, too, serves as an identity in statements like "#iammugclub" and "#MugClubForLife."

However, at the same time as they tie their own identities to Crowder, his supporters expressed hostility toward identity as a political category in a way consistent with conservative rejection of "identity politics." Thus, one tweeter said, "CONGRATS!!! ■ to @gaywonk for making June the LGBTQXYZ month about @scrowder! #Mugclub thanks you! @theblaze #PrideMonth #VoxAdpocalypse." This remark uses the common conservative tactic of delegitimating queer identities by creating fictitious ones to suggest that all such identities are equally made up. Another tweeter declared, "Long time watcher, just joined mug club because Pootube is apparently full of a bunch of green haired gender neutral basement dwellers." Colorful hair, too, is a frequent target of conservative ire, often linked to sexual and gender nonconformity, as in the meme "blue hair and pronouns,"[69] perhaps because of the rejection of the normative that it signals.

That this mockery is ultimately not about the idea of identity as ridiculous in general but antipathy toward particular, queer identities can be seen from the instances of calling Maza a "lispy queer," as in "#fightthelispyqueer," as well as the huge frequency of "fig," which is the seventh most common word, appearing in 13 percent of tweets in the corpus. The fiction that this is not a substitute for "fag" almost comes apart at times, with tweets like, "Much as I enjoy @scrowder, I didn't enjoy it enough I was willing to pay for Mug Club. @gaywonk changed that. Stay free, you FIG." The construction of this tweet uses "fig" as a slur, and it is not hard to figure out what it is replacing. There are also other instances of bowdlerization, as in, "People like that little ginger beer over at Vox make me very glad I joined #MugClub right off the jump." The unwillingness to use the terms these tweeters so clearly wish to use is fascinating alongside rhetoric about other people's excessive sensitivity, such as "#growapair #LwC #fuckyourfeelings." In such ways, they treat hurt feelings as mockable but also will not directly say what they mean, analogous to the "Let's Go Brandon" meme that became popular in 2021 as a way to say (but not say) "Fuck Joe Biden."[70] Putting these two approaches to identity politics alongside each other helps us see how, much as with the incoherent politics of Bernie Bros discussed in chapter 2, the construction of the ingroup is flexible in content but extremely rigid in its good guy/bad guy structure. Disavowing other people's identities while asserting their own is deeply bound up in flattening or even inverting the power structure, making themselves the victims of their actual victims. The notion that conservatives or free speech are under attack by being prohibited from cashing in on belittling marginalized people is a particularly clear manifestation of the logic that plays out throughout this book, in which identifying one's fan group as a victim (however inaccurately) justifies nearly endless vitriol.

7

"Teaching White Kids They're Bad"

Antifandom of Critical Race Theory and
Fannish Attachment to Whiteness

On March 15, 2021, conservative activist Christopher Rufo tweeted, "The goal is to have the public read something crazy in the newspaper and immediately think 'critical race theory.' We have decodified the term and will recodify it to annex the entire range of cultural constructions that are unpopular with Americans"; he bragged that "we have successfully frozen their brand— 'critical race theory'—into the public conversation and are steadily driving up negative perceptions. We will eventually turn it toxic, as we put all of the various cultural insanities under that brand category."[1] The fact that "critical race theory" has subsequently been used on the Right to describe everything from academic lectures about civil rights history to books by and about Black people shows that, as of this writing, this campaign has largely been successful.[2] But why should an academic theory primarily taught in law schools be the target of any activist campaign in the first place? The CRT panic does not really make a lot of sense unless you understand it as rooted in an emotional attachment to—and commitment to defending—whiteness. In particular, given that the CRT panic is structured through emotional attachments cultivated by like-minded communities telling each other interrelated stories based on a shared set of mediated texts, the tools of fan studies can help us understand the CRT panic.

In this chapter, I use the critical race theory panic that began in mid-2021 to understand how attachment to whiteness is structured like a fandom. I recognize that this juxtaposition might be jarring, so let me start with some definition work. I define "fandom" here as having three basic characteristics: public, collective affect, or feels; public, collective interpretation of shared text(s); and identity and community formation structured by affective ties and texts. To begin with feels, Louisa

Ellen Stein describes millennial fandom as a site of "feels culture," in which "emotions remain intimate but are no longer necessarily private; rather, they build a sense of an intimate collective, one that is bound together precisely by the processes of shared emotional authorship. In this equation, emotion fuels fan transformative creativity, and performances of shared emotion define fan authorship communities."[3] While feels are typically understood as love or affection, I argue that shared emotional creativity structured around hatred and anger functions much the same way. Second, there is a mediated text at the center of this phenomenon that gives rise to collective interpretation and transformative creativity. This is to use the fandom concepts of "canon" and "fanon"; canon, Kristina Busse notes, "tends to be defined as the collection of texts considered to be the authoritative source for fan creations."[4] Correspondingly, fanon, or fan-created canon, is the set of details and characteristics of the object of fannish attachment that are collectively agreed on in a fan community, but that do not actually appear anywhere in the source text.[5] These shared texts and interpretations drive feels and community, and I argue that they can do so regardless of what the mediated source text is. Third, fandoms are characterized by community and group identity—those feels and texts are public and collective and build ties among those with shared interests as well as a sense of self, including when those ties are rooted in grievance and a false sense of victimhood. Looking at the CRT panic in this way helps us understand the otherwise perplexing process of building an entire narrative edifice around a legal theory; how it draws people into community and shapes identity; and how it cultivates, maintains, and disguises affective attachments to whiteness itself.[6]

This is where I stretch this book's organizing principle all the way to—but hopefully not past—its breaking point. Here, as with electoral politics (see chapter 2), the disjuncture between being a fan as something related to media, on one hand, and more material instances of social power, on the other, is acute. As Lucy Miller notes in her discussion of Make America Great Again (MAGA) as a fandom, "Fans' actions are [. . .] seen as having an impact only within the fan community and on the bottom lines of those companies whose financial success depends on fan texts whereas the behavior of partisans is positioned as having clear impacts on the entire political system."[7] However, interpreting phenomena like

MAGA or the CRT panic as fannish means recognizing the artificiality of that divide. Online communities that involve intense emotional relationships to cultural texts have ways of spilling out into broader impacts, from widespread mis- and disinformation to (as discussed in the introduction) insurrection. Thus, similarly to my position here, Miller argues that "fandom provides a means for better understanding that engagement [with the political and civic spheres] when its origins do not lie within established political parties or ideologies."[8] Attachments to whiteness are similarly an amorphous form of engagement based on feels, texts, and community, not formal institutions, and that combination of features makes it useful to think about them using fan studies as a lens. In this way, the value of the feels, texts, and community framework for making sense of various cultural phenomena beyond media becomes clear. This case is therefore interesting both to push the limits of what fan studies can do and to show intensified versions of the same conflicts over racism and power that have run through the other case studies.

To examine the CRT panic, I used Google Trends to find when searches for the term rapidly increased to determine when it had entered widespread awareness, which was in May 2021. I then searched press database Nexis Uni for "critical race theory" from May through early July 2021. I sorted the results by relevance, grouped duplicates, and collected stories with the term in the headline or preview. I included TV broadcast transcripts and excluded blogs, international sources, and overtly white-nationalist sources like the *Daily Caller* (though I included Fox News). I collected the first one hundred results that met these criteria, which took me to result 307 overall. News stories provide a window into the public arguments made in the CRT panic. While this is different from other chapters looking at how fans talk to each other in fan spaces, the significantly astroturfed nature of the CRT panic means that it exists substantially or even primarily as public outrage rather than private conversations.

My analysis found exactly the kind of recodification "to annex the entire range of cultural constructions that are unpopular with [conservative, white] Americans" that Rufo proposed, with slippage from reasonable statements about racism to (deliberately or accidentally) extreme positions no one holds, from extreme positions back to cast doubt on reasonable ones, and from CRT to a variety of right-wing bogey-men from anti-Americanism to Marxism. These forms of slippage create outrage and anxiety, while slippage from racism and white supremacy as structures to individual racists and white people both demonstrates and cultivates feels and community around whiteness. Using fan studies tools makes clear that what is happening here is an intense and collec-tive affective relationship to a mediated narrative, but rather than creat-ing a positive attachment to a text that spawns collective interpretations (a fanon, or fan-created canon), CRT panickers create a negative attach-ment and collective interpretations in opposition to a text (what I call an antifanon). Collective, textual engagement with whiteness helps build a subcultural identity out of what is actually the dominant group, recruit-ing affective attachment, leveraging the desire to feel good about the self, and especially creating a sense of whiteness as embattled.

Background: CRT and Moral Panics Meet Contemporary Whiteness

To understand how whiteness functions in the CRT panic, it is impor-tant to understand how race is socially constructed in general. The construction of race happens through what sociologists Michael Omi and Howard Winant have named "racial formation"; they define it as "the sociohistorical process by which racial categories are created, inhabited, transformed, and destroyed."[9] This framework calls attention to the fact that race is constructed, but also that this is an ongoing pro-cess rather than a completed one. Particular moves in this process are then racial projects: "A racial project is simultaneously an interpretation, representation, or explanation of racial dynamics, and an effort to reor-ganize and redistribute resources along particular racial lines."[10] Under this model, the CRT panic is a racial project that seeks to interpret, rep-resent, and explain whiteness in a way that will facilitate redistributing resources—specifically, like other moments of backlash, rolling back "the scant economic and social progress made in the United States [. . .] by African Americans, women, and other racial, ethnic, and sexual minorities."[11]

Whiteness studies has traditionally conceptualized whiteness as invis-ible or transparent,[12] and in routine white supremacy that is true. But as Ruth Frankenberg notes, "It is only in those times and places where white supremacism has achieved hegemony that whiteness attains (usually unstable) unmarkedness"; by contrast, "In times and places when whiteness and white dominance are being built or reconfigured, they are highly visible, named, and asserted, rather than invisible or simply 'normative.'"[13] Our current moment is precisely one of whiteness as "visible, named, and asserted." This is not to say that white supremacy is not hegemonic in the contemporary moment (it surely remains so), but it *is* being reconfigured.

The trajectory I examine here began in backlash to Barack Obama's election as president, which troubled whiteness as the default of power; indeed, Stephanie Hartzell points out that "the term 'alternative right' was coined in November 2008—just weeks after the (first) election of Barack Obama."[14] Hartzell argues that the alt-right is "an extension of white nationalists' longstanding attempts to reach mainstream white U.S. American audiences through articulations between far-right and pro-white ideologies."[15] This round of attempts was largely successful, as white nationalism became a mainstream political force beginning in the mid-2010s, which Donald Trump, with his racist rhetoric, both represented and benefited from. As Hartzell describes, "The 'alt-right' burst onto the mainstream U.S. American political scene within this context of proliferating racism and proponents quickly positioned themselves among Trump's most fervent pro-white supporters. As others have noted, support between Trump and the 'alt-right' has been mutual."[16] This period of reconfiguration both made racism acceptable again (at least in some circles) and articulated a positive vision of whiteness—both in the sense of having a positive opinion about it and in the sense of having a positive existence rather than being defined by contrast as the allegedly neutral ground that constructs other races as lacking.

Contestation over the meaning of race reached fever pitch when the murder of George Floyd in summer 2020 resulted in widespread protests across the nation that made it radically less possible to operate from the white-default frame. The reconfiguration of whiteness that I am discussing can even be seen as a *response* to the invisibility of quotidian whiteness, a drive to shore up whiteness and define it as visible rather than default precisely as its hegemonic status is being contested. Self-conscious white supremacists have always seen whiteness, of course, but the late-2010s rise of the alt-right and white nationalism aims to create a sense of whiteness as a conscious community identity beyond those self-identified supremacists, taking these ideas out into broader culture. It is in this sense that white nationalism is a racial project, a concerted effort at reconfiguration of the racial system. It is also important to point out that whiteness's invisibility was only ever "the invisibility (for whites) of whiteness"[17]—people of color have long needed to see and understand whiteness, if only as a survival strategy.

Making sense of this particular racial project thus requires understanding both what the critical race theory (CRT) that they are panicking about is, and how moral panics function. To begin with the former, since the 1970s (though scholars did not consciously frame it as a movement until 1989), the scholarly project of CRT has shown how apparently neutral laws are in fact structured by the racial inequality endemic to US society.[18] As Richard Delgado and Jean Stefancic describe in the introduction to their collection of CRT scholarship, CRT responded to a sense that "the civil rights movement of the 1960s had stalled, and indeed that many of its gains were being rolled back. New approaches were needed to understand and come to grips with the more subtle, but just as deeply entrenched, varieties of racism that characterize our times."[19] Kimberlé Crenshaw, Neil Gotanda, Gary Peller, and Kendall Thomas, in their collection of the foundational CRT texts, put a finer point on it, saying that CRT seeks to interrogate "how a regime of white supremacy and its subordination of people of color have been created and maintained in America, and, in particular, to examine the relationship between that social structure and professed ideals such as 'the rule of law' and 'equal protection.'"[20] That is, the problem is not merely that law has not been neutrally applied to white people and people of color (though it hasn't), but rather that apparently neutral legal concepts are themselves structured by white supremacy.

To ask about entrenched racism and its manifestations in institutions such as law, "CRT begins with a number of basic insights. One is that racism is normal, not aberrant, in American society."[21] This is to say that racism is part of mundane attitudes and practices, not merely spectacular moments like Klan rallies. Recognizing this fact then shows that "formal equal opportunity [. . .] can thus remedy only the more extreme and shocking forms of injustice" and "can do little about the business-as-usual forms of racism that people of color confront every day and that account for much misery, alienation, and despair."[22] The civil rights movement's legal gains outlawed de jure forms of discrimination—which is usually represented in the popular imaginary as the end of racism. But de facto discrimination persisted, which was in large part what CRT was developed to explain. Moreover, CRT began from an activist orientation and was intended "not merely to understand the vexed bond between law and racial power but to change it," rejecting "the prevailing orthodoxy that scholarship should be or could be 'neutral' and 'objective.'"[23] Part of contesting the legal understandings up to that point, that is, was identifying them as representing not a neutral perspective but a particular, interested one: that of the existing power structure. In subsequent years, inroads have been made on subtler forms of taking whiteness as the default, beginning in scholarly work like that of CRT and other scholarship on race in the social sciences and humanities and subsequently taken up unevenly in the broader culture—though such forms of white supremacy remain powerful and hegemonic.

Given what CRT actually is, the level of anxiety around it shows that the anti-CRT fights are a moral panic. Stanley Cohen, who first described moral panics in 1972, describes them as "elite engineered."[24] Despite images of parents screaming at school boards, that is, the CRT panic is in fact generated top-down, originating not from ordinary concerned citizens but from employees of conservative think tanks (like the Manhattan Institute, where Rufo, quoted at the beginning of the chapter, is a senior fellow); political operatives, such as some who served in the Trump administration;[25] and free market absolutists funded by the Koch brothers.[26] In particular, moral panics tend to be stirred up by elites to facilitate political and social ends. This pattern holds in the CRT case; as one example, "Former top aides to President Donald Trump have begun an aggressive push to combat the teaching of critical race theory and capitalize on the issue politically, confident that a backlash will vault them back into power,"[27] and indeed the 2021 Virginia gubernatorial election went for Republican Glen Youngkin in part because he stirred up hysteria over CRT.[28]

From these elite figures and institutions, the moral panic is propagated out into the broader population. At a basic level, moral panics are characterized by a sense that social values are threatened.[29] Using this framework then directs our attention to what these values are. In this case, as I will show, it is white supremacy. Additionally, the perception of the threat is also disproportionate to the actual risk and harm, and therefore irrational.[30] Here, white dominance is in no way under immediate threat—though we might hope it is on the way out in the long term. This is not to say that there have not been shifts in white supremacy. Widespread protests in summer 2020 after the murder of George Floyd encouraged a society-wide engagement with concepts such as police brutality and systemic racism. While such engagement was often no more substantive than an Instagram post, there was potentially critical mass for a genuine reckoning with structural racism. This unsettled not just avowed white supremacists but a wide swath of white people, even some who might otherwise have thought of themselves as progressive. Contestation of white supremacy provoked anxiety around whiteness as an identity category, making a proportion of white people ripe for a moral panic about race, which those interested in shoring up whiteness then exploited.

Understanding both CRT and moral panics lets us see that the CRT panic is about collective emotional attachment to a thing and defending it against perceived attack. This is classic fan behavior. Yet despite its imaginary nature, the perceived threat in the moral panic is not arbitrary.[31] Moral panics happen along existing social fault lines, with "a suitable victim"—often, someone socially valued, in this case white children or white people in general—and a "suitable enemy: a soft target, easily denounced, with little power and preferably without even access to the battlefields of cultural politics"—like schoolteachers or people of color.[32] While the tenets of CRT—racism is structural and routine—are relatively uncontroversial statements at this end of history in the context of scholarship, the moral-panic machine got ahold of them and worked its usual transformative magic, ginning up fear of a nonexistent threat and transmuting something innocuous into a threat.

Moral panics are always and inevitably responding to imaginary threats, but their effects are nevertheless material. As one journalist noted, "While this conflict and panic is based on misinformation, the fear these people feel is real. We saw a woman cry real tears at the thought that her child was being taught to be ashamed for being white."[33] None of the CRT panic's claims bear any relationship to the actual arguments made by the body of scholarship known as CRT, but that is not the point. What matters in the CRT panic is how feels get attached to this text, how the text is the site of public collective engagement, and how those things encourage community and identity formation. Those emotions, and the affective attachments to being white that they ultimately signal, are what make fannish attachments a useful theoretical lens to make sense of this phenomenon.

CRT as Transmedia and Its Antifanon

Analyzing the CRT panic through fandom begins from understanding that it involves feels about a text. While overt white nationalism can directly attach value to whiteness, that is still largely taboo in the mainstream, where the color-blind model in which talking about race is impolite has been quite persistent.[34] When Black Lives Matter became a rallying cry after the murder of Michael Brown in Ferguson, Missouri, in 2014, for example, white people who were offended by this assertion (mostly) knew they should not say "White Lives Matter"; instead, the response to the assertion that Black people's lives were devalued by police and society was to recast the issue away from race with "All Lives Matter" or shore up the value of the police as an institution of white supremacy with a retort of "Blue Lives Matter."[35]

Similarly, what the CRT panic does is produce attachment to whiteness through rejection of CRT. This is an intense affective relationship to a text—a negative one—and can therefore usefully be thought of through the lens of antifandom, meaning "those who strongly dislike a given text or genre, considering it inane, stupid, morally bankrupt and/ or aesthetic drivel."[36] In this move, whiteness retains, or regains, some of its invisibility, being defined as an absence of race or distinctiveness. This is why "we must protect children from (knowing about) racism" only sometimes specifies that the children are white. I argue that this happens through treating CRT as a transmedia text—a set of texts spread across space and time and encountered through multiple media like tweets, Fox News broadcasts, or letters to the editor. As Henry Jenkins describes, "A transmedia story unfolds across multiple media platforms, with each new text making a distinctive and valuable contribution to the whole"[37]—and, substituting "important" for "valuable" here, that is what we see in how CRT is taken up and distorted. These various components are also, like other successful transmedia stories, modular. Jenkins points out that transmedia works best when "any given product is a point of entry into the franchise as a whole."[38] You do not have to consume all of these sources to engage with the CRT panic narrative, but it gets richer the more of them you do consume.

Importantly, the "CRT" of the CRT panic is actually (anti)fanon. This conceptualization builds from the concept of fanon, or fan-created canon, meaning the set of details and characteristics of the object of fannish attachment that are collectively agreed on in a fan community, but are the product of interpretation rather than actually arising from the source text. The "CRT" of the CRT panic bears almost no relation to the real thing, but that is irrelevant. What people believe it to be—the fanon—shapes how they engage it and what sense they make of it. Carol A. Stabile contends that "fear is subject to condensation and displacement" in moral panics,[39] as diffuse fears are concretized or fear is shifted from one thing onto another. The construction of fanon out of the transmedia narrative in the CRT panic is characterized by a related phenomenon—slippage, in which the actual claims of CRT are pushed several steps further to absurdity; outrage over caricatures of CRT is used to slide back and cast thoroughly mainstream concepts as similarly extreme; and CRT is mapped onto established culture war bogeymen to argue for its danger by analogy.

Caricaturing CRT: Slippage toward the Outrageous

To begin with slippage from reasonable to outrageous, it takes two forms. On one hand, the movement is toward the outrageous with respect to institutions such as the nation itself. Senator John Kennedy of Louisiana slides from CRT's actual argument that white supremacy has been baked in since the foundation of the United States to a claim that "critical race theory teaches that the primary reason that America was founded was to maintain white supremacy, not freedom, not rule of law, not equal opportunity, not personal responsibility but white supremacy."[40] Here, in addition to transmuting the real CRT claim into an overbroad one about the "primary reason" the United States was founded, Kennedy also tosses in a variety of other buzzwords like "freedom" and "personal responsibility" that are likely to generate a knee-jerk protective reaction in his conservative audience. A similar slippage in these discussions happens with critiques of the United States as a settler colony without legitimate claim to Indigenous people's lands, which were presented in sensationalist ways by one Fox News host: "The entire existence of the United States of America is the result of imperialism and colonialism by white Protestant Europeans who came into this continent and imposed their will and created this country, that the real natives, indigenous peoples of this area are south of the border, and so they have every right to come to this country. They're not illegal aliens. You're an illegal alien."[41] Such framing, identified by the host as "Lat/Crit, which is Latino critical race theory," evokes ever-present conservative anxiety and/or anger about Latine people crossing the border,[42] and then points it at CRT.

On the other hand, there is slippage toward caricatures of what CRT says about people. In September 2020, in response to the events of that summer but well before the CRT panic took off, the Trump administration issued a memo commanding federal agencies to cancel any "training or propaganda effort that teaches or suggests either (1) that the United States is an inherently racist or evil country or (2) that any race or ethnicity is inherently racist or evil."[43] While it is encouraging to see racism equated with evil, this memo does so in a way that not only slides from critiques of the United States and whiteness as institutions to hyperbolic statements about specific people being inherently evil but also implies that without evil there can be no racism, making mundane, polite, structural racism impossible to engage. At times, the slide is more overt, as when Sam Jones, a member of the College Republicans, announced that CRT teaches that "the way you are born contributes to the amount of success you can achieve in this country. [It] states that white people are born with everything and if you are not white, you are born with nothing."[44] The first sentence is absolutely correct, but the second engages in sleight-of-hand, treating "contributes" as identical to the overblown formation of "everything/nothing"—with a straight face. These dramatics are illogical, but are highly effective in producing feels about the CRT text.

Similarly, CRT concepts like intersectionality are caricatured to make them seem absurd. One writer of a letter to his local paper contended that "in Critical Race Theory, a white-skinned, heterosexual Christian male is considered to be part of a group of guilty oppressors. A black, gay, female transgender would be considered to be part of a group of innocent victims. As part of Critical Race Theory, intersectionality also teaches that those in the 'oppressed' group have greater moral superiority than those in the oppressor group."[45] This statement distorts the actual premise of intersectionality that all of these different social structures both (a) contribute to the life chances a person has and (b) interact with each other, and constructs caricatured "maximum privilege" and "maximum oppression" figures. Then it layers on the idea that privilege and oppression are matters of personal guilt or innocence rather than descriptors of structural positions. This exploits the ways that, as Hartzell argues, "the presumption of personal innocence for any lingering manifestations of racism has opened space for white folks to imagine themselves as victims of racial injustice by, for example, [. . .] interpreting discourse on racism as a personal attack on their good character."[46] To cap it all off, the letter to the editor ratchets that up even further to a claim of moral superiority. Each bit of the letter is more absurd than the last, but it casts that absurdity quite handily back onto the concept of intersectionality. Here again, the point is not to make a reasoned argument against the body of CRT scholarship but to have collective negative feelings about this body of text. The outlandish statement is a staple of this genre, as in the claim that CRT promotes "an idea that black people are incapable of achieving anything on their own,"[47] when any critical analysis of race would instead argue that Black people do achieve, but have to do so against the grain of systemic racism—working twice as hard for half the credit, as the saying goes. Thus, there is a consistent move to construct over-the-top arguments that enable dismissing all of CRT as ridiculous.

Reverse Motte and Bailey: Undermining the Reasonable

Another signature move of the CRT panic is the slide back the other way, from outrageous to reasonable. One anti-CRT screed contends that "the two-step CRT apologia described is thus willfully dishonest. It is a bad-faith argument, pure and simple. In formal logic, we would recognize it as a prototypical motte-and-bailey fallacy."[48] The "motte-and-bailey fallacy" conflates two different positions, arguing the controversial one (the outer edges, akin to the bailey in a medieval castle) while pretending to support the uncontroversial one (something centrist, like the motte in a castle). I contend that the anti-CRT argument can be understood as a reverse motte-and-bailey, trying to force proponents to defend a bailey not of their own making—the outlandish argument—in an attempt to overwhelm them and let the motte—actual analysis of racism—be overrun. This is what makes the CRT panic's other slippage more insidious, as opponents take outrage at caricatured CRT and point it back at formerly uncontroversial and ultimately centrist interventions in racism. For example, Florida's anti-CRT "law stipulates that educators cannot teach critical race theory, which it describes as 'the theory that racism is not merely the product of prejudice, but that racism is embedded in American society and its legal systems in order to uphold the supremacy of white persons.'"[49] Racism *is not* just individual prejudice. It *is* embedded in systems. These are uncontroversial social-scientific observations, and now, using the lever of the CRT panic, illegal in the nation's third largest state. A parent at a school board meeting in Pennsylvania made a particularly clear slide, arguing that "saying America is wholly racist, and White supremacy are [*sic*] the biggest threats to America, is like saying Big Foot is the biggest threat. It's a lie."[50] It is a clear caricature to say that America is "wholly" racist, but the outrage at that is then slid back to dismiss a claim about the threat white supremacists pose—an actual threat identified by the Department of Homeland Security during the Trump administration.[51] This comment also begins to suggest how the CRT panic can move people toward white nationalism, linking an attack on one with dismissing the danger of the other.

This move appears in many variations. For example, Fox News host Laura Ingraham says, "So if you're White, you are de facto guilty. Now, if you're not White, you're given special status and consideration. Now, they call this diversity, equity and inclusion, DEI, but it's really just plain old racism."[52] Ingraham, a leading source of white-supremacist talking points on Fox,[53] skillfully raises the specter of white guilt to then cast doubt on DEI, which, far from being radical, has often been critiqued as a superficial approach to antiracism that simply adds people of color into institutions without unsettling their structural whiteness.[54] Yet through Ingraham's rhetoric centering white feelings, even superficial diversity is deemed racist. In one of the most absurd—and therefore illustrative—examples, an Idaho state representative recounted a story told by one of her constituents, who complained about being asked to teach *To Kill a Mockingbird*:[55] "The message was clear: White people are bad, Black people are innocent victims. And the students were encouraged to believe there was an endless era of Black victimization"; as CNN pointed out, far from being a newfangled innovation of CRT, "To Kill a Mockingbird was published in 1960, has long been considered a literary classic, and its protagonists are a White lawyer and his precocious daughter,"[56] but what mattered to this CRT panicker was that it was a novel that unambiguously constructs racism as wrong, which to her was antiwhite. That is, while there is in fact ongoing mistreatment of Black people to this day, it is very much mainstream to claim that all racism was ended by the civil rights movement—which was still fighting in 1960 to secure most of the legal successes it would eventually have. Thus, contending that *To Kill a Mockingbird* falsely extends the "era of Black victimization" too far along the trajectory of history, when the novel describes the Jim Crow era, appears to contend that even the civil rights movement was not needed, let alone CRT, which arose to explain how racist outcomes persisted when formal equality under law was achieved. Through techniques of conflation and slippage, then, the CRT panic expands to ever more targets.

CRT as the Everybogeyman

The final way in which CRT is framed as dangerous is through slippage to conflate it with existing bogeymen, again trading on feels. To begin with a bogeyman that at least shares with CRT a focus on disrupting white supremacy, there are forty-four references to The 1619 Project in the data set. This journalistic project, released by the *New York Times Magazine* in August 2019, "aims to reframe the country's history by placing the consequences of slavery and the contributions of Black Americans at the very center of the United States' national narrative."[57] While there were some small-scale disputes of some of the arguments from academic historians, the project was widely viewed as a helpful reframing of the nation that emphasized how racism has been with us from the start—except among conservatives, who have campaigned against it.[58] Fox News reported that former president Donald Trump declared that "it should be positive school choice, teaching American history for real, abolishing the '1619 Project,' eliminating critical race theory,"[59] making just such a move to conflate the two. Setting aside the chilling implications of the state "abolishing" a piece of journalism from a private company or "eliminating" a field of academic inquiry, the move here is to associate the new thing conservatives do not like (CRT) with the thing they had not liked two years before.

A second conservative bogeyman leveraged against CRT is Marxism, which at least since the Cold War has been a floating signifier ready to take on the disliked event of the week, much as CRT became in 2021. A fellow at the conservative think tank the Ethics and Public Policy Center contended that "this is a warmed over latest version of Marxism, and they are trying to teach the kids to see the world through lenses of power, and become enemies with one another, ultimately attributing everything to either being a part of an oppressed class where Marx had economic oppression, the woke brought in the categories of oppression to include gender, sexuality, and race."[60] Unsurprisingly, this is not an accurate summary of Marx, who did want workers of the world to unite but did not think of class in terms of identity, instead defining category membership through the action of having surplus value extracted (proletariat) and doing the extracting (bourgeoisie). Nevertheless, much like the outlandish claims against CRT itself, what Marx really said is irrelevant because he is a text that generates feels. Another route of slippage arrives at Marxism via the Frankfurt School—who were, at least, Marxist. One Fox host claimed, "Not everybody remembers critical theory in the Frankfurt School of Marxism and so forth, which is where critical race theory came from. It's not just coincidence that they have very similar names."[61] On one level, this is amusing, because of course "not everybody remembers" a group of theorists rarely read outside of graduate programs in the humanities and social sciences. But it is also simply false. There is nothing particularly Marxist about CRT, and while it does draw from "continental social and political philosophy,"[62] there is not some root "critical theory" that then gives rise to branches of critical x, y, or z theory as proposed in this claim, but linking CRT to Marxism through the commonality of "critical + theory" achieves the desired end despite its falsity.

The notion of being "anti-American" is yet another bogeyman raised with CRT—ironically both conflating antiracist and anti-American and insisting that America is not racist. This maneuver has three key features. First, it is totalizing: CRT's argument that problems have been structured into society is transmuted into saying that problems are everything, everywhere. Thus, CRT proponents are alleged to claim that America is "inherently racist,"[63] or, as Texas senator Ted Cruz put it, "fundamentally racist and irredeemably racist."[64] That movement from "fundamentally" to "irredeemably" is characteristic of the CRT panic—saying something is systemic does not mean that it cannot be fixed, just that the way it gets fixed needs to act at the level of the system rather than nibbling around the edges at particular manifestations. Here we also see some of the other characteristic moves of the CRT panic—slippage from reasonable to over the top discussed above and a similar slide from structures down onto individuals (as in moving from critique of whiteness as a system to attributing guilt to individual white people, which I will discuss in the next section). The resistance to systemic thinking is sometimes direct: "We did not want our children to be taught that America is systemically racist."[65] This complaint demonstrates that the panic is not just about a mistaken impression about what CRT is and does but an objection to fundamental facts about how racism works that are uncontroversial to experts in the field.

On the other hand, the CRT panic is bound up in feelings about the United States. Commenters lament, as Florida governor Ron DeSantis does, that "critical race theory is teaching people to hate our country,"[66] or, as Missouri senator Josh Hawley does, that children who start out with "eyes full of hope and hearts full of pride in their country" have this destroyed by learning about CRT.[67] While it is commendable if learning about US racism troubles childlike uncritical reverence for the nation (it doesn't; people keep the reverence and jettison the history), feelings about the country are fundamentally irrelevant to the question of understanding how it functioned historically and functions today—but very relevant to provoking outrage. In such ways, treating CRT as an amorphous transmedia canon without clear boundaries positions it to be seized on as antifanon: distorted into caricature, used to undermine even centrist antiracism, and linked to bogeymen. In this way, it becomes a text that is tremendously powerful for evoking feels.

White People Tears: White Feelings and Constructing an Underdog Subculture

If CRT functions as a text that is the site of feels, then the collectivity of those feels, and the way they cultivate a community identity around this text, is both the other side of how fan studies is useful and, more importantly, how the CRT panic cultivates a collective identity of whiteness beyond self-identified white supremacists. In particular, the discourse makes three moves to leverage feelings about whiteness as community and identity. First, it asserts that white people are made to feel bad, in part through slippage from structural racism to individual racists. Second, white people feel attacked through slippage from CRT as opposing white supremacy to CRT as opposing white people. Third, white people want to feel good about being white people. Ultimately, this centering of white feelings shows that the threat of CRT is not to history or America or even white children, but whiteness as a means of distributing power.

To begin with emphasis on white people's hurt feelings, perhaps the most telling slippage in the CRT panic is from race as a system down to individual racists—usually, specifically individual white people as racists. For example, Ted Cruz claimed that "critical race theory says every white person is a racist."[68] "A racist" as an identifiable kind of person is irrelevant to questions about structural racism—but collapsing the distinction collapses the distance between the average white person who is a beneficiary of racism and the hood-wearing or tiki torch–carrying white supremacist invoked by "a racist." Because the white supremacist is still largely reviled, this collapse provokes a strong negative reaction in the average white person, but thinning that boundary also helps white supremacists tremendously—allowing an argument that "they say everything is racist anyway, so come join us." In a similar argument, centrist Damon Linker claims that "politicians and parents [. . .] do not want their children taught in state-run and state-funded schools that the country was founded on an ideology of white supremacy in which every white child and family today is invariably complicit regardless of their personal views of their Black fellow citizens."[69] Here, as so often, the move is down to individual people and their individual feelings and beliefs, never even pausing at (let alone taking seriously) the system level.

Paradoxically, even the universalizing moves use this logic, as when CRT is described as "committed to advancing profoundly un-American notions of collectivized and racially hierarchical guilt and innocence."[70] Collectivized guilt maps the guilt of some individuals onto all individuals, such that, in alleging it, individuals are still the point.

Fundamentally, the issue is about bad feelings. One writer of a letter to the editor in his local paper demonstrates a common framing: "A lot of White people, in particular, have grown weary and resentful of being called racist."[71] Racist, here, is a thing to be called, a bad or hurtful name—not an encouragement to examine one's own behavior or structural benefit. An author interviewed on Fox News took a similar position, saying, "It's a suggestion that even considering yourself above race is white,"[72] as if considering race a negative and "low" thing to want to be above did not rely on the fact that "because whiteness is unmarked, 'race' is often taken as a synonym for 'people of color,' and if people of color are who 'have' race, whiteness becomes race free, or, crucially, race neutral."[73] A desire to transcend a "low" thing associated with people of color is precisely white—and precisely about white feelings. Another common framing is that CRT is "teaching white people to hate themselves."[74]

In keeping with the CRT panic's focus on K–12 education, there is a swath of arguments specifically about bad feelings for children. One parent at a meeting covered by CNN declared, "We do not want our children to be taught that they are oppressed or they are oppressors by virtue of their color."[75] This notion of "an oppressor" is individualizing and helps provoke the feels integral to the CRT panic. Others characterize the situation more bluntly as "teaching white kids they are bad because they are white."[76] This often takes the form of allegations that CRT causes guilt, as when Tennessee Senate majority leader Jack Johnson called for teaching history "in a manner that doesn't leave a school child leaving the classroom feeling guilty because of who they are."[77] Another feeling CRT is frequently alleged to cause is shame, with former vice president Mike Pence declaring that "critical race theory teaches children as young as kindergarten to be ashamed of their skin color."[78] More dramatically, a member of anti-CRT group Parents Defending Education declares that "we should not be trying to shame and degrade children."[79]

In all of these instances, the feelings of white people, and specifically white children, are centered; the feels and the fanon entirely displace the substance of what CRT is and does—because only the feelings actually matter to these speakers. At a fundamental level, all of these claims are, of course, incorrect. The feelings of particular white people are irrelevant to the problem of systemic racism—this is how we can have "racism without racists" and why focusing on individual racists is unhelpful to actually solving racism.[80] Moreover, even if the project of CRT did focus on white feelings, guilt and shame and self-hatred are profoundly useless feelings when it comes to solving anything. Finally, and most importantly, the focus on white feelings recenters white people all over again when the whole point is to stop making white people the default perspective. This is a flow from a mediated text to collective feels to identity and community, and this structure is one key reason to think of this phenomenon through the lens of fan studies, well versed in making sense of such collective action based in intense affect.

This recurring focus on white people's bad feelings lends itself to understanding white people as under attack. Seeing the ingroup as an embattled underdog—even when it is not, like Gamergaters, Zach Snyder fans, or Sad Puppies—is a common feature of fandom.[81] Out of a similar formation, another site of slippage in the CRT panic is from opposition to racism or white supremacy to opposition to (or even violence toward) white people. One Fox News host simply terms CRT "anti-white propaganda."[82] A parent at an anti-CRT town hall covered by CNN was worried about what might happen to her (white) kids: "This is my taxpayer's money. I don't want it to go to indoctrinate kids that then are going to hate my kids because of the color of their skin and attack them because of the color of their skin. What happened in the summer, it twisted the minds of all kids. My kids can be attacked by Antifa kids or BLM kids if they're not black. They are white like my kids. But they are believing, they were indoctrinated."[83] Here, in addition to packaging together a variety of bogeymen—BLM (Black Lives Matter), mentioned a total of fifty-eight times in the overall data between abbreviated and spelled-out versions; Antifa, with nineteen overall mentions—and grievances (taxpayer dollars) with a belief that antiracist attitudes are a sign of indoctrination, this parent reveals a specific fear that CRT will lead to (possibly physical) "attacks" against white kids.[84] A document distributed at an anti-CRT forum claimed that "CRT's vision for our future mandates legal discrimination against white citizens."[85] One parent complained that when she posted a letter against CRT to Facebook, "she was 'literally lynched.' CNN suggested perhaps she was just figuratively lynched"; what she found to be akin to terrorist extrajudicial execution was "very harshly, obviously, calling me racist and bigot and demanding that my post would be removed."[86] These statements are unreasonable, but they are also sincerely believed.

It is less clear whether pundits making similar claims are sincere. One Fox News host claimed that to describe Black people as being at a structural disadvantage "is racist, not just towards white people, but towards black people."[87] Here, the very idea of structural inequality is treated as self-evidently racist against white people. At the extreme, radio host Michael Savage reportedly said that teaching CRT in schools was "exactly what was done to the Jews in Germany. And it's the road to the death camps for white people."[88] The (astonishingly extreme) claim here appears to be that talking about structural advantage to white people is the same as treating Jewish people as subhuman and murdering six million of them. In all of these ways, then, white people, though they are the dominant group in society, are transmuted into an embattled minority. Such claims, whether sincere or cynical, are rooted in a sense that civil rights are a zero-sum game—that more of them for Black people, Indigenous people, and other people of color means less for white people. But it also, at a deeper level, stumbles into the truth: whiteness *is* a product of white supremacy. Dismantling white supremacy will force a wholesale reconfiguration of what it means to be white, and white people *will* lose—but only our unearned sense of superiority.

Such arguments form a point of contact with the far Right. Hartzell argues that cultivating an underdog position is a tool of white nationalist affective recruitment: "Both white nationalist and 'alt-right' rhetoric attempt to promote pro-white racial consciousness and make space for overt celebrations of white pride in mainstream public discourse by disarticulating whiteness from its position of domination to reimagine white U.S. Americans as disadvantaged and disenfranchised."[89] That is, the self-identity as victims, underdogs, etc., can lead to seeking out collective spaces and communities in which to feel pride. Bridget Blodgett and Anastasia Salter similarly note that "the fictive identity which both

the alt-right and #GamerGate movements have established for themselves positions them as a weaker outsider to modern American culture.
They have created fictional enemies to represent the social power they
feel they lack in their regular lives."[90] As the mention of "fictional enemies" suggests, often, this is specifically a sense that they have been victimized by the gains of others. Blodgett and Salter describe the far Right
as "prone to adopting narratives of victimhood in which women and
non-white individuals are the aggressors and threats to a 'way of life.'"[91]
Frequently, as in the CRT panic, this alleged victimization is framed as
"reverse racism" or "reverse discrimination." While there is of course no
such thing, "given the European American experience—historically and
sociologically—equal opportunity for people of color feels like reverse
discrimination for whites."[92] In addition to matching people's feelings,
such claims also do cultural work: "Claiming white injury is a way of
protesting the erosions of white men's historical advantage while denying that advantage has ever existed."[93]

This then calls for greater attention to how notions of embattled whiteness drive radicalization. As Hamilton Carroll contends, "White injury
is clearly more perception than reality, but it is a perception that has extraordinary sociocultural heft."[94] Convincing white people to see themselves as victims as white people is the lever that gets some subset of them
to form a conscious attachment to whiteness. Loretta J. Ross and Mary
Ann Mauney, describing the recruitment tactics of white-supremacist
groups in the mid-1990s, say that "broadening the issues and using conservative buzzwords attract the attention of whites who may not consider
themselves racist but in their own minds are just patriotic Americans
concerned about the moral decay of 'their' country."[95] This move, to
loop in conservative buzzwords and concerns about weakness of the nation, is startlingly similar to the CRT panic's leveraging of conservatives'
most beloved and feared terms. The fact that these emotional moves to
evoke threats are designed to move people toward white supremacy then
casts raising the specter of harm to white children in a new light. That is,
there is a straight line from "white kids learning about racism in schools
are under attack" to the "14 words," the white-supremacist slogan that "we
must secure the existence of our people and a future for white children."[96]

This white-supremacist recruitment pathway works because, in the
face of feeling bad and attacked, CRT panickers—like other similarly

positioned white people—want to feel good. As Rebecca Lewis notes in her report on reactionary right YouTube, such figures and their videos "provide a likeminded community for those who feel like social underdogs for their rejection of progressive values, and they provide a sense of countercultural rebellion for those same audiences."[97] Both Bharath Ganesh and Lewis stress the role of identity in building these kinds of communities.[98] Jessie Daniels argued in her study of the early white-supremacist Internet that "it offers them something meaningful," particularly for those who "experience cultural alienation or anomie" that leaves them yearning for such a place.[99]

This is to underscore that one common response to feeling isolated and especially embattled as part of a group is to seek out community with those with similar interests. Ruth Frankenberg's study of white women found that being the default and not anything in particular can encourage people to "yearn for belonging to a bounded, nameable culture," or "emphasize the parts of their heritage that are bounded over the parts that are dominant"—such as knowing the European country one's ancestors immigrated from—noting that this risks "romanticizing the experience of being oppressed," as indeed recruiting membership in whiteness as oppressed does. Frankenberg cautions that "focusing on one's membership in a bounded group may mean failing to fully examine what it means to be part of a cultural and racial group that is dominant and normative," which is exactly the point in moves to cultivate a collective white identity.[100] This drive for a positive experience of whiteness—both as good and as bounded and named—is served by attachments to whiteness rooted in "common sense, communal belonging, and pride."[101] Ultimately, "As mainstream white audiences awaken to the contemporary significance of race, they are positioned to seek affectively positive formations of racial consciousness—ways of acknowledging race, in general, and whiteness, in particular, that feel good."[102] What the CRT panic tends toward is building a community based on the feels about this text. This allows a reverse flow from hating CRT back toward loving whiteness.

Conclusion

Ultimately, using the tools of fan studies to make sense of the CRT panic calls attention to several key features. First, the CRT panic is rooted in feels about a text—negative ones—and can therefore usefully be thought of through the lens of antifandom. Second, CRT itself is treated as a transmedia canon, and particularly one that is modular and can be drawn from selectively to create (anti)fanon. This process of fanon formation then includes some distinctive moves: the actual claims of CRT are pushed several steps further to absurdity, outrage over caricatures of CRT is used to slide back toward thoroughly mainstream concepts and cast them as similarly extreme, and CRT is mapped onto established culture-war bogeymen to argue for its danger by analogy. These moves recruit intense negative affective attachments to CRT, which then enable attachments to whiteness. Seeing the ingroup as an embattled underdog, even when it is not, is a common feature of fandom, and a frequent response to feeling isolated and especially embattled as part of a group is to seek out community. In this way, thinking the CRT panic alongside fandom helps us make sense of both the feels and the fanon of it—the emotional intensity and how unmoored that is from the facts of actual CRT scholarship. Through applying the lens of fan studies to something that by most definitions bears little resemblance to a fandom, we see both what the field has to offer and, more importantly, the power of feels, texts, and community in shaping contemporary culture.

Conclusion

Of Victimhood and Vitriol

As I said in the introduction, calling fandom "ugly" self-evidently requires specification rather than seeming in any way obvious. Now that I have spent seven chapters describing cases of fandom ugliness, we can see more clearly what, specifically, "ugly" means. Ugly fandom is fans of former US president Donald Trump and Bernie Bros—particularly aggressive fans of US senator Bernie Sanders—thinking that any election their candidate loses is rigged. Ugly fandom is fans who are willing to destroy what they love when it doesn't go the way they want, such as those who respond to fan fiction with hundreds or thousands of tags clogging up their experience on the Archive of Our Own by trying to render the site unusable in protest, as well as fans of *The 100* (The CW, 2014–2020) trying to get the show canceled because their favorite character was killed. Ugly fandom is thinking that queerness means you are downtrodden, no matter what else is going on, as seen in the homonormativity of slash fan fiction's focus on middle-class domesticity and whiteness; fans lashing out against the showrunner of *The 100* after Lexa's death; both sides of the fan fiction Anti Wars thinking their marginalization as queer—and their self-identification as fighting for other queer people—justifies their behavior; and the consistent failure of queer fandom to reckon with race. Ugly fandom is an argument that freedom of speech is not only absolute but a right to enjoy speech even (or even especially) if it is harmful to others, as in the anti-anti position that asserts a right to write, read, and enjoy fan fiction featuring underage sex, incest, and rape, as well as fans insisting that YouTuber Steven Crowder's racist and homophobic attacks on journalist Carlos Maza are funny jokes.

In more general terms, ugly fandom is fan mass harassment, a recurring feature of fandom in the last decade, including in #Gamergate, the campaign against feminists in video games; #Comicsgate, which opposed diversity in comics; #LexaDeservedBetter, the hashtag responding to the character's death in *The 100*; social media attacks on actor Kelly Marie Tran by *Star Wars* fans; and #VoxAdpocalypse, the outcry from fans of Crowder when he faced consequences for his harassment of Maza. This is, as these examples show, typically social media–based harassment, and the role of platform aggregation and amplification in scaling up ugliness to previously unseen levels should not be disregarded. Ugly fandom is also fans believing that there is no need to pull punches or think about who is on the other end of an angry social media post. Moreover, in most cases, the mass harassment seen in ugly fandom is specifically racist and sexist. This exclusionary tendency is related to the ways in which ugly fandom is often specifically collective action to resist attempts to increase the prevalence and prominence of people of color, women, and queer people in fandoms and as fan objects. Ugly fandom is also the ways fans often think only about their own (sometimes imagined) marginalization at the expense of others. At its extreme, ugly fandom is the violence of the August 2017 Unite the Right rally, which was fundamentally about fandom of the Confederacy and the white supremacy it represents, and it is the rally-turned-attempted-coup on January 6, 2021, which was bound up in Trump fandom. Ugly fandom is rooted in a dualistic moral framework that sharply distinguishes between the good "us" and the evil "them," whether this is an ingroup and outgroup of fans, fans and industry, or the "them" who have wronged "us," whomever they may be.

In this chapter, I highlight the underlying patterns in beliefs and behavior across types of ugly fandom toward making sense of why it appears where and when and how it does. I show that ugly fandom is rooted in beliefs about fans being victims—whether as fans, as queer people, or as white men; of industry, of other fans, or of social justice. Moreover, ugly fandom responds to actual social structures and situations that have been misunderstood. This is what makes it such an intractable problem, as fans may be misinterpreting what they see, and acting horribly in response, but they are not making it up. It is essential to take seriously the deeply affective nature of fan ugliness, and this is why fan studies is such an essential lens on contemporary power relations.

Hurt People Hurt People: How Fan Ugliness is Driven by Perceived Victimhood

Seeing the ingroup as an embattled underdog is a common feature of fandom. Lexa fans insisted they had been mistreated, quite possibly for ratings. Slash fans position themselves as transgressive and marginalized for their queer desires. Comicsgaters argue that they are devalued, disrespected, and even subject to attack. However, it is important to recognize that this self-perception as downtrodden can happen even when it is not true, as with Comicsgaters, Gamergaters, Zach Snyder fans feeling that they have been denied his true vision for *Justice League* (Warner Bros., 2017; *Zack Snyder's Justice League*, HBO Max, 2021), or campaigns to ensure that "traditional" white and masculinist science fiction won Hugo Awards by groups called Sad Puppies and Rabid Puppies. Indeed, it is especially important to pay attention to the victim narrative when it is not accurate. As legal scholar Mary Anne Franks argues, "Victim-claiming is a reversal technique that puts the powerful in the space of the vulnerable, the abuser in the space of the abused."[1] This is precisely what happens when fandoms dominated by straight white men like #Comicsgate, #VoxAdpocalypse, and the CRT panic make themselves out to be the victims of their actual victims. Across fandoms and flashpoints, there is a persistent inability to tell a powerful role from a powerless one, and this has everything to do with when ugly fandom happens and what it looks like.

This is to say that the excesses of fan reaction chronicled in this book are rooted in a belief in victimhood and fan powerlessness. As an organized group, or even a diffuse, angry mob, fans have incredible capacity to do harm, but each group/mob I have discussed is comprised of individuals who themselves do not have much power, particularly compared to the media industries and other institutions that are a frequent target of backlash. From the perspective of any given fan, they are David and the media industry is Goliath, and there are long odds of success. Fans' belief that the opposition is powerful and distant, someone they cannot really hurt, who will perhaps not even see their angry social media posts, was often true for any given fan in isolation, for #Gamergate and #Comicsgate as much as Lexa fans. As scholars such as Katie Wilson have shown, fans' belief that they are marginalized or even persecuted as fans, geeks, or nerds can serve as a radicalization pathway; reactionary backlash events, like Gamergate and the Sad Puppies, grow out of the fact that men's rights activism speaks to fans' sense of being "bullied" because negative stereotypes about fans feminize them.[2] What this book has shown is that a similar ratcheting up of harmful behavior can arise even without a far-right Internet subculture waiting to recruit (or receive) disaffected fans. While ugly fandom can certainly lead to political radicalization, it is important to understand even when it doesn't. Fundamentally, the belief in powerlessness is itself powerful, tending to lead fans to rationalize taking action by any means necessary and to underestimate their own impacts.

That is, identifying one's fan group as a victim (however inaccurately) is used to justify nearly endless vitriol. Within this framework, victim status is understood to excuse the response, used to elide questions of collateral damage and suppress attention to other forms of harm than the one fans are focused on. Because the opposition is seen as powerful and out of fans' reach, because they believe they are punching upward, and because they think of themselves as members of a marginalized group that has been harmed, there is a sense that anything and everything is permitted. This is clear from the fans who oppose mega-tagged fiction, who did not care that they were making AO3 worse but rather saw their campaign as noble because it was in the name of making the platform correct the design flaw that allowed mega-tagging. It is also precisely the logic by which "Gamergate participants adhered to a normatively white masculine subject position that viewed itself as being under attack from SJWs and feminists, and thus justified harassing behavior through a mantle of victimhood."[3] Across multiple types of fans, their (real or imagined) marginal position is understood to justify harassing behavior, and constraints they might (or might not) otherwise have felt disappear or become less salient as fan hurt authorizes hurting back.

Another reason why the ugly fan responses look the way they do is that fans feel that something they *should* have has been taken from them. This is what is often talked about in terms of fans being "entitled." In my 2019 book, I contended that "arguments that fans are entitled have accumulated in recent years and erupted in summer 2016; they are a sign of a backlash that could potentially roll back the (limited) progress of fan inclusion" in media-industry decision-making processes.[4] In that earlier work, I was interested in how the language of entitlement was used by media makers and journalists to flatten out the differences between activism and harassment in order to render all fan requests illegitimate. Here I want to view this concept at a different angle: these fans do feel entitled to different outcomes than they have received, but rather than using this fact to dismiss them, analysis has to take it seriously. Lexa fans felt entitled to have her survive and thrive because of the way *The 100* staff had interacted with them and hyped up the relationship. That did not come from nowhere. Indeed, white men fans feel entitled to being centered because they always have been. That comes from somewhere, too.

Much as Eve Ng's definition of queerbaiting notes that "the crucial element is [. . .] how satisfactorily queerness plays out in the canonical text relative to viewer expectations," a context that "changes over time,"[5] I am framing a model of entitlement here that makes sense of fan demands in relation to fan expectations in particular cases. The expectations may be (and often are) mistaken, but they shape what fans do, and for that reason they cannot be ignored. Bernie Bros felt that Sanders deserved the support of all progressives and that therefore Elizabeth Warren's campaign was underhanded. That is why they call her a snake. Antis feel that fan fiction should be a safe and inclusive space that does not reproduce the failures of dominant culture and therefore conclude that including troubling content is a breach of what they have agreed to in participating. The Fandom Is Beautiful narrative of fandom as a progressive, inclusive space is itself the reason why they act as though their consent has been violated by the existence of disturbing stories. Right-wing fandoms like #Comicsgate and #VoxAdpocalypse so frequently invoke the cuck, the man who does not have the power he ought, because they have anxiety about access to the power they feel is their due. This is a notion that white masculinity *should* be centered and powerful and that when it is not, something has gone wrong.[6] Taken to its extreme in the CRT panic, a sense that things are falling apart gives rise to seeing opposition to racism or white supremacy as opposition to (or even violence toward) white people, because people who formerly did not have to think about their whiteness and its value—let alone have either one questioned—suddenly do. This is not to say that any of them are *right* to have these expectations. But it is inescapable that they *do* have these expectations.

If fans see themselves as marginalized and as having had things taken from them, it is unsurprising that they might then look for a villain and that their sense of the situation might congeal into a stark black-and-white morality in which there is a specific person or group that has done the oppressing and must be resisted. Moreover, having such an external enemy works to solidify in-group ties and build community—which can then form a feedback loop as the filter bubble of fans with shared opinions convince each other that they are correct, that their opinion is widespread, and/or that their course of action is warranted. This is the source of the "you're either with us or you're against us" models that have recurred across the case studies in this book. As Matt Hills notes, "Toxic fan practices can be seen as 'good' by those carrying them out,"[7] and the roles of the "us" and "them" morality and of the mutually reinforcing echo chamber in convincing them of this goodness should not be underestimated. In conjunction with First Amendment fundamentalism, which "has transformed the right to free speech from a minimalist, negative protection from government into a super-right that allows the most powerful groups in society to defend affirmative accommodation for an increasingly expansive concept of speech, regardless of the costs to the rights of other groups,"[8] this dualistic view is the origin of the argument that there is only a binary—either anything goes in fan fiction or humor, or nothing is safe. Indeed, in the Anti Wars, both sides operate with a rigid dualistic morality: any inclusion of harmful content is endorsement, and any suggestion that troubling content be handled carefully is censorship. Similarly, asking straight white men heroes to share the spotlight—whether in comic books or history books—is seen as equivalent to eliminating them altogether. As this link to the CRT panic begins to suggest, such moral surety is a staple of the contemporary culture wars.

The sharp division of villain and victim is sustained in part through an expansive notion of victimhood. In such a model, harassing speech is free speech, which can never be in any way curtailed, but contesting it is harm done to the #Gamergate or #Comicsgate or #VoxAdpocalypse fan (as opposed to someone else exercising free speech in return). Likewise, these sorts of sweeping concepts of victimhood are how Comicsgaters identify themselves as being persecuted by SJWs and bad fans by having their pleasures contested or even just de-universalized. At a fundamental level, these incidents turn on questions of identity, in particular reactionary fans' identification as victims of the marginalized groups they both mock and see as extraordinarily powerful. Similarly, the CRT panic sees the diminution (a diminutive diminution at that!) of the centrality of white people in history, literature, and education more broadly as a harm. We do not have to concede that these are forms of harm (I think we shouldn't), but analysis can and should recognize how they arise from the combination of a victim identity and a sharp moral dualism—anything "they" do that "we" don't like is villainy.

In all of these ways, then, groups of fans with various levels of actual power are transmuted into an embattled minority (at least in their own minds). It is particularly important to understand how this imaginary embattlement then collides with actual marginalization. Queerness is seen as overriding all other marginalization across slash fiction, Lexa fans, and the Anti Wars, for example. This makes it impossible to address racism in these phenomena. Among reactionary fans, their sense of victimhood similarly precludes seeing how they victimize. Such claims, whether sincere or cynical, are rooted in a sense that media and political power are a zero-sum game—that more for Black people, Indigenous people, and other people of color, more for women, more for queer people, means less for straight white men. If the comic book industry does a run in which Thor is a woman or Spider-Man is Afro-Latino, they are abandoning their "loyal fan base"—geeky straight white men—to cater to "outsiders" who want to push liberal politics, even though these characters are always straight white men in another run later (or even concurrently). Importantly, this perception is often specifically a sense that fans have been victimized by the gains of others, much as Bridget Blodgett and Anastasia Salter describe the far Right as "prone to adopting narratives of victimhood in which women and non-white individuals are the aggressors and threats to a 'way of life.'"[9] Frequently, as in #Comicsgate and the CRT panic, inclusion is framed as "reverse racism" or "reverse discrimination." While there is of course no such thing as reverse racism, diminishing the unearned privilege that white people have historically had does often feel, experientially, like a loss. In addition to matching people's feelings that they have less than they used to, such claims also do cultural work: "Claiming white injury is a way of protesting the erosions of white men's historical advantage while denying that advantage has ever existed."[10] This is a position rooted in seeing straight white men as the cultural default and rejecting (often intensely) the inclusion of anyone else within the fannish community or fan object as an unwelcome imposition.

However, perhaps related to the sense that they *ought* to have certain kinds of social and cultural power, at the same time that ugly fandom has this strong attachment to a victim identity, fans also see their own collective action as powerful. In a seeming contradiction, this is a model in which fans are both downtrodden victims of whomever their nemesis happens to be *and* think of themselves as so central and important and powerful an audience segment that their boycott actions like those against *The 100* and YouTube, their buycotts such as that of Mug Club, and their large-scale hashtag campaigns like #Comicsgate and #LexaDeservedBetter and #VoxAdpocalypse will produce results. Fans think they are marginalized, but also that losing their patronage would devastate the media maker. It is hard to square this belief in their own power with the fact that they also believe they are so weak and downtrodden that they can go in guns blazing without having to think about consequences, but the attitudes do coexist.

A Case of Mistaken (Victim) Identity: Understanding Ugliness on Its Own Terms

In one way, fandom ugliness seems easy to dismiss: these idiots think they are victims when they're not? Write them off. In another way, it seems like an intractable problem: How can you reason with someone's hurt feelings? Rather than either of these approaches, I propose that the way out is through—interpretation must take seriously the deep affective attachments *and* the mistaken sense of victimhood. Analysis must understand where these feelings come from in order to respond to fandom ugliness, and in doing so will gain insight into the broader sociopolitical landscape of the contemporary moment. The points of contact across very different fandoms that I have demonstrated throughout this book show that fandom reflects and refracts broader relations of power—and, specifically, domination. In fact, it is precisely being enmeshed in these relations that produces the particular configuration of ugly fandom that arises. Fans often correctly identify that there is some kind of power relation happening to or near them—that they are mistreated or devalued or have had their power diminished—but equally often draw the wrong conclusion about its cause and solution. Antis correctly identify rape and incest and underage sex in fan fiction as troubling material, but incorrectly conclude that it can therefore never be addressed at all and that anyone who does so is condoning violence. Fans correctly identified that they had been wronged when they were manipulated into watching *The 100* with Lexa as the carrot when the writers knew they intended to kill her off, but incorrectly concluded that the right way to respond was mass harassment of Rothenberg. Both groups of fans are right that the situations they object to are legitimately upsetting, and this is why the responses—disproportionate as they are—make sense to them.

Similarly, fans do correctly identify that they do not have a great deal of power relative to media industries. Lexa fans certainly did not have the capacity to get Rothenberg fired, persuade the CW network or its advertisers to change course, or impact any other corporate entity involved—though not for lack of trying. Comicsgaters are not wrong that longtime fans and loyalty are not respected by media industries, but they blame marginalized creators and fans rather than the fact that comics, like every business, is pushed by the financialization of capital to ever more growth, not catering to the same fixed group. Crowder fans were not wrong that YouTube had a huge amount of power in the situation and could shut down any creator's livelihood at any time, but displaced this almost entirely onto Carlos Maza, who had no such power. Fans are right that they are relatively powerless in their interactions with industry, and this is why it makes sense to them to fight as ferociously as they do—even as from a more distant position these responses are easily recognized as excessive.

Finally, the sense in #Comicsgate and #VoxAdpocalypse and the CRT panic that white people, especially straight white men, are losing power is also not entirely wrong (if vastly overstated). Their formerly unquestioned superiority is being questioned in the mainstream rather than just by those left out. They remain both socially dominant as straight white men and the core demographic for nearly all media industry products, but they are not *as* dominant, and they are not the *only* demographic. Something has shifted, and they see that. Fans are right that power structures are changing, and this is why they react as intensely as they do. Ways of enacting domination on women, queer people, and people of color that were formerly uncontested now face pushback that is amplified enough by social or institutional media to be seen at scale. The reality of social structures of privilege that they used to be able to ignore is now visible not just to those who lack it (and have always known how privilege works) but to those whose experience was formerly silently conditioned for the better. Seeing themselves as downtrodden when they are actually still quite powerful is about perceiving the diminution of white masculine power relative to that of other groups as both far greater than it actually is and as a fundamental threat to white men,[11] and in that sense is mistaken, but there *has* been a shift. At a deeper level, the sense that resistance to white supremacy in comics, or slash fiction, or YouTube, or public culture writ large, is resistance to whiteness itself is not wrong. It is also not wrong to believe that dismantling white supremacy will force a wholesale reconfiguration of what it means to be white, and white people *will* lose—but only our unearned sense of superiority. This is why these people see whiteness as embattled. These fans do not fully understand the shifting landscape. They likely have only the vaguest sense. Certainly, seeing the shift in white masculine dominance as a crisis is incorrect. But the anxiety has a material referent, and this has everything to do with its power.

I am not saying we should not hold fans accountable for who they decide to blame and what they decide to do about it. Far from it. The harm they do—to other fans, to actors who dare to portray characters they wish had not been written, to gay Latino journalists, even to TV showrunners and elected officials with some level of institutional power and social media filtering—is significant and unacceptable no matter why it is that they are doing it. I am not even saying that we need to have compassion for fans and their hurt feelings. Indeed, at one point there was a subheading in chapter 5 that read "Everyone Is an Asshole." But I *am* saying that analysis has to reckon with the fact that there is a kernel of truth in these fan complaints. It is not possible to understand why these forms of ugliness are so recurring and persistent and impervious to logic without accounting for that iota of reality. Fans can see the impacts of various industry systems and social structures, after all. They are real. Analysis has to begin from this recognition. In such ways, by taking seriously the situations fans identify—even if thoroughly not endorsing their conclusions about them—research can understand where the victim identity comes from, why it is so persistent, and why people respond as they do.

But where do we go from there? In a situation where there is a relation of trust, where a group or some subset of its members might believe a scholar who tells them they have misinterpreted what they are seeing, making that educational move may be a productive intervention. But it would be naïve to think that every type of ugly fandom I have discussed in this book can be solved that way. What I want to suggest instead is that it might be possible to intervene before a full-blown eruption of ugly fandom by recognizing when group identity is structured around victimhood. This gives some predictive power for when a situation is likely to become explosive as the feeling of being downtrodden loosens restrictions on responses to disputes. They might be wrong that they are marginal—they often are!—but it is not possible to understand these campaigns, let alone intervene, without acknowledging that they *do* feel that way, and that it drives their responses. These feelings, right or wrong, matter because they have material effects. However, it is also important to attend to the risks of intervention. As pointed out by scholars of the far-right Internet, scholars who research such groups can become targets,[12] and the risks of collective social media action also lurk. Intervening in these situations is by no means a simple choice, but it is only possible when we understand them.

Fan Studies Is Beautiful . . . or, at Least, Useful

Ultimately, it is this taking seriously of the feels of it all that is the reason why the tools of fan studies improve understanding of these broader relations of power. Fan studies takes seriously the role of affect, specifically pleasure, in shaping communities and responses to texts. If fandom is what Louisa Ellen Stein calls a "feels culture," with public emotions that build connections between people and drive creation in community,[13] what this book has, hopefully, shown is that ugly fandom, too, is a feels culture bound together by shared, public, emotional creation of community and texts. Indeed, Stein notes that "some millennial fans seek to channel feels culture into professional or publicly visible social activist endeavors,"[14] and that is in many ways what a hashtag campaign is, regardless of whether the feeling involved is love or anger. Fan studies helps us understand refusing to consider the harms that one's pleasure in certain types of content might do, from underage, rape, and incest fan fiction to homophobic and racist jokes to (hi)stories in which all the heroes are straight white men. Thinking through fan studies and its attention to pleasure also encourages us to consider how the right to speak is often understood as a right to speak without discomfort, or even a right to pleasure in speech. Focusing on affect and pleasure helps us understand why discussions from the Anti Wars to the CRT panic circle around making people feel bad as the ultimate harm that overrides any harm those people themselves are doing, because contestation of these fictions (fan or racial) produces the absence of pleasure, and pleasure is the point.

Additionally, fan studies' attention to the affect that attaches specifically to objects of fandom helps us understand the parasocial intimacies that drive ugly fandom as much as they do any other sort. People loved a celebrity so much that they tried to overthrow the government; they concluded that he was speaking directly and intimately to them to encourage them to do so (and the congressional January 6 committee has perhaps proven that he really was).[15] The January 6 riot is deeply tied into parasocial relationships fans develop with objects of fandom. Such relationships are often facilitated or enhanced by the (perceived) intimacy of social media celebrity,[16] which is on display in #VoxAdpocalypse as much as the many people tweeting at and direct messaging Twitter owner Elon Musk (and his many impersonators) as I write this, seeing him as reachable because he is just like them—a troll who tweets whatever comes to mind, and especially when it can hurt an enemy—and hoping to get just a bit of his attention.[17] Parasocial intimacy flattens power relations, and this is why it has a concomitant effect of making figures like Trump and Crowder and Sanders seem less powerful than they are, which is important to the construction of these figures as victims who need fans to defend them that runs throughout fan responses.

Perhaps most importantly, fan studies calls attention to how these feelings are refracted and routed through attachment to texts. The

CRT panic is really about the anxiety of whiteness suddenly being questioned, but it is framed as a fight about novels and textbooks and libraries. So, too, #Comicsgate is about straight white men having slightly less power in society, but it is fought out on the terrain of comic books. For #VoxAdpocalypse, this same anxiety takes place around and through YouTube videos. The feelings of Bernie Bros are about the sense that the broad structural and institutional change they seek is blocked, but they displace their frustration with this blockage onto the figure of Elizabeth Warren. Lexa fans, in the face of lesbians being seen as unworthy of romantic happiness or even life, in the face of a present in which "straight time tells us that there is no future but the here and now of our everyday life," were making a demand for a future, for "the realm of potentiality that must be called on, and insisted on, if we are ever to look beyond the pragmatic sphere of the here and now, the hollow nature of the present,"[18] which the speculative nature of *The 100* and its writers' openness to writing queer characters and storylines seemed to suggest was possible. This is how their more existential hurt became a fight about a TV show. In the Anti Wars, one side sees all of the sexual violence and harm in the world and the media, but fights it out on the terrain of fan fiction. The other side of the Anti Wars sees queer pleasure and freedom being foreclosed by society, and they fight it out over fan fiction too. That these are textual engagements—rather than attached directly to identity—is why we need fan studies to understand them.

Ultimately, what I hope to have shown in *Fandom Is Ugly* is that fandom is both a site of articulation of power and a mode of articulation of power, both a thing that people feel intensely and act aggressively about, and the way those feels generate that aggression across a wide variety of mediated phenomena that may not necessarily look like fandoms. Holding on to these key aspects of fandom—feels and community and texts—provides important insight into a great many things that are otherwise hard to understand. Though at the inception of fan studies, "we got a narrative of 'fandom is progressive' because the particular academics who founded fan studies were themselves progressive—they chose those texts, joined those communities, and that was what was available for them to see," but also because "the people who set the stage were precisely the educated, middle-class, liberal white people fandom *was* open to,"[19] what I hope to have shown in this book is that this origin is not the field's destiny, and its tools can be turned to interrogate those same formations. As we move into its third decade, fan studies has much more to teach us.

ACKNOWLEDGMENTS

This book is better because of the assistance, advice, feedback, conversations, suggestions, and friendship of several people. Thank you to Rachel Marks for being the best research assistant ever. Thanks to Stephen Hopkins, AC Leith, and Lyle Skains for coming up with exactly the sources I needed at the right moment. My work with Megan Condis on reactionary group Comicsgate laid the foundation for chapter 1, and my work with Emily Tarvin on YouTube governance led me toward what became chapter 6, and both chapters are better for that past collaboration. Audiences at the Children's Literature Association 2017, Fan Studies Network North America 2018 and 2019, Society for Cinema and Media Studies 2021, 2022, and 2023, and Console-ing Passions 2023 conferences, as well as at Goethe University (Frankfurt, Germany) provided feedback on different parts of this project at various stages.

My writing group in the Department of English at the University of Central Florida has been a source of both camaraderie and thoughtful critique. Many thanks to Anastasia Salter, Anna Jones, Bill Fogarty, James Campbell, Pavithra Tantrigoda, Roni Joyner, Stephen Hopkins (again), and Tison Pugh for that and for being rad people I look forward to chatting with. Kristina Busse, Anne Jamison, and Lori Morimoto also gave key feedback at formative stages of this project. Thanks are due also to J. S. A. Lowe and Kristina Busse (again) for letting me turn up at odd times to bounce an idea off them. Much love to faculty group chat (The Illegibles) for always being down for "Did I read this right?" or "Help me edit the anger out of this email" or (sometimes gallows) humor about the absurdity of life. Anastasia Salter (again), Anne Sullivan, Emily Johnson, and John Murray have been the best friends anybody could ask for. John is the MVP this time around for helping me with APIs and scraping at various stages of this project. I have tremendous gratitude for all of these people, for all of their help in ways big and small. This book (and I) wouldn't be the same without you.

Portions of the introduction were previously published in Mel Stanfill, "Introduction: The Reactionary in the Fan and the Fan in the Reactionary," *Television & New Media* 21, no. 2 (2020): 123–34. Chapter 3 is partially adapted from Mel Stanfill, "The Unbearable Whiteness of Fandom and Fan Studies," in *A Companion to Fandom and Fan Studies*, edited by Paul Booth, 305–17 (Oxford, UK: Wiley-Blackwell, 2018). Chapter 3 is also partially adapted from Mel Stanfill, "Straight (White) Women Writing about Men Bonking? Complicating Our Understanding of Gender and Sexuality in Fandom," in *The Routledge Handbook of Gender and Communication*, edited by Marnel Niles Goins, Joan Faber McAlister, and Bryant Keith Alexander, 446–58 (New York: Routledge, 2020). Portions of chapter 7 were previously published as Mel Stanfill, "Antifandom of CRT as Fannish Attachment to Whiteness," *In Media Res*, March 28, 2022.

NOTES

INTRODUCTION

1 Gamergate protested the supposedly destructive influence of feminist game designers and critics. Supporters of Gamergate often defended their actions by arguing that their ire was about "ethics in games journalism," pointing to the movement's start in an accusation against indie game developer Zoë Quinn that she was "trading sexual favors with journalists for positive reviews of her game"— allegedly ill-gotten reviews that did not exist. Gray, Buyukozturk, and Hill, "Blurring the Boundaries," 2. However, as an investigation by *Newsweek* demonstrated, the vast majority of Gamergate's vitriol targeted women game developers and media makers, not journalists or media outlets. See Wofford, "Is GamerGate about Media Ethics or Harassing Women?"

2 Lind, "Unite the Right, the Violent White Supremacist Rally in Charlottesville, Explained."

3 Grady, "*Star Wars* Fans Harassed Kelly Marie Tran for Months."

4 Jane, "Beyond Antifandom," 186.

5 For a broader discussion of this narrative of fandom as progressive, see Stanfill, "Introduction."

6 See Gray, Sandvoss, and Harrington, "Introduction." Francesca Coppa pushed back at this argument in 2014, saying that "it's hard for me not to hear something patronizing, or perhaps just skeptical, in the labelling of that first wave as 'Fandom is Beautiful.' But as a fan as well as a scholar, I respond, 'Fuck yeah, Fandom Is Beautiful.'" Coppa, "Fuck Yeah, Fandom Is Beautiful," 74. Sandvoss, Gray, and Harrington clarified in 2017 that "we referred to this wave as 'Fandom Is Beautiful' to draw parallels to the early (and often rhetorically and inspirationally vital) stages of identity politics common for other groups hitherto Othered by mainstream society." Sandvoss, Gray, and Harrington, "Introduction," 3.

7 Proctor and Kies, "Editors' Introduction."

8 Gray, "New Audiences, New Textualities." See, for example, Gray, "Antifandom and the Moral Text"; Jane, "Beyond Antifandom"; Jones, "Antifan Activism as a Response to MTV's 'The Valleys'"; and the work collected in Click, ed., *Anti-Fandom.*

9 Stanfill, "Introduction."

10 Proctor and Kies, "Editors' Introduction," 137.

11 Hills, "An Extended Foreword," 111.

12 Scott, "Towards a Theory of Producer/Fan Trolling," 144.

13 Massanari, "#Gamergate and The Fappening," 333. See also Guerrero-Pico, Establés, and Ventura, "Killing Off Lexa"; Lamerichs et al., "Elite Male Bodies"; Proctor and Kies, "Editors' Introduction."

14 Proctor and Kies, "Editors' Introduction," 132.

15 O'Donnell, "Militant Meninism," 656.

16 Lawson, "Platform Vulnerabilities," 822.

17 Hills, "An Extended Foreword."

18 Scott, "Towards a Theory of Producer/Fan Trolling," 143.

19 Gray, "Antifandom and the Moral Text," 840–41.

20 On hate sites, see Gray, "New Audiences, New Textualities"; on hate blogs, see Fathallah, "Polyphony on Tumblr."

21 Jones, "#AskELJames, Ghostbusters, and #Gamergate," 416.

22 Jane, "Hating 3.0," 43.

23 Puar, *Terrorist Assemblages*; McRuer, *Crip Theory*.

24 To analyze how the January 6, 2021, invasion of the US Capitol was understood as an act of fandom, I searched press database Nexis Uni for "Trump + fan" on January 31, 2021, restricting the search only to results published on or after January 6. The results were sorted by relevance; I used the "group duplicates" feature, excluded any stories that had the same title with the same word count, and selected the longest version of stories with the same title from the same outlet with different word counts to avoid duplication. I proceeded through the search results until I had collected one hundred relevant stories, which took me to result number 270 overall.

25 Miller, "'Wolfenstein II' and MAGA as Fandom"; Dean, "Politicising Fandom"; Sandvoss, Gray, and Harrington, "Introduction."

26 Davisson, "Mashing Up, Remixing, and Contesting the Popular Memory of Hillary Clinton," para. 2.1.

27 Biesecker et al., "Records Show Fervent Trump Fans Fueled US Capitol Takeover."

28 "Tragedy of Trump on Show."

29 Sandvoss, "Toward an Understanding of Political Enthusiasm as Media Fandom," 253.

30 Hinck, *Politics for the Love of Fandom*, 6.

31 Waysdorf, "Placing Fandom," 285, 289.

32 Miller, "'Wolfenstein II' and MAGA as Fandom," para. 3.17.

33 At least until they realized these images were evidence of crimes and started deleting them.

34 "Reliable Sources."

35 Abdelmahmoud, "The Pro-Trump Mob Was Doing It for the 'Gram."

36 Norris and Bainbridge, "Intersections," para. 1.

37 On the connections of pseudo-Norse symbols to white supremacy, see Birkett, "US Capitol Riot." Thanks to Stephen Hopkins for pointing me in the right direction here.

38 "CNN International."
39 Forsey, "Donald Trump's 'Hypnotic Handshake' and 'Secret Weapon' He Uses to Win People Over."
40 Bucktin, "Overrun Run by Trump's Mob."
41 Smith, Goodin, and Sheets, "Hunt for the MAGA Cop Killer."
42 Ruiz, "'Take This Country Back.'"
43 "Tragedy of Trump on Show."
44 Romano, "The Internet's Most Beloved Fanfiction Site Is Undergoing a Reckoning"; Wilson, "How One Fanfic Is Breaking AO3 (and Fandom)."
45 Romano, "The Internet's Most Beloved Fanfiction Site Is Undergoing a Reckoning."
46 Busse, *Framing Fan Fiction*, 203.
47 Romano, "The Internet's Most Beloved Fanfiction Site Is Undergoing a Reckoning."
48 Busse, *Framing Fan Fiction*, 204.
49 Jackson, "Fanfic Writer Put Entirety of '1984' in the Tags of a Story."
50 For this analysis, I manually collected comments from the period when the mega-tagging was happening. The community is organized as a series of moderator-created posts, on which community members comment, creating individual threads about different topics. Starting from the February 21, 2021, post, at the height of the mass tagging, I read comments and manually collected those that specifically addressed deliberately posting massive quantities of tags until I reached one hundred relevant posts.
51 Throughout the book, all social media post spellings and abbreviations are reproduced as is, with emendations in brackets as needed for clarity. I acknowledge that direct quotation means the text of the posts may be found by search engine, but by not directly naming users or linking posts, I am adding a level of protection to avoid exposing individual posters to scrutiny they may not have anticipated.
52 All posts on FFA are anonymous, and while there is an elaborate code for labeling identities such as "same anon," "not the anon you replied to," etc., posts may or may not signal their author's identity in this way. It is therefore impossible to know how many people were involved in the thread, nor, indeed, whether there was sock puppetry involved.
53 Organization for Transformative Works, "Application."
54 Bullard, "Motivating Invisible Contributions," 184–85.
55 Organization for Transformative Works, "The OTW Is Recruiting for AO3 Documentation Staff, Graphic Designers, Policy & Abuse Staff, Strategic Planning Staff, and Translation Volunteers."
56 Either C or D could also be A responding again; it is impossible to tell.
57 Notably, in August 2021, AO3 announced that it was changing the policy to limit the number of tags on a work to seventy-five, and while this change was not explicitly explained as a response to *STWW* or the other mega-tagging, these

incidents likely played a role. See Archive of Our Own, "Upcoming Limit on Tags per Work."

58 For an examination of the anti (and its counterpart, the anti-anti), see chapter 5.

59 The term "alternative right" was coined in 2008 by Paul Gottfried. See Hartzell, "Alt-White." However, "alt-right" was popularized in the run-up to the 2016 election. See Google Trends, "Google Trends: Alt-Right." On links of Gamergate to the alt-right, see Condis, *Gaming Masculinity*; Lewis, "Alternative Influence"; Massanari, "Rethinking Research Ethics, Power, and the Risk of Visibility in the Era of the 'Alt-Right' Gaze"; Massanari and Chess, "Attack of the 50-Foot Social Justice Warrior"; Salter, "From Geek Masculinity to Gamergate."

60 Malmgren, "Don't Feed the Trolls"; Marwick and Lewis, "Media Manipulation and Disinformation Online"; Blodgett and Salter, "*Ghostbusters* Is for Boys"; Lawson, "Platform Vulnerabilities"; O'Donnell, "Militant Meninism."

61 Blodgett and Salter, "*Ghostbusters* Is for Boys," 134.

62 Marwick and Lewis, "Media Manipulation and Disinformation Online," 46.

63 Ganesh, "The Ungovernability of Digital Hate Culture," 34.

64 Daniels, *Cyber Racism*, 55.

65 Hartzell, "Alt-White," 130.

66 Costley White, *The Branding of Right-Wing Activism*, 20.

67 Jenkins, *Convergence Culture*.

68 Blodgett and Salter, "*Ghostbusters* Is for Boys," 136.

69 Jane, "Beyond Antifandom," 186.

70 Hartzell, "Whiteness Feels Good Here," 137.

71 Miller, "'Wolfenstein II' and MAGA as Fandom"; Dean, "Politicising Fandom"; Sandvoss, Gray, and Harrington, "Introduction."

72 Miro, "Who Are the People?"

73 Coppa, "Fuck Yeah, Fandom Is Beautiful," 77.

74 Tushnet, "'I'm a Lawyer, Not an Ethnographer, Jim,'" 22.

75 On fans as industry's target audiences, see Scott, *Fake Geek Girls*; Stanfill, *Exploiting Fandom*.

76 Salter and Blodgett, *Toxic Geek Masculinity in Media*.

77 Wilson, "Red Pillers, Sad Puppies, and Gamergaters."

78 Pande, "Who Do You Mean by 'Fan'?" 330.

79 Pande, "Who Do You Mean by 'Fan'?" 320. On unacknowledged whiteness in fandom and fan studies, see also Stanfill, "The Unbearable Whiteness of Fandom and Fan Studies"; Turk, "Interdisciplinarity in Fan Studies."

80 Woo, "The Invisible Bag of Holding," 245.

81 Wanzo, "African American Acafandom and Other Strangers," para. 1.4.

82 There is also a growing body of excellent research on the distinctive experiences and practices of fans of color that is outside my scope here. See, for example, Seymour, "Racebending and Prosumer Fanart Practices in Harry Potter Fandom"; Wanzo, "African American Acafandom and Other Strangers"; Warner, "If Loving

Olitz Is Wrong, I Don't Wanna Be Right"; Warner, "ABC's Scandal and Black Women's Fandom"; Warner, "(Black Female) Fans Strike Back."

83 Johnson, "Transformative Racism," para. 2.3.

84 Jenkins, "Negotiating Fandom"; Morimoto, "Ontological Security and the Politics of Transcultural Fandom"; Stanfill, "The Unbearable Whiteness of Fandom and Fan Studies."

85 De Kosnik, *Rogue Archives*; Pande, "Who Do You Mean by 'Fan'?"

86 Johnson, "Transformative Racism," para. 5.3.

87 Busse, "Geek Hierarchies, Boundary Policing, and the Gendering of the Good Fan."

88 Scott, *Fake Geek Girls*, 14, 13.

89 centreoftheselights, "AO3 Ship Stats 2022."

90 Busse, *Framing Fan Fiction*; Tushnet, "'I'm a Lawyer, Not an Ethnographer, Jim.'"

91 Gonzalez, "Swan Queen, Shipping, and Boundary Regulation in Fandom."

92 Russo, "The Queer Politics of Femslash," 160.

93 Coker and Viars, "Welcoming the Dark Side?"

94 Rico, "Fans of Columbine Shooters Eric Harris and Dylan Klebold," para. 6.3.

95 Jones, "#AskELJames, Ghostbusters, and #Gamergate," 424.

96 Wilson, "Red Pillers, Sad Puppies, and Gamergaters."

97 Driessen, "'For the Greater Good?'" 26.

98 On cybervigilantism, see Jung, "Fan Activism, Cybervigilantism, and Othering Mechanisms in K-Pop Fandom"; on digital vigilantes, see Driessen, "'For the Greater Good?'"

99 Foucault, *The Archaeology of Knowledge and the Discourse on Language.*

100 Bingham, "Talking about Twitch."

101 Navar-Gill and Stanfill, "'We Shouldn't Have to Trend to Make You Listen.'"

102 Demšar et al., "Orange."

CHAPTER 1. WHAT REAL FANS WANT IS STRAIGHT WHITE HEROES

1 Gamergate, a similarly structured movement of fans within video game culture, protested the supposedly destructive influence of feminist game designers and critics beginning in 2014. It included conspiracy theories about collusion between journalists and academics in the wake of a series of articles questioning the relevance of the "gamer" identity (see Mortensen, "Anger, Fear, and Games") and a discussion of feminism in games at an academic conference (see Chess and Shaw, "A Conspiracy of Fishes"). Doxing is the posting of private information online for the purpose of harassment. On Comicsgate's tactics, see Elbein, "#Comicsgate"; Pitts Jr., "Comicsgate."

2 A subreddit is an online community on the website Reddit where people gather to discuss a particular topic. Subreddits are created and governed by volunteer users called moderators, who set the rules for participation and can delete posts or even ban users from the community for violating those rules.

3 Emmett, "From Batgirl to Comicgate?"

4 Pitts Jr., "Comicsgate."

5 Burbank, "Chelsea Cain Leaves Twitter Following Sexist Harassment."

6 Francisco, "What Is Comicsgate?" As their disproportionate representation in three of these four flashpoints already begins to suggest, in the aggregate, Marvel generates much more discussion from Comicsgaters than DC, with 1,026 mentions in the posts from r/WerthamInAction, compared to 338 for DC (just 32 percent as many).

7 Stanfill, "Introduction," 125.

8 "PRAW." Many thanks to John Murray for his invaluable help with this process. The earliest extracted comment is from four days after the subreddit's creation on March 17, 2015. It is not clear whether this is the case because the subreddit sat empty for a few days after creation, or earlier posts have been deleted, or the API did not return earlier posts due to reaching the cap on permissible data extraction. However, given that there are so few days missing, the data is a very close approximation of complete at the time of collection. This data was originally scraped for a coauthored project with Megan Condis. See Condis and Stanfill, "Debating with Wertham's Ghost." My overview of Comicsgate in the introduction to this chapter owes much to this project and to Megan.

9 Anthony, "AntConc."

10 Hills, "An Extended Foreword," 105.

11 Scott, *Fake Geek Girls*, 4.

12 See Hadas, "The Web Planet"; Bennett, "Discourses of Order and Rationality"; Stanfill, "'They're Losers, but I Know Better'"; Yodovich, "'A Little Costumed Girl at a Sci-Fi Convention.'"

13 Theodoropoulou, "The Anti-Fan within the Fan"; Lopez and Lopez, "Deploying Oppositional Fandom"; Mortensen, "Anger, Fear, and Games."

14 Blodgett and Salter, "*Ghostbusters* Is for Boys," 136.

15 For the SJW in Gamergate discourse, see Chess and Shaw, "A Conspiracy of Fishes"; Braithwaite, "It's about Ethics in Games Journalism?"; Salter, "From Geek Masculinity to Gamergate." For responses from other groups of fans, see Blodgett and Salter, "*Ghostbusters* Is for Boys"; Scott, *Fake Geek Girls*.

16 Nakamura, "'Putting Our Hearts into It,'" 36.

17 Massanari and Chess, "Attack of the 50-Foot Social Justice Warrior," 526.

18 Massanari and Chess, "Attack of the 50-Foot Social Justice Warrior," 527.

19 "*Yaoi*," a Japanese term for media content featuring same-sex desire among men, "is an abbreviated form of 'yama nashi, ochi nashi, imi nashi' ('no climax, no point, no meaning') in Japanese." See Yang and Bao, "Queerly Intimate," 862. "Slash" is the corresponding term in anglophone fandom and "refers to the convention of employing a stroke or 'slash' to signify a same-sex relationship between two characters." See Jenkins, *Textual Poachers*, 186. In Japanese, "*senpai*" refers to a more senior student, but it is often used by fans of Japanese media to indicate a crush due to the anime and manga trope of seeking *senpai*'s approval. See

"Urban Dictionary: Senpai," Urban Dictionary, accessed November 4, 2023, www
.urbandictionary.com.

20 A snowclone is a "phrase that has a standard pattern in which some of the words
can be freely replaced"; examples include "X is the new Y." Macmillan Dictionary,
"Snowclone."

21 Massanari, "#Gamergate and The Fappening," 335.

22 These critiques also apply fairly neatly to Comicsgaters, who are eager to
be outraged, invested in rejecting diversity at all costs, and resistant to alternate
views.

23 Bennett, "Discourses of Order and Rationality," 215.

24 Massanari, "#Gamergate and The Fappening," 333.

25 See Chess and Shaw, "A Conspiracy of Fishes"; Gray, Buyukozturk, and Hill,
"Blurring the Boundaries"; Nakamura, "Putting Our Hearts into It."

26 Massanari and Chess, "Attack of the 50-Foot Social Justice Warrior," 528.

27 Busse, "Beyond Mary Sue," 160.

28 Mjolnir is the name of Thor's hammer.

29 Notably, this is one of many instances where the scope of the subreddit's complaints exceeds comics to encompass other "geek" media.

30 I am sympathetic to this critique. See chapter 3's discussion of the strange politics
of exalting women's sexual attraction to men as subversive.

31 Indeed, other posts in the subreddit complain when women characters are insufficiently sexy. For a discussion see Condis and Stanfill, "Debating with Wertham's
Ghost."

32 Surplus audiences are those "for whom producers had not built a business model,"
who are not part of the calculation of who is intended to consume the product.
See Jenkins, Ford, and Green, *Spreadable Media*, 14.

33 See, for example, Rosenberg, "Mike White on Why Men Won't Watch Women
on TV." This does not seem to be an empirically tested reality in media, though
a study of fiction books found that approximately 83 percent of men preferred
books with men as protagonists, while 65 percent of women had no preference for
the gender of the protagonist. See Summers, "Adult Reading Habits and Preferences in Relation to Gender Differences." Thanks to Lyle Skains for alerting me to
this source. However, while I could not find any such studies about media, media
industry conventional wisdom seems to believe in these gender preferences,
which shapes decisions to center stories on men.

34 Busse, "Geek Hierarchies, Boundary Policing, and the Gendering of the Good
Fan," 84.

35 Williams, "The Saturday Interview."

36 Johnson, "Fan-Tagonism," 290.

37 Moore, *Watchmen*.

38 It is also, of course, deeply ironic from a member of a backlash movement known
for doxing, harassment, and violent threats. See Elbein, "#Comicsgate"; Pitts Jr.,
"Comicsgate."

39 Peppard, "'A Cross Burning Darkly, Blackening the Night,'" 62–64. Though, as
    Anna F. Peppard also notes, this representation does not entirely escape racist
    tropes, as "Black Panther's name and powerset, which includes enhanced senses
    and agility inspired by his namesake and manifests in various slinking, stalking,
    and crouching movements across the pages, are obviously animalistic."
40 Harmon, "'Star Wars' Fan Films Come Tumbling Back to Earth."
41 See Young, "Race in Online Fantasy Fandom"; Gonzalez, "Swan Queen, Shipping,
    and Boundary Regulation in Fandom." Notably, as seen from the way Comic-
    sgaters define creators from marginalized groups as being hired to write bad
    fanfic, canon is only above reproach when it meets the community consensus of
    acceptability.
42 Jenkins, *Textual Poachers.*
43 See Massanari, "#Gamergate and The Fappening"; Salter and Blodgett, *Toxic Geek
    Masculinity in Media*; Salter, "From Geek Masculinity to Gamergate"; Scott, *Fake
    Geek Girls*; Wilson, "Red Pillers, Sad Puppies, and Gamergaters."
44 Scott, *Fake Geek Girls*, 17.
45 See Lawson, "Platform Vulnerabilities"; Ging, "Alphas, Betas, and Incels";
    O'Donnell, "Militant Meninism."
46 See Carroll, *Affirmative Reaction*; Hartzell, "Alt-White"; Hartzell, "Whiteness Feels
    Good Here."
47 Blodgett and Salter, "*Ghostbusters* Is for Boys."
48 Salter, "From Geek Masculinity to Gamergate"; Proctor and Kies, "Editors' Intro-
    duction"; Scott, *Fake Geek Girls.*
49 Carroll, *Affirmative Reaction*, 5.
50 On shared politics, see Salter, "From Geek Masculinity to Gamergate"; Scott, *Fake
    Geek Girls*; Ganesh, "The Ungovernability of Digital Hate Culture"; Ging, "Alphas,
    Betas, and Incels." On connections of fandom to misogynist website Return of
    Kings, see Johnson, "Fantagonism, Franchising, and Industry Management of
    Fan Privilege." On Breitbart employee Milo Yiannopoulos's role in the harassment
    campaign against Black actress Leslie Jones, see Blodgett and Salter, "*Ghostbusters*
    Is for Boys"; Lawson, "Platform Vulnerabilities."

CHAPTER 2. "#SENATORKAREN BACK STABBED BERNIE"
 1 Dean, "Politicising Fandom," 411.
 2 Hinck, *Politics for the Love of Fandom*, 6. For similar work, see the 2012 special
    issue of *Transformative Works and Cultures* on Transformative Works and Fan
    Activism, particularly Brough and Shresthova, "Fandom Meets Activism"; Hinck,
    "Theorizing a Public Engagement Keystone"; Jenkins, "'Cultural Acupuncture'";
    Neta Kligler-Vilenchik et al., "Experiencing Fan Activism."
 3 Zoonen, "Popular Culture as Political Communication," 6.
 4 See Davisson, "Mashing Up, Remixing, and Contesting the Popular Memory of
    Hillary Clinton"; Miro, "Who Are the People?"; Sandvoss, "Toward an Under-
    standing of Political Enthusiasm as Media Fandom."

5 Miro, "Who Are the People?" 64.

6 See Sandvoss, "Toward an Understanding of Political Enthusiasm as Media Fandom."

7 See Wilson, "Playing with Politics."

8 See Lamerichs et al., "Elite Male Bodies."

9 On political fanvids, see Davisson, "Mashing Up, Remixing, and Contesting the Popular Memory of Hillary Clinton." On political fan fiction, see Winter, "Fanon Bernie Sanders."

10 See Davisson, "Mashing Up, Remixing, and Contesting the Popular Memory of Hillary Clinton"; Dean, "Politicising Fandom"; Lamerichs et al., "Elite Male Bodies"; Miller, "'Wolfenstein II' and MAGA as Fandom"; Sandvoss, "The Politics of Against"; Winter, "Fanon Bernie Sanders."

11 On fandom of Obama, see Sandvoss, "Toward an Understanding of Political Enthusiasm as Media Fandom." On Sanders fandom, see Winter, "Fanon Bernie Sanders."

12 See Miro, "Who Are the People?"; Lamerichs et al., "Elite Male Bodies"; Miller, "'Wolfenstein II' and MAGA as Fandom"; Sandvoss, "The Politics of Against."

13 Journalists, too, were curious. See, for example, Ellis, "Why Elizabeth Warren's Feeds Are Flooded with Snake Emoji."

14 Gray, "New Audiences, New Textualities," 70.

15 Sandvoss, "The Politics of Against," 131, 129.

16 Mitchell, "Politics on Twitter."

17 See Lawson, "Platform Vulnerabilities"; Trice and Potts, "Building Dark Patterns into Platforms."

18 Hawksey, "Twitter Archiving Google Sheet."

19 The first spike of tweets kicked off when Representative Ro Khanna (D-CA), a frequent legislative collaborator with Sanders, posted a positive statement about Warren's book on May 7, 2021, and was met with intense negative response. Ro Khanna [@RoKhanna], "I Was Late to My Morning Meeting." The tweets intensified when he admonished those replying to him for using the snake emoji. Ro Khanna [@RoKhanna], "Enough with the Snakes in the Comments!" There does not appear to have been a specific precipitating event on October 31, and that spike was also smaller. The minimum number of tweets in a day was zero. The maximum was 907. The median was 4. The average was 11.2. The standard deviation was 53.2. One standard deviation above the mean was 64.4 tweets or more per day. Five days exceeded this number of tweets: 5/7/2021: 161 tweets; 5/8/2021: 907 tweets; 5/9/2021: 238 tweets; 5/10/2021: 241 tweets; 10/31/2021: 76 tweets. At a total of 1623 tweets, these five days account for 74 percent of all unique tweets in the data set.

20 Gephi.org, "Gephi."

21 Demšar et al., "Orange."

22 The average number of instances of a word was 3.5; the standard deviation was 14.65. Three standard deviations above the mean was 47.5 uses. Forty-three words met this criterion.

23 Anthony, "AntConc."

24 The term "hate-watching" was coined by journalist Emily Nussbaum in 2012. See Nussbaum, "Hate-Watching 'Smash.'"

25 The most frequent word was "rokhanna," representing the tokenized version of Twitter username @RoKhanna, with 1,194 instances.

26 Sandvoss, "Toward an Understanding of Political Enthusiasm as Media Fandom," 266.

27 It is certainly possible that these accounts tweeting against Warren and for Sanders are not run by genuine Sanders fans. However, given that the eleven-month period in which tweets were collected did not coincide with any election cycles for either senator, it is not clear what would be gained from falsification at the scale necessary to produce the pattern observed in the data.

28 Sandvoss, "Toward an Understanding of Political Enthusiasm as Media Fandom," 263.

29 Ro Khanna [@RoKhanna], "Enough with the Snakes in the Comments!"

30 Butler, *Bodies That Matter*, ix.

31 Anderson, "Presidential Pioneer or Campaign Queen?" 533.

32 Anderson, "Presidential Pioneer or Campaign Queen?" 532.

33 Epstein, "Bernie Sanders Vows to Stay on Upcoming Ballots and Continue to Gather Delegates so He Can 'Exert Significant Influence over the Party Platform.'"

34 Ro Khanna [@RoKhanna], "Enough with the Snakes in the Comments!"

35 "Cosplay," from "costume play," refers to dressing up as a character. "LARP" is "live-action roleplay," engaging in a roleplaying game that also involves acting out what is occurring, as opposed to a model more like *Dungeons & Dragons* in which players just tell the story.

36 Puzzanghera, "Book Advance Helped Boost Income for Elizabeth Warren and Her Husband to Nearly $900,000 Last Year, Financial Disclosures Show."

37 Forbes, "The Forbes 400 2021." As it happens, Sanders, with a net worth around $3 million, is also in the 1 percent. Dennison, "How Rich Is Bernie Sanders?"

38 This is similar to the notion of the "anti" wanting to prohibit all allegedly problematic content in fan fiction. See chapter 5.

39 "Elon Musk Charged with Securities Fraud for Misleading Tweets."

40 McKay, "Report."

41 Levin, "Elon Musk Calls British Diver in Thai Cave Rescue 'Pedo' in Baseless Attack."

42 Schroeder, "Warren."

43 Kurtzleben, "Here's How Many Bernie Sanders Supporters Ultimately Voted for Trump."

44 Penney, "Social Media and Citizen Participation in 'Official' and 'Unofficial' Electoral Promotion," 417.

45 Sandvoss, "Toward an Understanding of Political Enthusiasm as Media Fandom," 253.

46 Miller, "'Wolfenstein II' and MAGA as Fandom," para. 1.4.

47 Sandvoss, "Toward an Understanding of Political Enthusiasm as Media Fandom," 288.

48 McManus, "Elizabeth Warren's Pivot on 'Medicare for All' Shows the Tricky Politics of Healthcare."

49 Khalid, "Warren Apologizes to Cherokee Nation for DNA Test."

50 It is not clear what advantages Warren actually sought or gained, but she did list herself as a minority faculty member from 1986 to 1995. See Hicks, "Did Elizabeth Warren Check the Native American Box When She 'Applied' to Harvard and Penn?"

51 Samuels, "Rachel Dolezal's True Lies."

52 Penney, "Social Media and Citizen Participation in 'Official' and 'Unofficial' Electoral Promotion," 405.

53 Davisson, "Mashing Up, Remixing, and Contesting the Popular Memory of Hillary Clinton," para. 1.1.

54 Miro, "Who Are the People?" 63.

55 See Theodoropoulou, "The Anti-Fan within the Fan"; Lopez and Lopez, "Deploying Oppositional Fandom."

CHAPTER 3. ON THE HOMONORMATIVITY OF SLASH, FROM
CURTAIN FIC TO CANONICITY

1 Penley, *NASA/Trek*; Elizabeth Woledge, "Intimatopia"; Tosenberger, "'The Epic Love Story of Sam and Dean.'"

2 Jenkins, *Textual Poachers*; Penley, *NASA/Trek*.

3 Bacon-Smith, *Enterprising Women*.

4 For more recent examples of arguments that fan fiction is a queer space or a space particularly welcoming to queer people, see Hampton, "Bound Princes and Monogamy Warnings; Massey, "Borderland Literature, Female Pleasure, and the Slash Fic Phenomenon"; Duggan, "Transformative Readings."

5 McRuer, *Crip Theory*, 30.

6 Russo, "The Queer Politics of Femslash," 160.

7 Pande, "Squee from the Margins," 211.

8 Scodari, "Resistance Re-Examined," 10.

9 The exception is if same-sex love and sex is in a book for kids or teens, as the wave of book banning that began in 2021 demonstrates. See Mazariegos and Sullivan, "Efforts to Ban Books Jumped an 'Unprecedented' Four-Fold in 2021, ALA Report Says."

10 Russo, "The Queer Politics of Femslash," 159.

11 Anders et al., "The Heteronormativity Theory of Low Sexual Desire in Women Partnered with Men," 402.

12 Busse, "Geek Hierarchies, Boundary Policing, and the Gendering of the Good Fan," 75, 88.

13 See Kies, "One True Threesome"; Hampton, "Bound Princes and Monogamy Warnings"; Schmidt, "Monstrous Melodrama."

14 Busse, "My Life Is a WIP on My LJ," 208.
15 Lackner, Lucas, and Reid, "Cunning Linguists," 201.
16 De Kosnik, *Rogue Archives*, 151. Original emphasis.
17 In a survey conducted with Lauren Rouse, we found that 53.77 percent of fans who use AO3 self-identify as cisgender women. See Rouse and Stanfill, "Fan Demographics on Archive of Our Own."
18 Coppa, "Women, 'Star Trek,' and the Early Development of Fannish Vidding," 2.1.
19 Penley, "Interview with Constance Penley," 372.
20 Scodari, "'Nyota Uhura Is Not a White Girl,'" 337.
21 Scodari, "Resistance Re-Examined," 114.
22 It is not necessarily transgressive of the source text—as many have pointed out, we should not assume the text is straight. For such arguments in media studies, see Doty, *Making Things Perfectly Queer*; Jones, "The Sex Lives of Cult Television Characters." In fan studies, see Åström, "'Let's Get Those Winchesters Pregnant'"; Ng, "Between Text, Paratext, and Context"; Tosenberger, "'The Epic Love Story of Sam and Dean.'"
23 Jones, "The Sex Lives of Cult Television Characters," 81.
24 See Hampton, "Bound Princes and Monogamy Warnings"; Melissa A. Hofmann, "Johnlock Meta and Authorial Intent in Sherlock Fandom."
25 See Jenkins, *Textual Poachers*; Penley, *NASA/Trek*.
26 Tosenberger, "The Epic Love Story of Sam and Dean," para. 1.2. Jenkins, *Textual Poachers*, 187.
27 Notably, there are periods in the source text when Rogers is small and weak compared to Barnes, when Rogers was a technologically enhanced super-soldier and Barnes a much less powerful human, and when both are super-soldiers, and in stories set in each period there is a tendency to map roles back onto physical strength and weakness, showing how, in practice, the fact that the writers of these genres are steeped in cultural norms that essentialize sexuality means that stories end up reproducing those norms at least some of the time. Thanks to JSA Lowe for encouraging me to clarify this.
28 Lackner, Lucas, and Reid, "Cunning Linguists," 194.
29 Green, Jenkins, and Jenkins, "Normal Female Interest in Men Bonking," 19.
30 Duggan, *The Twilight of Equality?* 50.
31 Crenshaw, "Beyond Racism and Misogyny," 114.
32 Cohen, "Punks, Bulldaggers, and Welfare Queens," 439.
33 Ferguson, "Race-Ing Heteronormativity," 53.
34 Puar, *Terrorist Assemblages*, 31–32.
35 See Åström, "'Let's Get Those Winchesters Pregnant'"; Kies, "One True Threesome"; Flegel and Roth, "Annihilating Love and Heterosexuality without Women."
36 See Kies, "One True Threesome"; Hunting, "'Queer as Folk' and the Trouble with Slash"; Busse, *Framing Fan Fiction*.
37 See Hunting, "'Queer as Folk' and the Trouble with Slash"; Callis, "Homophobia, Heteronormativity, and Slash Fan Fiction"; Busse, *Framing Fan Fiction*.

38 Åström, "'Let's Get Those Winchesters Pregnant,'" para. 7.1.

39 See Jenkins, *Textual Poachers*; Scodari, "Resistance Re-Examined"; Åström, 'Let's Get Those Winchesters Pregnant.'"

40 See Hunting, "'Queer as Folk' and the Trouble with Slash"; Callis, "Homophobia, Heteronormativity, and Slash Fan Fiction."

41 In "Homophobia, Heteronormativity, and Slash Fan Fiction," Callis states that she "analyzed the frequency that heteronormativity was written into K/S stories, both from the 1970s–1980s and in stories written since 2005. I found that in my older sample of K/S, heteronormativity was present in 60 percent of the stories. In contrast, heteronormativity was only found in 28 percent of newer stories. Situations I coded as heteronormative included, among other things, assuming that sex was only about procreation, assuming that Vulcans would find homosexuality illogical, and discussing the 'reason for' or 'cause' of homosexuality. Each of these themes was found at least three times as often in older stories versus new" (para. 6.1).

42 Busse, *Framing Fan Fiction*, 64.

43 Tosenberger, "'The Epic Love Story of Sam and Dean,'" paras. 4.2, 4.4.

44 Flegel and Roth, "Annihilating Love and Heterosexuality without Women," para. 1.4.

45 Busse, *Framing Fan Fiction*, 76.

46 Jenkins, *Textual Poachers*, 219.

47 Busse, *Framing Fan Fiction*, 89.

48 Scodari, "Nyota Uhura Is Not a White Girl," 343. Notably, Scodari is a strong advocate of heterosexual pairings in fan fiction, such that, while her recentering of women can help counteract slash's misogyny, it can also reintroduce heteronormativity.

49 Indeed, as Jones points out, the structure of same-sex buddies who travel around together and eschew permanent entanglements lends itself to slash. Jones, "The Sex Lives of Cult Television Characters."

50 Åström, "'Let's Get Those Winchesters Pregnant.'"

51 Certainly, there has long been critique of the "women in refrigerators" trope in which violence against women is a plot device to provide trauma to a man. See Scott, "Fangirls in Refrigerators."

52 See Jenkins, *Textual Poachers*; Penley, *NASA/Trek*; Busse, *Framing Fan Fiction*.

53 Scodari, "Nyota Uhura Is Not a White Girl," 343.

54 Because the essay is available only to people with user accounts at the Archive of Our Own, because the intended audience was fandom rather than academics or the broader public, and because obtaining informed consent would be impossible, I am not naming or directly quoting this essay but rather speaking in general terms.

55 The question of proportionality is arguable because the prevalence of white men may be proportionate to media itself, but simply reproducing the faults of media would of course undermine the alleged transgression of slash.

56 Pande, "Who Do You Mean by 'Fan'?" 330.
57 Coker and Viars, "Welcoming the Dark Side?"
58 Penley, *NASA/Trek*, 145.
59 Johnson, "Transformative Racism," para. 5.3.
60 See TWC Editor, "Pattern Recognition"; Pande, "Squee from the Margins"; Stanfill, "Fans of Color in Femslash"; TWC Editor, "What Is an Anti?"
61 See Stanfill, *Exploiting Fandom*.
62 Pande, "Squee from the Margins"; Stanfill, "Fans of Color in Femslash."
63 Pande, "Who Do You Mean by 'Fan'?" 330.
64 TWC Editor, "Pattern Recognition"; Stanfill, "Fans of Color in Femslash."
65 TWC Editor, "Pattern Recognition."
66 "We're Not Gay, We Just Love Each Other—Fanlore."
67 Busse, *Framing Fan Fiction*, 163.
68 Coleman, "Writing with Impunity in a Space of Their Own."
69 Mel Stanfill, *Rock This Way*.
70 Gonzalez, "Swan Queen, Shipping, and Boundary Regulation in Fandom."
71 Ng and Russo, "Envisioning Queer Female Fandom."
72 centreoftheselights, "AO3 Ship Stats 2022."
73 Ng and Russo, "Envisioning Queer Female Fandom," para. 2.8.
74 Kumar, "'Carmilla' Fandom as a Lesbian Community of Feeling," para. 3.11.
75 Busse, *Framing Fan Fiction*, 27.
76 Willis, "Keeping Promises to Queer Children," 156.
77 Russo, "The Queer Politics of Femslash," 161.
78 Marks, "Fan Perspectives of Queer Representation in DC's *Legends of Tomorrow* on Tumblr and AO3"; Pande and Moitra, "'Yes, the Evil Queen Is Latina!'"; Stanfill, "Fans of Color in Femslash."
79 Russo, "The Queer Politics of Femslash," 161.
80 Ng, "Between Text, Paratext, and Context," 1.2.
81 Scott, "Towards a Theory of Producer/Fan Trolling." See chapter 4 for a discussion of one such flareup of conflict.
82 Russo, "The Queer Politics of Femslash," 161.
83 Allington, "'How Come Most People Don't See It?'" 49.
84 Gonzalez, "Swan Queen, Shipping, and Boundary Regulation in Fandom," 4.2.
85 Busse, *Framing Fan Fiction*, 104.
86 Pande, "Who Do You Mean by 'Fan'?" 323. For an in-depth discussion of this fandom's inattention to racism, see chapter 4.
87 Gonzalez, "Swan Queen, Shipping, and Boundary Regulation in Fandom," 4.8.
88 Ng, "Between Text, Paratext, and Context," 9.8.

CHAPTER 4. HELL HATH NO FURY LIKE A FAN QUEERBAITED

1 See chapter 1.
2 Romano, "Justice League's Snyder Cut Saga Reminds Us Which Fans' Voices Get Heard."

3 Know Your Meme, "Get Woke Go Broke."

4 Bourdaa, "'May We Meet Again,'" 388. Original emphasis.

5 Cameron, "Toxic Regulation," 4.

6 Cameron, "Toxic Regulation," 4.

7 McNutt, "'The 100' and the Social Contract of Social TV," para. 2.2.

8 Jason Rothenberg [@JRothenbergTV], "You Guys Know I Don't Ship."

9 Cameron, "Toxic Regulation," 5.

10 Stanfill, *Exploiting Fandom*.

11 Piester, "The 100 Boss Apologizes for How Lexa Died in Open Letter to Fans."

12 Ryan, "What TV Can Learn From 'The 100' Mess."

13 McNutt, "'The 100' and the Social Contract of Social TV," para. 3.6.

14 McNutt, "'The 100' and the Social Contract of Social TV," para. 2.2.

15 See Giroux, "Twitter Data Scraping Jupyter Notebook"; and Salter and Stanfill, eds., "Understanding Digital Culture." The data scrape targeted the one-month period after the episode aired, March 3 to April 2, 2016. Therefore, I believe that the data represents the earliest instance of each hashtag, as it took some time for the fan movement to coalesce. The tool then ran until it reached the designated endpoint (#LGBTFansDeserveBetter) or reached the tool's capacity of 10,000 tweets (#LexaDeserveBetter). There were a total of 3,445 unique users across the two data sets.

16 Guerrero-Pico, Establés, and Ventura, "Killing Off Lexa," 312.

17 Stanfill, "From #LGBTFansDeserveBetter to the Clexa Youth."

18 On TV production staff Twitter engagement with fans, see Navar-Gill, "From Strategic Retweets to Group Hangs." On Twitter's role in activism, see Jackson, Bailey, and Welles, *#HashtagActivism*; Korn, "#FuckProp8"; Tufekci, *Twitter and Tear Gas*.

19 Hills, "An Extended Foreword," 111.

20 Guerrero-Pico, Establés, and Ventura, "Killing Off Lexa," 316.

21 Johnson, "Fan-Tagonism," 287.

22 Hills, "An Extended Foreword," 114.

23 Guerrero-Pico, Establés, and Ventura, "Killing Off Lexa," 319.

24 Bourdaa, "'May We Meet Again,'" 389.

25 Waggoner, "Bury Your Gays and Social Media Fan Response," 1884.

26 Waggoner, "Bury Your Gays and Social Media Fan Response," 1888. Internal citation removed.

27 Waggoner, "Bury Your Gays and Social Media Fan Response," 1888.

28 Braithwaite, "It's about Ethics in Games Journalism?," 7. Internal citation removed. Intel later backtracked and created a $300 million Diversity in Technology Initiative to "increase the representation of women and underrepresented minorities in the workplace and our industry." Gilbert, "The Most Important News at CES Is a $300 Million Response to GamerGate." I cannot find any news articles that discuss Gamergate's response to this shift, but I would imagine they make the threat to Maybelline look tame.

29 Guerrero-Pico, Establés, and Ventura, "Killing Off Lexa," 319.

30 Navar-Gill and Stanfill, "'We Shouldn't Have to Trend to Make You Listen,'" 86.

31 Navar-Gill and Stanfill, "'We Shouldn't Have to Trend to Make You Listen,'" 90.

32 Guerrero-Pico, Establés, and Ventura, "Killing Off Lexa," 319.

33 Waggoner, "Bury Your Gays and Social Media Fan Response."

34 On the role of technology in enabling Gamergate, see O'Donnell, "Militant Me-
    ninism"; Salter, "From Geek Masculinity to Gamergate."

35 Trice and Potts, "Building Dark Patterns into Platforms," 3.

36 Marwick and Lewis, "Media Manipulation and Disinformation Online," 8.

37 Braithwaite, "It's about Ethics in Games Journalism?" 4.

38 See Guerrero-Pico, Establés, and Ventura, "Killing Off Lexa."

39 Massanari, "Rethinking Research Ethics, Power, and the Risk of Visibility in the
    Era of the 'Alt-Right' Gaze," 4.

40 "Filtering Mentions." Many thanks to AP Leith, who helped me locate this source.

41 Waggoner, "Bury Your Gays and Social Media Fan Response," 1884.

42 See Choyce, "The Aftermath of the Death of Lexa."

43 Butler, *Bodies That Matter*, ix.

44 Bourdaa, "'May We Meet Again,'" 389.

45 Fans also engaged in collective action to raise money for the Trevor Project,
    "the world's largest suicide prevention and crisis intervention organization for
    lesbian, gay, bisexual, transgender, queer, and questioning (LGBTQ) young
    people." The Trevor Project, "The Trevor Project." The campaign donated nearly
    $180,000. See "Fundraising for The Trevor Project." This can be seen as an instan-
    tiation of what Ashley Hinck calls "fan-based citizenship": "public engagement
    that emerges from a commitment to a fan object." Hinck, *Politics for the Love of
    Fandom*, 6.

46 As Waggoner notes, "While fans also tweeted #CancelThe100, their efforts here
    were too late. (The CW announced the renewal the next day, a decision that
    would have been made already.)" Waggoner, "Bury Your Gays and Social Media
    Fan Response," 1884.

47 Indeed, "the Lexa Pledge, a promise for better LGBTQ representation written
    by TV creators in consultation with fans," which "was designed to spread and
    gather signatures," did not get traction; "those in the television industry who have
    spoken about not signing it point to a perceived infringement on creative free-
    dom; they do not want to be told what kind of stories they can and cannot tell."
    Cameron, "Toxic Regulation," 11, 12.

48 Cameron, "Toxic Regulation," 2.

49 Bourdaa, "'May We Meet Again,'" 389.

50 Waggoner, "Bury Your Gays and Social Media Fan Response," 1884.

51 On the "us" versus "them" mentality of Gamergate, see Miller, "'Wolfenstein II'
    and MAGA as Fandom"; Trice and Potts, "Building Dark Patterns into Platforms."

52 Waggoner, "Bury Your Gays and Social Media Fan Response," 1886.

53 Cameron, "Toxic Regulation," 5.

54 Guerrero-Pico, Establés, and Ventura, "Killing Off Lexa," 317.
55 On Gamergate's version of the No True Scotsman argument, see Massanari, "#Gamergate and The Fappening"; Mortensen, "Anger, Fear, and Games."
56 Cameron, "Toxic Regulation," 2.
57 Bourdaa, "'May We Meet Again,'" 385.
58 Guerrero-Pico, Establés, and Ventura, "Killing Off Lexa," 319.
59 The odds of electrocution from a phone that is not plugged in seem to be rather low. Greenfield, "How Likely Is Death by IPhone Electrocution?"
60 Cameron, "Toxic Regulation," 3.
61 Marwick and Caplan, "Drinking Male Tears," 547.
62 Trice and Potts, "Building Dark Patterns into Platforms," 6.
63 Pande, "Who Do You Mean by 'Fan'?" 323.
64 Pande, "Who Do You Mean by 'Fan'?" 323.
65 Braithwaite, "It's about Ethics in Games Journalism?" 7.
66 Salter, "From Geek Masculinity to Gamergate," 251–52.
67 See Jasser et al., "Controversial Information Spreads Faster and Further Than Non-Controversial Information in Reddit."

CHAPTER 5. THE ANTI WARS

1 Gray, "New Audiences, New Textualities," 70.
2 Click, Anti-Fandom.
3 Alexis Lothian in TWC Editor, "What Is an Anti?" 3.4.
4 "Ships," short for "relationships," refers to romantic pairings in fandom. A shipper is someone who variously enjoys, supports, or advocates for (and which one of these is, in fact, a site of contestation) a particular ship. "To ship," or "shipping," is the act of enjoying, supporting, or advocating for a particular ship.
5 Rouse, "Voltron," 155.
6 Stein, Millennial Fandom, 158. In addition to this commentary function, tagging with "anti-" creates what Winter et al. call a "content space" in platforms that otherwise do not have them (unlike Facebook Groups or subreddits) by organizing all related posts into a single, browsable body. Winter et al., "A Taxonomy of User Actions on Social Networking Sites."
7 Stitch in TWC Editor, "What Is an Anti?" para. 3.2.
8 Doxing or doxxing is posting identifying information online for the purpose of harassment.
9 Jess H, "A Statement on Malicious Email Attacks against OTW Volunteers." I am not quoting the internal message directly because it is not public, but I received it as the editor of Transformative Works and Cultures.
10 Stitch in TWC Editor, "What Is an Anti?" para. 5.4.
11 Giroux, "Twitter Data Scraping Jupyter Notebook"; Demšar et al., "Orange."
12 Both tools started from the time of collection and worked backwards until they reached their maximum capacity. For the Jupyter Notebook, in which the start date can be adjusted, I iteratively searched backward using the earliest date in

each set as the start for the subsequent search. For Orange, there were three single collections of five thousand each on August 30.

13 Lothian in TWC Editor, "What Is an Anti?" para. 7.10.

14 Lothian in TWC Editor, "What Is an Anti?" para. 4.2.

15 Historically, "fanon" referred to "a series of details and characteristics that are shared by most slash stories, but have no factual basis in the original media text." Stasi, "The Toy Soldiers from Leeds," 121. It was fan-developed canon that people accepted as true or correct. Like many fandom terms, it has shifted over time, and "in fanon" now tends to refer to something more like "in fan space" or "in fan interpretation," retaining the notion of having no basis in the source but losing the sense of collectively making up a new fact.

16 See obsession_inc, "Affirmational Fandom vs. Transformational Fandom."

17 It is also a fond wish of media companies everywhere. See Consalvo, "Cyber-Slaying Media Fans"; Stanfill, *Exploiting Fandom*. However, as we saw in chapter 3, taking this approach is increasingly common.

18 Stanfill, "The Fan Fiction Gold Rush, Generational Turnover, and the Battle for Fandom's Soul."

19 Gonzalez, "Swan Queen, Shipping, and Boundary Regulation in Fandom," paras. 4.2, 4.4.

20 Warner, "(Black Female) Fans Strike Back," 257.

21 Gonzalez, "Swan Queen, Shipping, and Boundary Regulation in Fandom," 5.1.

22 See, for example, Jenkins, *Textual Poachers*; Bacon-Smith, *Enterprising Women*; Penley, *NASA/Trek*. Importantly, this story that fan studies has told about fans—and fans have told about themselves—was only ever partially true, as seen in the homophobia described above as well as discussions of the prevalence of racism in fandom. See Johnson, "Transformative Racism"; Pande, "Squee from the Margins"; Pande, "Who Do You Mean by 'Fan'?"; TWC Editor, "Pattern Recognition."

23 See Coppa, "An Editing Room of One's Own"; De Kosnik, "*Fifty Shades* and the Archive of Women's Culture"; Lothian, Busse, and Reid, "'Yearning Void and Infinite Potential.'"

24 Warner, "ABC's *Scandal* and Black Women's Fandom," 35, 39.

25 Ng, "Between Text, Paratext, and Context."

26 While there is not a corresponding argument about increased acceptability of nonwhite characters over time—not least because race and sexuality, though they can sometimes be analogized, are quite different systems—Warner does identify downplaying of both the challenges of representing interracial relationships and cultural resistance to treating Black women as desirable. Eliding these cultural realities hides the fact that such depictions still face an uphill battle. Warner, "ABC's *Scandal* and Black Women's Fandom."

27 Lothian in TWC Editor, "What Is an Anti?" para. 8.2.

28 Weber, "What's Wrong with Be(Com)Ing Queer?" 682.

29 For example, the ruling in *Obergefell v. Hodges*, the case that secured the right of same-sex couples to marry throughout the United States, said that "the right to

marry is a fundamental right inherent in the liberty of the person, and under the Due Process and Equal Protection Clauses of the Fourteenth Amendment couples of the same-sex may not be deprived of that right and that liberty," and that laws prohibiting same-sex marriage were "invalid to the extent they exclude same-sex couples from civil marriage on the same terms and conditions as opposite-sex couples."

30 Busse, *Framing Fan Fiction*, 27.

31 Barthes, "The Death of the Author," 146.

32 Rubin, "Thinking Sex," 6.

33 Rubin, "Thinking Sex," 11, 14.

34 In *Avatar: The Last Airbender*, the Fire Nation is an imperialistic society that has committed genocide against other nations.

35 See Vance, "Negotiating Sex and Gender in the Attorney General's Commission on Pornography."

36 As Rubin notes, feminists were joined by the law in making this argument, as in a case where "a man was convicted of aggravated assault for a whipping administered in an S/M scene. There was no complaining victim. The session had been filmed and he was prosecuted on the basis of the film" because, the court reasoned, "a normal person in full possession of his mental faculties does not freely consent to the use, upon himself, of force likely to produce great bodily injury," and therefore the recipient could not have consented. Rubin, "Thinking Sex," 31.

37 MacKinnon, "Feminism, Marxism, Method, and the State," 652.

38 MacKinnon, "Feminism, Marxism, Method, and the State," 532.

39 "Fujo" is short for "*fujoshi*," or "rotten girls," in Japanese, a term in which "fantasizing male-male romance and eroticism is self-mockingly characterized as rotten, fallen, and up to no good." Wei, "Iron Man in Chinese Boys' Love Fandom." "*Fujoshi*," similarly to "weeb," has been weaponized in English-language fandom as a way to single out "wrong" engagement with Japanese popular culture, prompting debates about authentic or inauthentic uses of "*fujoshi*" by both those who self-describe as such and critics (Lori Morimoto, private communication, February 7, 2021).

40 Rubin, "Thinking Sex," 13.

41 Lothian in TWC Editor, "What Is an Anti?" 7.6.

42 Rubin, "Thinking Sex," 28.

43 Busse, *Framing Fan Fiction*, 198, 209.

44 Lothian and Stanfill, "An Archive of Whose Own?" para. 4.3.

45 Busse, *Framing Fan Fiction*, 198.

46 For discussion of a similar argument in the context of the critical race theory panic, see chapter 7.

47 Franks, *The Cult of the Constitution*, 12.

48 "Squick" is a fannish term for being "grossed out," connoting personal taste rather than a sense that something is objectively harmful. Busse and Hellekson, "Introduction," 11.

49 Lothian and Stanfill, "An Archive of Whose Own?" para. 7.2.

50 Franks, *The Cult of the Constitution*, 13.

51 Franks, *The Cult of the Constitution*, 106.

52 Sneha Kumar in TWC Editor, "What Is an Anti?" para. 5.5.

53 Lothian and Stanfill, "An Archive of Whose Own?" para. 1.1.

54 Stanfill, *Exploiting Fandom*, 24.

55 Bonilla-Silva, *Racism without Racists*, 8.

56 Lothian and Stanfill, "An Archive of Whose Own?" para. 2.1.

57 Massanari and Chess, "Attack of the 50-Foot Social Justice Warrior," 526.

58 Butler, *Gender Trouble*, 182.

59 See Pande, "Who Do You Mean by 'Fan'?"; Stanfill, *Exploiting Fandom*; Wanzo, "African American Acafandom and Other Strangers"; Warner, "If Loving Olitz Is Wrong, I Don't Wanna Be Right"; Warner, "ABC's Scandal and Black Women's Fandom."

60 Pande, "Squee from the Margins," 182.

61 For a discussion of antiracist reckoning in fandom in relation to Floyd's murder, see Lothian and Stanfill, "An Archive of Whose Own?"

62 Stitch in TWC Editor, "What Is an Anti?" para. 6.3.

63 Lothian and Stanfill, "An Archive of Whose Own?" para. 2.2.

64 Stitch in TWC Editor, "What Is an Anti?" para. 8.13.

65 Rufo, "@ConceptualJames We Have Successfully Frozen Their Brand"; Rufo, "@ConceptualJames the Goal Is to Have the Public."

66 Stitch in TWC Editor, "What Is an Anti?" para. 4.4.

67 Similarly, for all that the Anti Wars frequently turn on questions of underage sex, they actually do not engage the question of what the harms might be of invoking the negative stereotype of gay men as pederasts. Instead, the question circles around whether the stories eroticize children. Thanks to Tison Pugh for raising this angle on the argument about underage sex.

68 Matsuda, "Public Response to Racist Speech," 47.

69 On Haiti earthquake fiction, see Busse, "The Ethics of Studying Online Fandom." On inventing white characters, see Coker and Viars, "Welcoming the Dark Side?" Franks, *The Cult of the Constitution*, 112.

70 Matsuda, "Public Response to Racist Speech," 18.

71 Lawrence, "If He Hollers Let Him Go," 80.

72 Lothian and Stanfill, "An Archive of Whose Own?" para. 1.1.

CHAPTER 6. "I JUST JOINED THE #MUGCLUB!"

1 McKay, "YouTube"; O'Donovan, "YouTube Has Finally Admitted That Steven Crowder Mocking Someone for Being a Gay Latino Is Not OK."

2 McKay, "YouTube."

3 McKay, "YouTube."

4 Lopatto, "Bowing to Pressure, YouTube Will Reconsider Its Harassment Policies."

5 Asarch, "What Is the Vox Adpocalypse?"

6 "Official YouTube Blog: Taking a Harder Look at Harassment."

7 "Official YouTube Blog: Taking a Harder Look at Harassment."

8 Asarch, "What Is the Vox Adpocalypse?"

9 "Official YouTube Blog: Our Ongoing Work to Tackle Hate."

10 "Official YouTube Blog: Our Ongoing Work to Tackle Hate."

11 Asarch, "What Is the Vox Adpocalypse?"

12 Tarvin and Stanfill, "'YouTube's Predator Problem,'" 824.

13 Asarch, "What Is the Vox Adpocalypse?"

14 Cunningham and Craig, *Social Media Entertainment*, 112.

15 McKay, "YouTube."

16 "Louder with Crowder on BlazeTV."

17 Many thanks to John Murray for helping me with this scraping—and with converting the resulting JSON to a usable format.

18 Demšar et al., "Orange."

19 Crawford, *Consuming Sport*, 113.

20 Hills, *Fan Cultures*; Sandvoss, *Fans*.

21 Stanfill, *Exploiting Fandom*, 89, 91.

22 Costley White, *The Branding of Right-Wing Activism*, 11.

23 Crawford, *Consuming Sport*.

24 Jenkins, *Convergence Culture*, 222.

25 Jenkins, "Interactive Audiences?" 141.

26 Jenkins, *Convergence Culture*, 91.

27 Jenkins, "Cultural Acupuncture," para. 1.6.

28 Neilson, "Boycott or Buycott?" 214.

29 Hoffmann et al., "Under Which Conditions Are Consumers Ready to Boycott or Buycott?" 169. Micheletti and Oral, "Problematic Political Consumerism," 705.

30 See Ted Cruz [@tedcruz], "Goya Is a Staple of Cuban Food"; and Aleem, "The Goya Foods Boycott Controversy, Explained."

31 Zengerle, "Can the Black Rifle Coffee Company Become the Starbucks of the Right?"

32 Micheletti and Oral, "Problematic Political Consumerism"; Neilson, "Boycott or Buycott?"

33 "BlazeTV."

34 The Daily Wire, "About."

35 "Steven Crowder's Twitter Monthly Stats."

36 "Filtering Mentions."

37 On intimacy, see Berryman and Kavka, "'I Guess a Lot of People See Me as a Big Sister or a Friend'"; Berryman and Kavka, "Crying on YouTube"; Jerslev, "In The Time of the Microcelebrity"; Raun, "Capitalizing Intimacy." On access, see Berryman and Kavka, "'I Guess a Lot of People See Me as a Big Sister or a Friend'"; Berryman and Kavka, "Crying on YouTube"; García-Rapp and Roca-Cuberes, "Being

an Online Celebrity"; Hou, "Social Media Celebrity and the Institutionalization of YouTube"; Jerslev, "In the Time of the Microcelebrity"; Raun, "Capitalizing Intimacy."

38 See Geraghty, "It's Not All about the Music."

39 Stanfill, *Exploiting Fandom*, 90.

40 Macuk, "What's Up with That T-Shirt?"

41 Macuk, "What's Up with That T-Shirt?" I do confess that part of me appreciates the meta angle of using an actual fig leaf as a fig leaf to pretend that he is not being homophobic.

42 See Lawson, "Platform Vulnerabilities"; Ging, "Alphas, Betas, and Incels"; O'Donnell, "Militant Meninism."

43 See Carroll, *Affirmative Reaction*; Hartzell, "Alt-White"; Hartzell, "Whiteness Feels Good Here."

44 Blodgett and Salter, "*Ghostbusters* Is for Boys."

45 Franks, *The Cult of the Constitution*, xiii.

46 Franks, *The Cult of the Constitution*, 106.

47 Heredia and Stanfill, "Reactionary Influencers and the Construction of White Conservative Victimhood."

48 On Bennett's transphobia, see: Tobin and Austin, "'Gun Girl' Claims a Riot at Ohio University, but Her Old Adversary at UK Isn't Buying It." On antisemitism, see: Zoellner, "'Gun Girl' Kaitlin Bennett Accused of Making Anti-semitic Statements in Leaked Messages."

49 Walker, "The Shifting Symbolism of the Gadsden Flag."

50 Hesse, "'Make Liberals Cry Again' Became the Battle Hymn of the Republicans under Trump."

51 Lulz are a "particular kind of unsympathetic ambiguous laugher. Lulz is similar to Schadenfreude—loosely translated from German as reveling in the misfortune of someone you dislike—but has much sharper teeth." Phillips, *This Is Why We Can't Have Nice Things*, 2, 1, 24.

52 Crosset, Tanner, and Campana, "Researching Far Right Groups on Twitter."

53 "Words We're Watching: 'Streisand Effect.'"

54 A 2019 post on a firearms enthusiast website notes that Walther Arms had "been sponsoring him for quite a while." See CarolinaFirearmsForum, "Walther Goes Louder with Crowder." Walther's Facebook page has a video featuring Crowder using one of its guns posted in 2017. See "Walther Arms, Inc."

55 Hogg and Corin, "Parkland Survivors."

56 Cook, "The NRA Should Send Obama a 'Thank You' Card."

57 Franks, *The Cult of the Constitution*, 108.

58 Alexander, "Creators Aren't Surprised That YouTube Won't Enforce Its Own Policies against Harassment."

59 Franks, *The Cult of the Constitution*, 116.

60 Franks, *The Cult of the Constitution*, 115.

61 Franks, *The Cult of the Constitution*, 112.

62 Doxing is the posting of private information online for the purpose of harassment.

63 Franks, *The Cult of the Constitution*, 115.

64 Gillespie, "The Politics of 'Platforms.'"

65 Shapiro "Facts, Episode 3."

66 Beauchamp, "Jordan Peterson, the Obscure Canadian Psychologist Turned Right-Wing Celebrity, Explained."

67 Franks, *The Cult of the Constitution*, 198.

68 Tarvin, "YouTube Fandom Names in Channel Communities and Branding," para. 1.2.

69 Know Your Meme, "Of Course You Have Blue Hair and Pronouns."

70 Long, "How 'Let's Go Brandon' Became Code for Insulting Joe Biden."

CHAPTER 7. "TEACHING WHITE KIDS THEY'RE BAD"

1 Rufo, "@ConceptualJames the Goal Is to Have the Public"; Rufo, "@Conceptual-James We Have Successfully Frozen Their Brand."

2 On civil rights lectures, see: Harrison, "Local Professor Speaks Out after School District Cancels Civil Rights Lecture over CRT Concerns." On books by and about Black people, see: Bellamy-Walker, "Book Bans in Schools Are Catching Fire."

3 Stein, *Millennial Fandom*, 156.

4 Busse, *Framing Fan Fiction*, 101.

5 Busse and Hellekson, "Introduction"; Stasi, "The Toy Soldiers from Leeds."

6 It is important that we not run this both directions; while the CRT panic cultivates a fannish attachment to whiteness, this does not mean that these are the only fans with an affective attachment to whiteness. To the contrary, as discussed earlier in the book, there is also white supremacy in regular old media fandom.

7 Miller, "'Wolfenstein II' and MAGA as Fandom," para. 3.1.

8 Miller, "'Wolfenstein II' and MAGA as Fandom," para. 3.9.

9 Omi and Winant, *Racial Formation in the United States*, 55.

10 Omi and Winant, *Racial Formation in the United States*, 56.

11 Savran, *Taking It like a Man*, 3.

12 On whiteness as invisible, see Dyer, *White*; Frankenberg, *White Women, Race Matters*; Hill, "Can Whiteness Speak?"; McIntosh, "White Privilege and Male Privilege"; Newitz and Wray, "Introduction." On whiteness as transparent, see Flagg, "'Was Blind, but Now I See.'"

13 Frankenberg, "Introduction," 5.

14 Hartzell, "Alt-White," 16–17.

15 Hartzell, "Alt-White," 16.

16 Hartzell, "Alt-White," 15.

17 Newitz and Wray, "Introduction," 3.

18 Delgado and Stefancic, "Introduction," xvi.

19 Delgado and Stefancic, "Introduction," xvi.

20 Crenshaw et al., "Introduction," xiii.

21 Delgado and Stefancic, "Introduction," xvi.

22 Delgado and Stefancic, "Introduction," xvi.

23 Crenshaw et al., "Introduction," xiii.

24 Cohen, "Whose Side Were We On?" 241. See also Cohen, *Folk Devils and Moral Panics*; McRobbie and Thornton, "Rethinking 'Moral Panic' for Multi-Mediated Social Worlds"; Miller, "A Risk Society of Moral Panic."

25 "'The Tea Party to the 10th Power.'"

26 Banks, "The Radical Capitalist behind the Critical Race Theory Furor."

27 "The Tea Party to the 10th Power."

28 Smith, "How Did Republicans Turn Critical Race Theory into a Winning Electoral Issue?"

29 See Baker, "Moral Panic and Alternative Identity Construction in Usenet"; Cohen, *Folk Devils and Moral Panics*; Miller, "A Risk Society of Moral Panic."

30 See Cohen, *Folk Devils and Moral Panics*; Marwick, "To Catch a Predator?"; Young, "Moral Panics and the Transgressive Other."

31 Young, "Moral Panics and the Transgressive Other."

32 Cohen, *Folk Devils and Moral Panics*, xii.

33 "CDC: Delta Variant Now Makes Up More Than Half of U.S. Cases."

34 On color-blind racism, see Bonilla-Silva, *Racism without Racists*.

35 Thanks to Stephen Hopkins for raising this parallel.

36 Gray, "New Audiences, New Textualities," 70.

37 Jenkins, *Convergence Culture*, 95–96.

38 Jenkins, *Convergence Culture*, 96.

39 Stabile, "Conspiracy or Consensus?" 260.

40 "New York Police Join Forces with ATF Agents."

41 "Interview with Sen. Tom Cotton (R–AR)."

42 As feminists have long pointed out, using the masculine "Latino" universally, while grammatically correct in Spanish, is exclusionary; recently, nonbinary people have argued that "Latino/Latina" is exclusionary as well. I use "Latine" as a gender-neutral option that, unlike "Latinx," is pronounceable in Spanish.

43 Vought, "Training in the Federal Government."

44 "CDC: Delta Variant Now Makes Up More Than Half of U.S. Cases."

45 Bradley, "Letter."

46 Hartzell, "Whiteness Feels Good Here," 130.

47 "Gutfeld."

48 Hammer, "Yes, We Should Ban Critical Race Theory from Our Schools."

49 Camera, "Bills Banning Critical Race Theory Advance in States Despite Its Absence in Many Classrooms."

50 Reeve, Guff, and Brunswick, "The Critical Race Theory Panic Has White People Afraid That They Might Be Complicit in Racism."

51 Sands, "White Supremacists Remain Deadliest US Terror Threat, Homeland Security Report Says."

52 "Schools Have Become Cesspools for Radical Thought."

53 Darcy, "Fox News Stands by Laura Ingraham after She Defends White Supremacist, Other Extremists on Her Prime Time Show."

54 For one key instance of this critique, see Ahmed, *On Being Included*.

55 Lee, *To Kill a Mockingbird*.

56 Reeve, Guff, and Brunswick, "The Critical Race Theory Panic Has White People
Afraid That They Might Be Complicit in Racism." Indeed, in 2022 it was removed
from the curriculum in Yakima, Washington, in part over complaints about its
"white savior complex." See Kent, "Mukilteo School District Votes to Remove 'To
Kill a Mockingbird' from Required Reading."

57 "The 1619 Project."

58 Serwer, "The Fight over the 1619 Project Is Not about the Facts."

59 "Chipman Admits He Favors Actual Gun Grabs."

60 "Joe Biden Signs Order Targeting Big Businesses."

61 "Tlaib Calls to Defund Immigration Agencies."

62 Delgado and Stefancic, "Introduction," xvi.

63 "Chicago Mayor Meets with Biden amid Increasing Violence."

64 "Critical Race Theory Panel."

65 "CDC: Delta Variant Now Makes Up More Than Half of U.S. Cases."

66 "CDC: Delta Variant Now Makes Up More Than Half of U.S. Cases."

67 "Vote to Advance Sweeping Voting Rights Bill Fails to Overcome GOP Filibuster."

68 "CDC: Delta Variant Now Makes Up More Than Half of U.S. Cases."

69 Linker, "The Left Is Anti-Anti-Critical Race Theory."

70 Hammer, "Yes, We Should Ban Critical Race Theory from Our Schools."

71 Page, "Can the Left Defend Critical Race Theory?"

72 "Gutfeld."

73 Stanfill, *Exploiting Fandom*, 24.

74 "How Critical Race Theory Went from Harvard Law to Fox News."

75 Reeve, Guff, and Brunswick, "The Critical Race Theory Panic Has White People
Afraid That They Might Be Complicit in Racism."

76 "Biden Announces Door-to-Door Vaccine Push."

77 Duncan, "Battle over Critical Race Theory Heats Up."

78 "Interview With Rep. Ruben Gallego (D–AZ)."

79 "Schools Have Become Cesspools for Radical Thought."

80 Bonilla-Silva, *Racism without Racists*.

81 On Gamergate, see Chess and Shaw, "A Conspiracy of Fishes"; Condis, *Gaming
Masculinity*; Gray, Buyukozturk, and Hill, "Blurring the Boundaries"; Massanari,
"#Gamergate and The Fappening"; Salter and Blodgett, *Toxic Geek Masculinity in
Media*. On Snyder's fans, see Salter and Stanfill, *A Portrait of the Auteur as Fanboy*.
On the Puppies, see Oleszczuk, "Sad and Rabid Puppies"; Wilson, "Red Pillers,
Sad Puppies, and Gamergaters."

82 "An Inside Look into Jesse Watters' Book."

83 "CDC: Delta Variant Now Makes Up More Than Half of U.S. Cases."

84 "Antifa" is the name for a loose confederation of often-combative activists whose "ideology is rooted in the belief that the Nazi party would never have been able to come to power in Germany if people had more aggressively fought them in the streets in the 1920s and 30s." See Anti-Defamation League, "Who Are Antifa?"
85 "History Repeated."
86 Reeve, Guff, and Brunswick, "The Critical Race Theory Panic Has White People Afraid That They Might Be Complicit in Racism."
87 "An Inside Look into Jesse Watters' Book."
88 "Uncovering Who Is Driving the Fight against Critical Race Theory in Schools."
89 Hartzell, "Alt-White," 11.
90 Blodgett and Salter, "*Ghostbusters* Is for Boys," 142.
91 Blodgett and Salter, "*Ghostbusters* Is for Boys," 136.
92 Wellman, "Minstrel Shows, Affirmative Action Talk, and Angry White Men."
93 Carroll, *Affirmative Reaction*, 5.
94 Carroll, *Affirmative Reaction*, 5.
95 Ross and Mauney, "The Changing Faces of White Supremacy," 555.
96 Anti-Defamation League, "14 Words."
97 Lewis, "Alternative Influence," 16.
98 Ganesh, "The Ungovernability of Digital Hate Culture"; Lewis, "Alternative Influence."
99 Daniels, *Cyber Racism*, 55, 54.
100 Frankenberg, *White Women, Race Matters*, 230.
101 Hartzell, "Whiteness Feels Good Here," 131.
102 Hartzell, "Whiteness Feels Good Here," 130.

CONCLUSION
1 Franks, *The Cult of the Constitution*, xiii.
2 Wilson, "Red Pillers, Sad Puppies, and Gamergaters."
3 Marwick and Caplan, "Drinking Male Tears," 547.
4 Stanfill, *Exploiting Fandom*, 184.
5 Ng, "Between Text, Paratext, and Context," para. 2.8.
6 Notably, this is a belief often shared by media industries and representations, as I have discussed elsewhere. See Stanfill, "Doing Fandom, (Mis)Doing Whiteness."
7 Hills, "An Extended Foreword," 114.
8 Franks, *The Cult of the Constitution*, 181.
9 Blodgett and Salter, "*Ghostbusters* Is for Boys," 136.
10 Carroll, *Affirmative Reaction*, 5.
11 See Salter, "From Geek Masculinity to Gamergate"; Proctor and Kies, "Editors' Introduction"; Scott, *Fake Geek Girls*.
12 See Chess and Shaw, "A Conspiracy of Fishes"; Massanari, "Rethinking Research Ethics, Power, and the Risk of Visibility in the Era of the 'Alt-Right' Gaze"; Rambukkana, "The Politics of Gray Data."
13 Stein, *Millennial Fandom*, 156.

14 Stein, *Millennial Fandom*, 170.
15 See Khardori, "The Odds Are Going Up That Trump Could Be Charged."
16 See Berryman and Kavka, "'I Guess a Lot of People See Me as a Big Sister or a Friend'"; Berryman and Kavka, "Crying on YouTube"; García-Rapp and Roca-Cuberes, "Being an Online Celebrity"; Hou, "Social Media Celebrity and the Institutionalization of YouTube"; Jerslev, "In the Time of the Microcelebrity"; Raun, "Capitalizing Intimacy."
17 For one such example, see elon musk [@soniasaraiya], "Thank You for DMing Me, the Ceo of Twitter." As of this writing, Saraiya, after changing her display name to "Elon Musk," has posted images of people DMing her to ask for jobs at Musk's companies and make suggestions (and demand credit if they are implemented). Thanks to Anastasia Salter for bringing this to my attention.
18 Muñoz, *Cruising Utopia*, 22, 21.
19 Stanfill, "Introduction," 126.

BIBLIOGRAPHY

Abdelmahmoud, Elamin. "The Pro-Trump Mob Was Doing It for the 'Gram." *BuzzFeed News*, January 7, 2021. www.buzzfeednews.com.

Ahmed, Sara. *On Being Included: Racism and Diversity in Institutional Life.* Durham, NC: Duke University Press, 2012.

Aleem, Zeeshan. "The Goya Foods Boycott Controversy, Explained." *Vox*, July 12, 2020. www.vox.com.

Alexander, Julia. "Creators Aren't Surprised That YouTube Won't Enforce Its Own Policies against Harassment." *The Verge*, June 5, 2019. www.theverge.com.

Allington, Daniel. "'How Come Most People Don't See It?': Slashing *The Lord of the Rings.*" *Social Semiotics* 17, no. 1 (2007): 43–62. https://doi.org/10.1080/10350330601124650.

"An Inside Look into Jesse Watters' Book." *Watters World.* Fox News, July 10, 2021.

Anders, Sari M. van, Debby Herbenick, Lori A. Brotto, Emily A. Harris, and Sara B. Chadwick. "The Heteronormativity Theory of Low Sexual Desire in Women Partnered with Men." *Archives of Sexual Behavior* 51, no. 1 (2022): 391–415. https://doi.org/10.1007/s10508-021-02100-x.

Anderson, Karrin Vasby. "Presidential Pioneer or Campaign Queen? Hillary Clinton and the First-Timer/Frontrunner Double Bind." *Rhetoric and Public Affairs* 20, no. 3 (2017): 525–38. https://doi.org/10.14321/rhetpublaffa.20.3.0525.

Anthony, Laurence. "AntConc." Laurence Anthony's Website, Tokyo, Japan: Waseda University, 2022. www.laurenceanthony.net.

Anti-Defamation League. "14 Words." Accessed August 26, 2021. www.adl.org.

———. "Who Are Antifa?" Accessed August 14, 2021. https://www.adl.org.

Archive of Our Own. "Upcoming Limit on Tags per Work." August 24, 2021. https://archiveofourown.org.

Asarch, Steven. "What Is the Vox Adpocalypse? YouTubers Weigh in on Controversial New Rules." *Newsweek*, June 6, 2019. www.newsweek.com.

Åström, Berit. "'Let's Get Those Winchesters Pregnant': Male Pregnancy in 'Supernatural' Fan Fiction." *Transformative Works and Cultures* 4 (2010). https://doi.org/10.3983/twc.v4i0.135.

Bacon-Smith, Camille. *Enterprising Women: Television Fandom and the Creation of Popular Myth.* Philadelphia: University of Pennsylvania Press, 1991.

Baker, Paul. "Moral Panic and Alternative Identity Construction in Usenet." *Journal of Computer-Mediated Communication* 7, no. 1 (2001). https://doi.org/10.1111/j.1083-6101.2001.tb00136.x.

Banks, Jasmine. "The Radical Capitalist behind the Critical Race Theory Furor." *The Nation*, August 13, 2021. www.thenation.com.

Barthes, Roland. "The Death of the Author." In *Image-Music-Text*, translated by Stephen Heath, 142–48. New York: Hill and Wang, 1978.

Beauchamp, Zack. "Jordan Peterson, the Obscure Canadian Psychologist Turned Right-Wing Celebrity, Explained." *Vox*, March 26, 2018. www.vox.com.

Bellamy-Walker, Tat. "Book Bans in Schools Are Catching Fire: Black Authors Say Uproar Isn't about Students." *NBC News*, January 6, 2022. www.nbcnews.com.

Bennett, Lucy. "Discourses of Order and Rationality: Drooling R.E.M. Fans as 'Matter out of Place.'" *Continuum* 27, no. 2 (2013): 214–27. https://doi.org/10.1080/10304312.2013.766313.

Berryman, Rachel, and Misha Kavka. "Crying on YouTube: Vlogs, Self-Exposure, and the Productivity of Negative Affect." *Convergence* 24, no. 1 (2018): 85–98. https://doi.org/10.1177/1354856517736981.

———. "'I Guess a Lot of People See Me as a Big Sister or a Friend': The Role of Intimacy in the Celebrification of Beauty Vloggers." *Journal of Gender Studies* 26, no. 3 (2017): 307–20. https://doi.org/10.1080/09589236.2017.1288611.

"Biden Announces Door-to-Door Vaccine Push." *Ingraham Angle*. Fox News, July 7, 2021.

Biesecker, Michael, Michael Kunzelman, Gillian Flauccus, and Jim Mustian. "Records Show Fervent Trump Fans Fueled US Capitol Takeover." *Associated Press*, January 11, 2021, sec. Political News.

Bingham, Christopher M. "Talking about Twitch: Dropped Frames and a Normative Theory of New Media Production." *Convergence* 26, no. 2 (2020): 269–86. https://doi.org/10.1177/1354856517736974.

Birkett, Tom. "US Capitol Riot: The Myths behind the Tattoos Worn by 'QAnon Shaman' Jake Angeli." *The Conversation*, January 11, 2021. http://theconversation.com.

"BlazeTV | News and Entertainment for People Who Love America." Accessed October 8, 2022. https://subscribe.blazetv.com/.

Blodgett, Bridget, and Anastasia Salter. "*Ghostbusters* Is for Boys: Understanding Geek Masculinity's Role in the Alt-Right." *Communication, Culture and Critique* 11, no. 1 (2018): 133–46. https://doi.org/10.1093/ccc/tcx003.

Bonilla-Silva, Eduardo. *Racism without Racists: Color-Blind Racism and the Persistence of Racial Inequality in the United States*. Lanham, MD: Rowman & Littlefield, 2003.

Bourdaa, Mélanie. "'May We Meet Again': Social Bonds, Activities, and Identities in the #Clexa Fandom." In *A Companion to Fandom and Fan Studies*, edited by Paul Booth, 385–99. Oxford, UK: Wiley-Blackwell, 2018.

Bradley, Michael. "Letter: Critical Race Theory Should Not Be Taught in Schools." *Whidbey News-Times*, June 29, 2021, sec. Letters.

Braithwaite, Andrea. "It's about Ethics in Games Journalism? Gamergaters and Geek Masculinity." *Social Media + Society* 2, no. 4 (2016): 1-10. https://doi.org/10.1177/2056305116672484.

Brough, Melissa, and Sangita Shresthova. "Fandom Meets Activism: Rethinking Civic and Political Participation." *Transformative Works and Cultures* 10 (2012). https://doi.org/10.3983/twc.2012.0303.

Bucktin, Christopher. "Overrun Run by Trump's Mob." *Daily Mirror*, January 7, 2021, 2nd edition, National Edition, sec. News.

Bullard, Julia. "Motivating Invisible Contributions: Framing Volunteer Classification Design in a Fanfiction Repository." In *Proceedings of the 19th International Conference on Supporting Group Work*, 181–93. Sanibel Island, FL: ACM, 2016. https://doi.org/10.1145/2957276.2957295.

Burbank, Megan. "Chelsea Cain Leaves Twitter Following Sexist Harassment." *Portland Mercury*, November 2, 2016. www.portlandmercury.com.

Busse, Kristina. "The Ethics of Studying Online Fandom." In *The Routledge Companion to Media Fandom*, edited by Melissa A. Click and Suzanne Scott, 9–17. New York: Routledge, 2017.

———. *Framing Fan Fiction: Literary and Social Practices in Fan Fiction Communities.* Iowa City: University of Iowa Press, 2017.

———. "Beyond Mary Sue: Fan Representation and the Complex Negotiation of Gendered Identity." In *Seeing Fans: Representations of Fandom in Media and Popular Culture*, edited by Lucy Bennett and Paul Booth, 159–68. New York: Bloomsbury Academic, 2016.

———. "Geek Hierarchies, Boundary Policing, and the Gendering of the Good Fan." *Participations* 10, no. 1 (2013): 73–91.

———. "My Life Is a WIP on My LJ: Slashing the Slasher and the Reality of Celebrity and Internet Performances." In *Fan Fiction and Fan Communities in the Age of the Internet: New Essays*, edited by Karen Hellekson and Kristina Busse, 207–24. Jefferson, NC: McFarland, 2006.

Busse, Kristina, and Karen Hellekson. "Introduction: Work in Progress." In *Fan Fiction and Fan Communities in the Age of the Internet: New Essays*, edited by Karen Hellekson and Kristina Busse, 5–40. Jefferson, NC: McFarland, 2006.

Butler, Judith. *Bodies That Matter: On the Discursive Limits of "Sex."* New York: Routledge, 1993.

———. *Gender Trouble: Feminism and the Subversion of Identity.* New York: Routledge, 1990.

Callis, April S. "Homophobia, Heteronormativity, and Slash Fan Fiction." *Transformative Works and Cultures* 22 (2016). https://doi.org/10.3983/twc.2016.0708.

Camera, Lauren. "Bills Banning Critical Race Theory Advance in States Despite Its Absence in Many Classrooms." *US News & World Report*, June 23, 2021, sec. News; Education News.

Cameron, Kelsey. "Toxic Regulation: From TV's Code of Practices to '#Bury Your Gays.'" *Participations: Journal of Audience and Reception Studies* 15, no. 1 (2018): 1–14.

CarolinaFirearmsForum. "Walther Goes Louder with Crowder." November 22, 2019. https://carolinafirearmsforum.com.

Carroll, Hamilton. *Affirmative Reaction: New Formations of White Masculinity.* Durham, NC: Duke University Press, 2011.

"CDC: Delta Variant Now Makes Up More Than Half of U.S. Cases." *Erin Burnett Outfront.* CNN, July 6, 2021.

centreoftheselights. "AO3 Ship Stats 2022." August 4, 2022. https://archiveofourown.org.

Chess, Shira, and Adrienne Shaw. "A Conspiracy of Fishes; or, How We Learned to Stop Worrying about #GamerGate and Embrace Hegemonic Masculinity." *Journal of Broadcasting & Electronic Media* 59, no. 1 (2015): 208–20. https://doi.org/10.1080/08838151.2014.999917.

"Chicago Mayor Meets with Biden amid Increasing Violence." *Fox Special Report with Bret Baier.* Fox News, July 7, 2021.

"Chipman Admits He Favors Actual Gun Grabs." *Ingraham Angle.* Fox News, May 26, 2021.

Choyce, Mel. "The Aftermath of the Death of Lexa." *Medium* (blog), March 25, 2016. https://medium.com/@melchoyce/the-aftermath-of-the-death-of-lexa-a846fc003067.

Click, Melissa A., ed. *Anti-Fandom: Dislike and Hate in the Digital Age.* New York: New York University Press, 2019.

"CNN International." *CNN International.* CNN, January 14, 2021.

Cohen, Cathy J. "Punks, Bulldaggers, and Welfare Queens: The Radical Potential of Queer Politics?" *GLQ: A Journal of Lesbian and Gay Studies* 3, no. 4 (1997): 437–65.

Cohen, Stanley. "Whose Side Were We On? The Undeclared Politics of Moral Panic Theory." *Crime, Media, Culture* 7, no. 3 (2011): 237–43. https://doi.org/10.1177/1741659011417603.

———. *Folk Devils and Moral Panics.* New York: Routledge, 1972.

Coker, Cait, and Karen Viars. "Welcoming the Dark Side? Exploring Whitelash and Actual Space Nazis in TFA Fanfiction." *NANO: New American Notes Online* 12 (2017). https://nanocrit.com.

Coleman, James Joshua. "Writing with Impunity in a Space of Their Own: On Cultural Appropriation, Imaginative Play, and a New Ethics of Slash in Harry Potter Fan Fiction." *Jeunesse: Young People, Texts, Cultures* 11, no. 1 (2019): 84–111. https://doi.org/10.3138/jeunesse.11.1.84.

Condis, Megan. *Gaming Masculinity: Trolls, Fake Geeks, and the Gendered Battle for Online Culture.* 1st edition. Iowa City: University of Iowa Press, 2018.

Condis, Megan, and Mel Stanfill. "Debating with Wertham's Ghost: Comic Books, Culture Wars, and Populist Moral Panics." *Cultural Studies* 36, no. 2 (2021): 1–28. https://doi.org/10.1080/09502386.2021.1946579.

Consalvo, Mia. "Cyber-Slaying Media Fans: Code, Digital Poaching, and Corporate Control of the Internet." *Journal of Communication Inquiry* 27, no. 1 (2003): 67–86.

Cook, Lindsey. "The NRA Should Send Obama a 'Thank You' Card." *US News & World Report,* June 23, 2015. www.usnews.com.

Coppa, Francesca. "Fuck Yeah, Fandom Is Beautiful." *Journal of Fandom Studies* 2, no. 1 (2014): 73–82. https://doi.org/10.1386/jfs.2.1.73_1.

———. "An Editing Room of One's Own: Vidding as Women's Work." *Camera Obscura: Feminism, Culture, and Media Studies* 26, no. 2 (2011): 123–30. https://doi.org/10.1215/02705346-1301557.

———. "Women, 'Star Trek,' and the Early Development of Fannish Vidding." *Transformative Works and Cultures* 1 (2008).

Costley White, Khadijah. *The Branding of Right-Wing Activism: The News Media and the Tea Party.* Oxford, UK: Oxford University Press, 2018.

Crawford, Garry. *Consuming Sport: Fans, Sport, and Culture.* New York: Routledge, 2004.

Crenshaw, Kimberlé Williams. "Beyond Racism and Misogyny: Black Feminism and 2 Live Crew." In *Words That Wound: Critical Race Theory, Assaultive Speech, and the First Amendment,* 111–32. Boulder, CO: Westview Press, 1993.

Crenshaw, Kimberlé, Neil Gotanda, Gary Peller, and Kendall Thomas. "Introduction." In *Critical Race Theory: The Key Writings That Formed the Movement,* xiii–xxxii. New York: New Press, 1996.

"Critical Race Theory Panel." ABC, June 20, 2021.

Crosset, Valentine, Samuel Tanner, and Aurélie Campana. "Researching Far-Right Groups on Twitter: Methodological Challenges 2.0." *New Media & Society* 21, no. 4 (2019): 939–61. https://doi.org/10.1177/1461444818817306.

Cunningham, Stuart, and David Craig. *Social Media Entertainment: The New Intersection of Hollywood and Silicon Valley.* New York: New York University Press, 2019.

The Daily Wire. "About." Accessed October 8, 2022. www.dailywire.com.

Daniels, Jessie. *Cyber Racism: White Supremacy Online and the New Attack on Civil Rights.* Lanham, MD: Rowman & Littlefield, 2009.

Darcy, Oliver. "Fox News Stands by Laura Ingraham after She Defends White Supremacist, Other Extremists on Her Prime Time Show." *CNN,* May 31, 2019. www.cnn.com.

Davisson, Amber. "Mashing up, Remixing, and Contesting the Popular Memory of Hillary Clinton." *Transformative Works and Cultures* 22 (2016). https://doi.org/10.3983/twc.2016.0965.

De Kosnik, Abigail. *Rogue Archives: Digital Cultural Memory and Media Fandom.* Cambridge, MA: MIT Press, 2016.

———. "*Fifty Shades* and the Archive of Women's Culture." *Cinema Journal* 54, no. 3 (2015): 116–25. https://doi.org/10.1353/cj.2015.0037.

Dean, Jonathan. "Politicising Fandom." *British Journal of Politics and International Relations* 19, no. 2 (2017): 408–24. https://doi.org/10.1177/1369148117701754.

Delgado, Richard, and Jean Stefancic. "Introduction." In *Critical Race Theory: The Cutting Edge,* edited by Richard Delgado and Jean Stefancic, 2nd edition, xv–xix. Philadelphia: Temple University Press, 2000.

Demšar, Janez, Tomaž Curk, Aleš Erjavec, Črt Gorup, Tomaž Hočevar, Mitar Milutinovič, Martin Možina, et al. "Orange: Data Mining Toolbox in Python." *Journal of Machine Learning Research* 14 (2013): 2349–53.

Dennison, Sean. "How Rich Is Bernie Sanders?" *Yahoo!Finance*, July 23, 2021. https://finance.yahoo.com.

Doty, Alexander. *Making Things Perfectly Queer: Interpreting Mass Culture*. Minneapolis: University of Minnesota Press, 1993.

Driessen, Simone. "'For the Greater Good?': Vigilantism in Online Pop Culture Fandoms." In *Introducing Vigilant Audiences*, edited by Daniel Trottier, Rashid Gabdulhakov, and Qian Huang, 25–48. England: Open Book Publishers, 2020.

Duggan, Jennifer. "Transformative Readings: Harry Potter Fan Fiction, Trans/Queer Reader Response, and J. K. Rowling." *Children's Literature in Education* 53 (2022): 147–68. https://doi.org/10.1007/s10583-021-09446-9.

Duggan, Lisa. *The Twilight of Equality? Neoliberalism, Cultural Politics, and the Attack on Democracy*. Boston: Beacon Press, 2004.

Duncan, Jericka. "Battle over Critical Race Theory Heats Up." *CBS Evening News*, June 27, 2021, Sunday edition, sec. News; Domestic.

Dyer, Richard. *White*. London: Routledge, 1997.

Elbein, Asher. "#Comicsgate: How an Anti-Diversity Harassment Campaign in Comics Got Ugly—and Profitable." *Daily Beast*, April 2, 2018, sec. Entertainment. www.thedailybeast.com.

Ellis, Emma Grey. "Why Elizabeth Warren's Feeds Are Flooded with Snake Emoji." *Wired*, January 15, 2020. www.wired.com.

elon musk [@soniasaraiya]. "Thank You for DMing Me, the CEO of Twitter." *Twitter*, November 4, 2022. https://twitter.com/soniasaraiya/status/1588628862988353536.

"Elon Musk Charged with Securities Fraud for Misleading Tweets." Press Release, US Securities and Exchange Commission, September 27, 2018. www.sec.gov.

Emmett, N. "From Batgirl to Comicgate? The Variant Cover Controversy." *Sequart Organization Magazine*, May 2, 2015. http://sequart.org/magazine/.

Epstein, Kayla. "Bernie Sanders Vows to Stay on Upcoming Ballots and Continue to Gather Delegates So He Can 'Exert Significant Influence over the Party Platform.'" *Business Insider*, April 8, 2020. Accessed May 1, 2022. www.businessinsider.com.

Fathallah, Judith May. "Polyphony on Tumblr: Reading the Hate Blog as Pastiche." *Transformative Works and Cultures* 27 (2018). https://journal.transformativeworks.org.

Ferguson, Roderick A. "Race-ing Heteronormativity: Citizenship, Sociology, and Gay Identity." In *Black Queer Studies: A Critical Anthology*, edited by E. Patrick Johnson and Mae G. Henderson, 52–67. Durham, NC: Duke University Press, 2005.

"Filtering Mentions." Twitter, September 12, 2013. https://blog.twitter.com/en_us/a/2013/filtering-mentions.

Flagg, Barbara J. "'Was Blind, but Now I See': White Race Consciousness and the Requirement of Discriminatory Intent." In *Critical White Studies: Looking behind the Mirror*, edited by Richard Delgado and Jean Stefancic, 629–31. Philadelphia: Temple University Press, 1997.

Flegel, Monica, and Jenny Roth. "Annihilating Love and Heterosexuality without Women: Romance, Generic Difference, and Queer Politics in Supernatural Fan

Fiction." *Transformative Works and Cultures* 4 (2010). https://doi.org/10.3983/twc
.2010.0133.

Forbes. "The Forbes 400 2021." October 5, 2021. www.forbes.com.

Forsey, Zoe. "Donald Trump's 'Hypnotic Handshake' and 'Secret Weapon' He Uses to
Win People Over." *Mirror*, January 20, 2021, 1st edition, sec. Politics. www.mirror.uk
.com.

Foucault, Michel. *The Archaeology of Knowledge and the Discourse on Language*. New
York: Pantheon, 1972.

Francisco, Eric. "What Is Comicsgate? The Newest Geek Controversy, Explained."
Inverse, February 9, 2018. www.inverse.com.

Frankenberg, Ruth. "Introduction: Local Whiteness, Localizing Whiteness." In *Displacing Whiteness: Essays in Social and Cultural Criticism*, edited by Ruth Frankenberg,
1–34. Durham, NC: Duke University Press, 1997.

———. *White Women, Race Matters: The Social Construction of Whiteness*. Minneapolis: University of Minnesota Press, 1993.

Franks, Mary Anne. *The Cult of the Constitution*. Stanford, CA: Stanford University
Press, 2019.

"Fundraising for The Trevor Project." The Trevor Project. Accessed September 10, 2022.
https://give.thetrevorproject.org.

Ganesh, Bharath. "The Ungovernability of Digital Hate Culture." *Journal of International Affairs* 71, no. 2 (2018): 30–49.

García-Rapp, Florencia, and Carles Roca-Cuberes. "Being an Online Celebrity: Norms
and Expectations of YouTube's Beauty Community." *First Monday* 22, no. 7 (2017).
https://doi.org/10.5210/fm.v22i7.7788.

Gephi.org. "Gephi—The Open Graph Viz Platform." Gephi, 2019. https://gephi.org.

Geraghty, Lincoln. "It's Not All about the Music: Online Fan Communities and Collecting Hard Rock Café Pins." *Transformative Works and Cultures* 16 (2014).

Gilbert, B. "The Most Important News at CES Is a $300 Million Response to Gamer-
Gate." *Engadget*, January 8, 2015. www.engadget.com.

Gillespie, Tarleton. "The Politics of 'Platforms.'" *New Media & Society* 12, no. 3 (2010):
347–64. https://doi.org/10.1177/1461444809342738.

Ging, Debbie. "Alphas, Betas, and Incels: Theorizing the Masculinities of the Manosphere." *Men and Masculinities* 22, no. 4 (2019): 638–57. https://doi.org/10.1177
/1097184X17706401.

Giroux, Amy Larner. "Twitter Data Scraping Jupyter Notebook." Humanities Commons, 2020. https://hcommons.org.

Gonzalez, Victoria M. "Swan Queen, Shipping, and Boundary Regulation in Fandom."
Transformative Works and Cultures 22 (2016). http://journal.transformativeworks.org.

Google Trends. "Google Trends: Alt-Right." Accessed June 13, 2021. https://trends
.google.com.

Grady, Constance. "*Star Wars* Fans Harassed Kelly Marie Tran for Months: She Just
Deleted Her Instagram Posts." *Vox*, June 5, 2018. www.vox.com.

Gray, Jonathan. "Antifandom and the Moral Text." *American Behavioral Scientist* 48, no. 7 (2005): 840–58. https://doi.org/10.1177/0002764204273171.

———. "New Audiences, New Textualities." *International Journal of Cultural Studies* 6, no. 1 (2003): 64–81. https://doi.org/10.1177/1367877903006001004.

Gray, Jonathan, Cornel Sandvoss, and C. Lee Harrington. "Introduction: Why Study Fans?" In *Fandom: Identities and Communities in a Mediated World*, edited by Jonathan Gray, Cornel Sandvoss, and C. Lee Harrington, 1–16. New York: New York University Press, 2007.

Gray, Kishonna L., Bertan Buyukozturk, and Zachary G. Hill. "Blurring the Boundaries: Using Gamergate to Examine 'Real' and Symbolic Violence against Women in Contemporary Gaming Culture." *Sociology Compass* 11, no. 3 (2017): e12458. https://doi.org/10.1111/soc4.12458.

Green, Shoshanna, Cynthia Jenkins, and Henry Jenkins. "Normal Female Interest in Men Bonking: Selections from the Terra Nostra Underground and Strange Bedfellows." In *Theorizing Fandom: Fans, Subculture, and Identity*, edited by Cheryl Harris and Alison Alexander, 9–38. Creskill, NJ: Hampton Press, 1998.

Greenfield, Rebecca. "How Likely Is Death by IPhone Electrocution?" *The Atlantic*, July 15, 2013. www.theatlantic.com.

Guerrero-Pico, Mar, María-José Establés, and Rafael Ventura. "Killing Off Lexa: 'Dead Lesbian Syndrome' and Intra-Fandom Management of Toxic Fan Practices in an Online Queer Community." *Participations: Journal of Audience and Reception Studies* 15, no. 1 (2018): 311–33.

"Gutfeld: We Are Losing This War against the Critical Race Theory 'Cult.'" *The Greg Gutfeld Show*. Fox News, June 24, 2021.

Hadas, Leora. "The Web Planet: How the Changing Internet Divided 'Doctor Who' Fan Fiction Writers." *Transformative Works and Cultures* 3 (2009). https://doi.org/10.3983/twc.v3i0.129.

Hammer, Josh. "Yes, We Should Ban Critical Race Theory from Our Schools." Editorial. *Newsweek*, July 1, 2021.

Hampton, Darlene Rose. "Bound Princes and Monogamy Warnings: Harry Potter, Slash, and Queer Performance in LiveJournal Communities." *Transformative Works and Cultures* 18 (2015). https://doi.org/10.3983/twc.2015.0609.

Harmon, Amy. "'Star Wars' Fan Films Come Tumbling Back to Earth." *New York Times*, April 28, 2002, sec. Movies. www.nytimes.com.

Harrison, Haley. "Local Professor Speaks Out after School District Cancels Civil Rights Lecture over CRT Concerns." *First Coast News*, January 11, 2022. www.firstcoastnews.com.

Hartzell, Stephanie L. "Whiteness Feels Good Here: Interrogating White Nationalist Rhetoric on Stormfront." *Communication and Critical/Cultural Studies* 17, no. 2 (2020): 129–48. https://doi.org/10.1080/14791420.2020.1745858.

———. "Alt-White: Conceptualizing the 'Alt-Right' as a Rhetorical Bridge between White Nationalism and Mainstream Public Discourse." *Journal of Contemporary Rhetoric* 8, no. 1–2 (2018): 6–25.

Hawksey, Martin. "Twitter Archiving Google Sheet." TAGS. Accessed February 11, 2021. https://tags.hawksey.info/.

Heredia, Erika M., and Mel Stanfill. "Reactionary Influencers and the Construction of White Conservative Victimhood." *Flow: A Critical Forum on Media and Culture* 27, no. 3 (2021). www.flowjournal.org.

Hesse, Monica. "'Make Liberals Cry Again' Became the Battle Hymn of the Republicans under Trump." *Washington Post*, November 5, 2020, sec. Perspective. www.washingtonpost.com.

Hicks, Josh. "Did Elizabeth Warren Check the Native American Box When She 'Applied' to Harvard and Penn?" *Washington Post* (blog), September 28, 2012. www.washingtonpost.com.

Hill, Mike. "Can Whiteness Speak? Institutional Antinomies, Ontological Disasters, and Three Hollywood Films." In *White Trash: Race and Class in America*, edited by Annalee Newitz and Matt Wray, 155–73. New York: Routledge, 1997.

Hills, Matt. "An Extended Foreword: From Fan Doxa to Toxic Fan Practices?" *Participations: Journal of Audience and Reception Studies* 15, no. 1 (2018): 105–26.

———. *Fan Cultures*. London: Routledge, 2002.

Hinck, Ashley. *Politics for the Love of Fandom: Fan-Based Citizenship in a Digital World*. Baton Rouge: Louisiana State University Press, 2019.

———. "Theorizing a Public Engagement Keystone: Seeing Fandom's Integral Connection to Civic Engagement through the Case of the Harry Potter Alliance." *Transformative Works and Cultures* 10 (2012). https://doi.org/10.3983/twc.2012.0311.

"History Repeated: In Guilford's Debate over the Teaching of Critical Race Theory, Echoes of the KKK and Other Racist Hate Groups Are Loud and Clear." *Hartford Courant*, July 4, 2021, 1st edition, sec. Other; C.

Hoffmann, Stefan, Ingo Balderjahn, Barbara Seegebarth, Robert Mai, and Mathias Peyer. "Under Which Conditions Are Consumers Ready to Boycott or Buycott? The Roles of Hedonism and Simplicity." *Ecological Economics* 147 (May 1, 2018): 167–78. https://doi.org/10.1016/j.ecolecon.2018.01.004.

Hofmann, Melissa A. "Johnlock Meta and Authorial Intent in Sherlock Fandom: Affirmational or Transformational?" *Transformative Works and Cultures* 28 (2018). https://doi.org/10.3983/twc.2018.1465.

Hogg, David, and Jaclyn Corin. "Parkland Survivors: It's Time Republican Cowards Ditched the NRA and Voted for Gun Checks." *Daily Beast*, January 8, 2019, sec. Politics. www.thedailybeast.com.

Hou, Mingyi. "Social Media Celebrity and the Institutionalization of YouTube." *Convergence* 25, no. 3 (2019): 534–53. https://doi.org/10.1177/1354856517750368.

"How Critical Race Theory Went from Harvard Law to Fox News." *Consider This from NPR*. NPR, July 6, 2021.

Hunting, Kyra. "'Queer as Folk' and the Trouble with Slash." *Transformative Works and Cultures* 11 (2012). https://doi.org/10.3983/twc.2012.0415.

"Interview with Rep. Ruben Gallego (D-AZ)." *Anderson Cooper 360 Degrees*. CNN, June 18, 2021.

"Interview with Sen. Tom Cotton (R-AR)." *Life, Liberty, Levin*. Fox News, June 27, 2021.

Jackson, Gita. "Fanfic Writer Put Entirety of '1984' in the Tags of a Story." *Vice*, February 26, 2021. www.vice.com.

Jackson, Sarah J., Moya Bailey, and Brooke Foucault Welles. *#HashtagActivism: Networks of Race and Gender Justice*. Illustrated edition. Cambridge, MA: MIT Press, 2020.

Jane, Emma A. "Hating 3.0: Should Anti-Fan Studies Be Renewed for Another Season?" In *Anti-Fandom: Dislike and Hate in the Digital Age*, edited by Melissa A. Click, 42–61. New York: New York University Press, 2019.

———. "Beyond Antifandom: Cheerleading, Textual Hate, and New Media Ethics." *International Journal of Cultural Studies* 17, no. 2 (2014): 175–90. https://doi.org/10.1177/1367877913514330.

Jason Rothenberg [@JRothenbergTV]. "You Guys Know I Don't Ship. But I Gotta Admit, #Clexa Is Seaworthy. #justsaying #The100 @miselizajane @debnamcarey." Tweet. *Twitter*, January 29, 2015. https://twitter.com/JRothenbergTV/status/560632588571009025.

Jasser, Jasser, Ivan Garibay, Steve Scheinert, and Alexander V. Mantzaris. "Controversial Information Spreads Faster and Further than Non-Controversial Information in Reddit." *Journal of Computational Social Science* 5, no. 1 (2022): 111–22. https://doi.org/10.1007/s42001-021-00121-z.

Jenkins, Henry. "Negotiating Fandom: The Politics of Racebending." In *The Routledge Companion to Media Fandom*, edited by Melissa A. Click and Suzanne Scott, 383–94. New York: Routledge, 2017.

———. "'Cultural Acupuncture': Fan Activism and the Harry Potter Alliance." *Transformative Works and Cultures* 10 (2012): n.p. https://doi.org/10.3983/twc.2012.0305.

———. *Convergence Culture: Where Old and New Media Collide*. New York: New York University Press, 2006.

———. "Interactive Audiences? The 'Collective Intelligence' of Media Fans." In *Fans, Bloggers, and Gamers: Exploring Participatory Culture*, 134–51. New York: New York University Press, 2006.

———. *Textual Poachers: Television Fans and Participatory Culture*. New York: Routledge, 1992.

Jenkins, Henry, Sam Ford, and Joshua Green. *Spreadable Media: Creating Value and Meaning in a Networked Culture*. New York: New York University Press, 2013.

Jerslev, Anne. "In The Time of the Microcelebrity: Celebrification and the YouTuber Zoella." *International Journal of Communication* 10 (2016): 19.

Jess H. "A Statement on Malicious Email Attacks against OTW Volunteers." Organization for Transformative Works, May 7, 2022. www.transformativeworks.org.

"Joe Biden Signs Order Targeting Big Businesses." *Fox Business Tonight*. Fox News, July 9, 2021.

Johnson, Derek. "Fantagonism, Franchising, and Industry Management of Fan Privilege." In *The Routledge Companion to Media Fandom*, edited by Melissa A. Click and Suzanne Scott, 395–405. New York: Routledge, 2017.

———. "Fan-Tagonism: Factions, Institutions, and Constitutive Hegemonies of Fandom." In *Fandom: Identities and Communities in a Mediated World*, edited by Jonathan Gray, Cornel Sandvoss, and C. Lee Harrington, 285–300. New York: New York University Press, 2007.

Johnson, Poe. "Transformative Racism: The Black Body in Fan Works." *Transformative Works and Cultures* 29 (2019). https://doi.org/10.3983/twc.2019.1669.

Jones, Bethan. "#AskELJames, Ghostbusters, and #Gamergate: Digital Dislike and Damage Control." In *A Companion to Fandom and Fan Studies*, edited by Paul Booth, 415–30. Oxford, UK: Wiley-Blackwell, 2018.

———. "Antifan Activism as a Response to MTV's 'The Valleys.'" *Transformative Works and Cultures* 19 (2015). http://journal.transformativeworks.org.

Jones, Sara Gwenllian. "The Sex Lives of Cult Television Characters." *Screen* 43, no. 1 (2002): 79–90. https://doi.org/10.1093/screen/43.1.79.

Jung, Sun. "Fan Activism, Cybervigilantism, and Othering Mechanisms in K-Pop Fandom." *Transformative Works and Cultures* 10 (June 15, 2012). https://doi.org/10.3983/twc.2012.0300.

Kent, Jackie. "Mukilteo School District Votes to Remove 'To Kill a Mockingbird' from Required Reading." *KIMA*, January 27, 2022. https://kimatv.com.

Khalid, Asma. "Warren Apologizes to Cherokee Nation for DNA Test." *NPR*, February 1, 2019, sec. Politics. www.npr.org.

Khardori, Ankush. "The Odds Are Going Up That Trump Could Be Charged." *Intelligencer*, June 29, 2022. https://nymag.com.

Kies, Bridget. "One True Threesome: Reconciling Canon and Fan Desire in 'Star Trek: Voyager.'" *Transformative Works and Cultures* 8 (2011). https://doi.org/10.3983/twc.2011.0248.

Kligler-Vilenchik, Neta, Joshua McVeigh-Schultz, Christine Weitbrecht, and Chris Tokuhama. "Experiencing Fan Activism: Understanding the Power of Fan Activist Organizations through Members' Narratives." *Transformative Works and Cultures* 10 (2012). https://doi.org/10.3983/twc.2012.0322.

Know Your Meme. "Of Course You Have Blue Hair and Pronouns." Accessed October 22, 2022. https://knowyourmeme.com.

———. "Get Woke Go Broke." Accessed September 5, 2022. https://knowyourmeme.com.

Korn, Jenny Ungbha. "#FuckProp8: How Temporary Virtual Communities around Politics and Sexuality Pop Up, Come Out, Provide Support, and Taper Off." In *Hashtag Publics: The Power and Politics of Discursive Networks*, edited by Nathan Rambukkana, new edition, 127–37. New York: Peter Lang, 2015.

Kumar, Sneha. "'Carmilla' Fandom as a Lesbian Community of Feeling." *Transformative Works and Cultures* 36 (2021). https://doi.org/10.3983/twc.2021.2007.

Kurtzleben, Danielle. "Here's How Many Bernie Sanders Supporters Ultimately Voted for Trump." *NPR*, August 24, 2017, sec. Politics. www.npr.org.

Lackner, Eden, Barbara Lynn Lucas, and Robin Anne Reid. "Cunning Linguists: The Bisexual Erotics of Words/Silence/Flesh." In *Fan Fiction and Fan Communities in the Age of the Internet: New Essays*, edited by Karen Hellekson and Kristina Busse, 189–206. Jefferson, NC: McFarland, 2006.

Lamerichs, Nicolle, Dennis Nguyen, Mari Carmen Puerta Melguizo, Radmila Rado-jevic, and Anna Lange-Böhmer. "Elite Male Bodies: The Circulation of Alt-Right Memes and the Framing of Politicians on Social Media." *Participations: Journal of Audience and Reception Studies* 15, no. 1 (2018): 27.

Lawrence, Charles R., III. "If He Hollers Let Him Go: Regulating Racist Speech on Campus." In *Words That Wound: Critical Race Theory, Assaultive Speech, and the First Amendment*, 53–88. Boulder, CO: Westview Press, 1993.

Lawson, Caitlin E. "Platform Vulnerabilities: Harassment and Misogynoir in the Digital Attack on Leslie Jones." *Information, Communication & Society* 21, no. 6 (2018): 818–33. https://doi.org/10.1080/1369118X.2018.1437203.

Lee, Harper. *To Kill a Mockingbird*. Philadelphia: Lippincott, 1960.

Levin, Sam. "Elon Musk Calls British Diver in Thai Cave Rescue 'Pedo' in Baseless Attack." *The Guardian*, July 16, 2018. www.theguardian.com.

Lewis, Rebecca. "Alternative Influence: Broadcasting the Reactionary Right on YouTube." Data & Society, September 18, 2018. https://datasociety.net.

Lind, Dara. "Unite the Right, the Violent White Supremacist Rally in Charlottesville, Explained." *Vox*, August 12, 2017. www.vox.com.

Linker, Damon. "The Left Is Anti-Anti-Critical Race Theory." *The Week*, June 25, 2021. https://theweek.com.

Long, Colleen. "How 'Let's Go Brandon' Became Code for Insulting Joe Biden." *AP News*, October 30, 2021. https://apnews.com.

Lopatto, Elizabeth. "Bowing to Pressure, YouTube Will Reconsider Its Harassment Policies." *The Verge*, June 6, 2019. www.theverge.com.

Lopez, Lori Kido, and Jason Kido Lopez. "Deploying Oppositional Fandom: Activists' Use of Sports Fandom in the Redskins Controversy." In *Fandom, Second Edition: Identities and Communities in a Mediated World*, edited by Jonathan Gray, Cornel Sandvoss, and C. Lee Harrington, 2nd edition, 174–88. New York: New York University Press, 2017.

Lothian, Alexis, Kristina Busse, and Robin Anne Reid. "'Yearning Void and Infinite Potential': Online Slash Fandom as Queer Female Space." *English Language Notes* 45, no. 2 (2007): 103–11.

Lothian, Alexis, and Mel Stanfill. "An Archive of Whose Own? White Feminism and Racial Justice in Fan Fiction's Digital Infrastructure." *Transformative Works and Cultures* 36 (2021). https://doi.org/10.3983/twc.2021.2119.

"Louder with Crowder on BlazeTV." BlazeTV, accessed October 8, 2022. https://get.blazetv.com.

MacKinnon, Catharine A. "Feminism, Marxism, Method, and the State: Toward Feminist Jurisprudence." *Signs* 8, no. 4 (1983): 635–58.

———. "Feminism, Marxism, Method, and the State: An Agenda for Theory." *Signs* 7, no. 3 (1982): 515–44.

Macmillan Dictionary. "Snowclone." Accessed April 20, 2020. www
 .macmillandictionary.com.

Macuk, Anthony. "What's Up with That T-shirt?" *Columbian Blogs*, August 22, 2019.
 https://blogs.columbian.com.

Malmgren, Evan. "Don't Feed the Trolls." *Dissent* 64, no. 2 (2017): 9–12. https://doi.org
 /10.1353/dss.2017.0042.

Marks, Rachel. "Fan Perspectives of Queer Representation in DC's *Legends of Tomorrow* on Tumblr and AO3." *Transformative Works and Cultures* 40 (2023).

Marwick, Alice E. "To Catch a Predator? The MySpace Moral Panic." *First Monday* 13,
 no. 6 (2008). www.firstmonday.dk.

Marwick, Alice E., and Robyn Caplan. "Drinking Male Tears: Language, the Manosphere, and Networked Harassment." *Feminist Media Studies* 18, no. 4 (2018): 543–
 59. https://doi.org/10.1080/14680777.2018.1450568.

Marwick, Alice, and Rebecca Lewis. "Media Manipulation and Disinformation Online." *Data & Society* (blog), 2017. https://datasociety.net/output/media
 -manipulation-and-disinfo-online/.

Massanari, Adrienne. "Rethinking Research Ethics, Power, and the Risk of Visibility in
 the Era of the 'Alt-Right' Gaze." *Social Media + Society* 4, no. 2 (2018): 1–10. https:
 //doi.org/10.1177/2056305118768302.

———. "#Gamergate and The Fappening: How Reddit's Algorithm, Governance, and
 Culture Support Toxic Technocultures." *New Media & Society* 19, no. 3 (2017): 329–46.
 https://doi.org/10.1177/1461444815608807.

Massanari, Adrienne L., and Shira Chess. "Attack of the 50-Foot Social Justice Warrior:
 The Discursive Construction of SJW Memes as the Monstrous Feminine." *Feminist
 Media Studies* 18, no. 4 (2018): 525–42. https://doi.org/10.1080/14680777.2018.1447333.

Massey, Erica Lyn. "Borderland Literature, Female Pleasure, and the Slash Fic Phenomenon." *Transformative Works and Cultures* 30 (2019). https://doi.org/10.3983
 /twc.2019.1390.

Matsuda, Mari J. "Public Response to Racist Speech: Considering the Victim's Story." In
 *Words That Wound: Critical Race Theory, Assaultive Speech, and the First Amend-
 ment*, 17–52. Boulder, CO: Westview Press, 1993.

Mazariegos, Miranda, and Meghan Collins Sullivan. "Efforts to Ban Books Jumped
 an 'Unprecedented' Four-Fold in 2021, ALA Report Says." *NPR*, April 4, 2022, sec.
 Book News & Features. www.npr.org.

McIntosh, Peggy. "White Privilege and Male Privilege: A Personal Account of Coming to See Correspondences through Work in Women's Studies." In *Critical White
 Studies: Looking behind the Mirror*, edited by Richard Delgado and Jean Stefancic,
 291–99. Philadelphia: Temple University Press, 1997.

McKay, Tom. "Report: Elon Musk Is Kind of a Dick." *Gizmodo*, November 11, 2020.
 Accessed May 7, 2022. https://gizmodo.com/.

———. "YouTube: No, We Won't Remove These Videos of Racist, Anti-Gay Harassment
 Because It's Just 'Debating.'" *Gizmodo*, June 5, 2019. https://gizmodo.com.

McManus, Doyle. "Elizabeth Warren's Pivot on 'Medicare for All' Shows the Tricky Politics of Healthcare." *Los Angeles Times*, November 20, 2019. www.latimes.com.

McNutt, Myles. "'The 100' and the Social Contract of Social TV." *Transformative Works and Cultures* 26 (2018). https://doi.org/10.3983/twc.2018.1297.

McRobbie, Angela, and Sarah L. Thornton. "Rethinking 'Moral Panic' for Multi-Mediated Social Worlds." *British Journal of Sociology* 46, no. 4 (1995): 559–74. https://doi.org/10.2307/591571.

McRuer, Robert. *Crip Theory: Cultural Signs of Queerness and Disability*. New York: New York University Press, 2006.

Micheletti, Michele, and Didem Oral. "Problematic Political Consumerism: Confusions and Moral Dilemmas in Boycott Activism." In *The Oxford Handbook of Political Consumerism*, edited by Magnus Boström, Michele Micheletti, and Peter Oosterveer. Oxford: Oxford University Press, 2019. https://doi.org/10.1093/oxfordhb/9780190629038.013.31.

Miller, Lucy. "'Wolfenstein II' and MAGA as Fandom." *Transformative Works and Cultures* 32 (2020). https://doi.org/10.3983/twc.2020.1717.

Miller, Toby. "A Risk Society of Moral Panic: The US in the Twenty-First Century." *Cultural Politics* 2, no. 3 (2006): 299–318.

Miro, Clara Juarez. "Who Are the People? Using Fandom Research to Study Populist Supporters." *Annals of the International Communication Association* 45, no. 1 (2021): 59–74. https://doi.org/10.1080/23808985.2021.1910062.

Mitchell, Travis. "Politics on Twitter: One-Third of Tweets from U.S. Adults Are Political." *Pew Research Center—U.S. Politics & Policy* (blog), June 16, 2022. https://www.pewresearch.org/politics/2022/06/16/politics-on-twitter-one-third-of-tweets-from-u-s-adults-are-political/.

Moore, Alan. *Watchmen*. New York: DC Comics, 1987.

Morimoto, Lori. "Ontological Security and the Politics of Transcultural Fandom." In *A Companion to Fandom and Fan Studies*, edited by Paul Booth, 257–75. Oxford: Wiley-Blackwell, 2018.

Mortensen, Torill Elvira. "Anger, Fear, and Games: The Long Event of #GamerGate." *Games and Culture* 13, no. 8 (2018): 787–806. https://doi.org/10.1177/1555412016640408.

Muñoz, Jose Esteban. *Cruising Utopia: The Then and There of Queer Futurity*. New York: New York University Press, 2009.

Nakamura, Lisa. "'Putting Our Hearts into It': Gaming's Many Social Justice Warriors and the Quest for Accessible Games." In *Diversifying Barbie and Mortal Kombat: Intersectional Perspectives and Inclusive Designs in Gaming*, edited by Yasmin B. Kafai, Brendesha M. Tynes, and Gabriela T. Richard, 35–47. Pittsburgh: Carnegie Mellon: ETC Press, 2016.

Navar-Gill, Annemarie. "From Strategic Retweets to Group Hangs: Writers' Room Twitter Accounts and the Productive Ecosystem of TV Social Media Fans." *Television & New Media* 19, no. 5 (July 1, 2018): 415–30. https://doi.org/10.1177/1527476417728376.

Navar-Gill, Annemarie, and Mel Stanfill. "'We Shouldn't Have to Trend to Make You Listen': Queer Fan Hashtag Campaigns as Production Interventions." *Journal of Film and Video* 70, no. 3–4 (2018): 85–100.

Neilson, Lisa A. "Boycott or Buycott? Understanding Political Consumerism." *Journal of Consumer Behaviour* 9, no. 3 (2010): 214–27. https://doi.org/10.1002/cb.313.

"New York Police Join Forces with ATF Agents." *Fox Special Report with Bret Baier*. Fox News, July 6, 2021.

Newitz, Annalee, and Matt Wray. "Introduction." In *White Trash: Race and Class in America*, edited by Annalee Newitz and Matt Wray, 1–12. New York: Routledge, 1997.

Ng, Eve. "Between Text, Paratext, and Context: Queerbaiting and the Contemporary Media Landscape." *Transformative Works and Cultures* 24 (2017). http://journal.transformativeworks.org.

Ng, Eve, and Julie Levin Russo. "Envisioning Queer Female Fandom." *Transformative Works and Cultures* 24 (2017). https://doi.org/10.3983/twc.2017.01168.

Norris, Craig, and Jason Bainbridge. "Intersections: Selling Otaku? Mapping the Relationship between Industry and Fandom in the Australian Cosplay Scene." *Intersections: Gender and Sexuality in Asia and the Pacific*, no. 20 (2009). http://intersections.anu.edu.au.

Nussbaum, Emily. "Hate-Watching 'Smash.'" *New Yorker*, April 27, 2012. www.newyorker.com.

Obergefell v. Hodges, 576 U.S. 644 (2015).

obsession_inc. "Affirmational Fandom vs. Transformational Fandom." June 1, 2009. https://obsession-inc.dreamwidth.org.

O'Donnell, Jessica. "Militant Meninism: The Militaristic Discourse of Gamergate and Men's Rights Activism." *Media, Culture & Society* 42, no. 5 (2019). https://doi.org/10.1177/0163443719876624.

O'Donovan, Caroline. "YouTube Has Finally Admitted That Steven Crowder Mocking Someone for Being a Gay Latino Is Not OK." *BuzzFeed News*, June 5, 2019. www.buzzfeednews.com.

"Official YouTube Blog: Our Ongoing Work to Tackle Hate." June 5, 2019. https://web.archive.org/web/20190605161610/https:/youtube.googleblog.com/2019/06/our-ongoing-work-to-tackle-hate.html.

"Official YouTube Blog: Taking a Harder Look at Harassment." June 6, 2019. https://web.archive.org/web/20190606043101/https:/youtube.googleblog.com/2019/06/taking-harder-look-at-harassment.html.

Oleszczuk, Anna. "Sad and Rabid Puppies: Politicization of the Hugo Award Nomination Procedure." *New Horizons in English Studies* 2, no. 1 (2017): 127–35.

Omi, Michael, and Howard Winant. *Racial Formation in the United States: From the 1960s to the 1990s*. 2nd edition New York: Routledge, 1994.

Organization for Transformative Works. "Application: Tag Wrangling Volunteer." Accessed April 17, 2021. www.transformativeworks.org.

———. "The OTW Is Recruiting for AO3 Documentation Staff, Graphic Designers, Policy & Abuse Staff, Strategic Planning Staff, and Translation Volunteers." February 17, 2021. www.transformativeworks.org.

Page, Clarence. "Can the Left Defend Critical Race Theory? Or Is the Goal to Merely Oppose Its Critics?" *Telegraph Herald*, July 5, 2021, sec. A.

Pande, Rukmini. "Who Do You Mean by 'Fan'? Decolonizing Media Fandom Identity." In *A Companion to Fandom and Fan Studies*, edited by Paul Booth, 319–32. Oxford, UK: Wiley-Blackwell, 2018.

———. "Squee from the Margins: Racial/Cultural/Ethnic Identity in Global Media Fandom." In *Seeing Fans: Representations of Fandom in Media and Popular Culture*, edited by Lucy Bennett and Paul Booth, 209–20. New York: Bloomsbury Academic, 2016.

Pande, Rukmini, and Swati Moitra. "'Yes, the Evil Queen Is Latina!': Racial Dynamics of Online Femslash Fandoms." *Transformative Works and Cultures* 24 (2017). http://journal.transformativeworks.org.

Penley, Constance. "Interview with Constance Penley." *European Journal of Cultural Studies* 15, no. 3 (2012): 360–79. https://doi.org/10.1177/1367549412440522.

———. *NASA/Trek: Popular Science and Sex in America*. New York: Verso, 1997.

Penney, Joel. "Social Media and Citizen Participation in 'Official' and 'Unofficial' Electoral Promotion: A Structural Analysis of the 2016 Bernie Sanders Digital Campaign." *Journal of Communication* 67, no. 3 (2017): 402–23. https://doi.org/10.1111/jcom.12300.

Peppard, Anna F. "'A Cross Burning Darkly, Blackening the Night': Reading Racialized Spectacles of Conflict and Bondage in Marvel's Early Black Panther Comics." *Studies in Comics* 9, no. 1 (June 1, 2018): 59–85. https://doi.org/10.1386/stic.9.1.59_1.

Phillips, Whitney. *This Is Why We Can't Have Nice Things: Mapping the Relationship between Online Trolling and Mainstream Culture*. Cambridge, MA: MIT Press, 2015.

Piester, Laura. "The *100* Boss Apologizes for How Lexa Died in Open Letter to Fans." *E! Online*, March 24, 2016. www.eonline.com.

Pitts, Leonard, Jr. "Comicsgate: Alt-Right Fan Boys Go after Women in World of Comics." *Miami Herald*, December 28, 2018. www.miamiherald.com.

"PRAW: The Python Reddit API Wrapper." Python. 2010. Reprint, Python Reddit API Wrapper Development, February 1, 2022. https://github.com.

Proctor, William, and Bridget Kies. "Editors' Introduction: On Toxic Fan Practices and the New Culture Wars." *Participations* 15, no. 1 (2018): 127–42.

Puar, Jasbir K. *Terrorist Assemblages: Homonationalism in Queer Times*. Durham, NC: Duke University Press, 2007.

Puzzanghera, Jim. "Book Advance Helped Boost Income for Elizabeth Warren and Her Husband to Nearly $900,000 Last Year, Financial Disclosures Show." *Boston Globe*, May 14, 2021. www.bostonglobe.com.

Rambukkana, Nathan. "The Politics of Gray Data: Digital Methods, Intimate Proximity, and Research Ethics for Work on the 'Alt-Right.'" *Qualitative Inquiry* 25, no. 3 (2019): 312–23. https://doi.org/10.1177/1077800418806601.

Raun, Tobias. "Capitalizing Intimacy: New Subcultural Forms of Micro-Celebrity Strategies and Affective Labour on YouTube." *Convergence* 24, no. 1 (2018): 99–113. https://doi.org/10.1177/1354856517736983.

Reeve, Elle, Samantha Guff, and Deborah Brunswick. "The Critical Race Theory Panic Has White People Afraid That They Might Be Complicit in Racism." *CNN Wire*, July 7, 2021.

"Reliable Sources." *Reliable Sources*. CNN, January 10, 2021.

Rico, Andrew Ryan. "Fans of Columbine Shooters Eric Harris and Dylan Klebold." *Transformative Works and Cultures* 20 (September 15, 2015). https://doi.org/10.3983/twc.2015.0671.

Ro Khanna [@RoKhanna]. "Enough with the Snakes in the Comments! Disagree Vehemently. But Social Media Should Not Be a Forum for Sexism or Gratuitous Meanness. We Need to Call That Out When We See It. @warren Has Been a Champion for Progressive Values." Tweet. *Twitter*, May 7, 2021. https://twitter.com/RoKhanna/status/1390728166080143361.

———. "I Was Late to My Morning Meeting Because I Couldn't Put down @ewarren Book Persist. She's an Intellectual Who Makes the Case That the Fight Is as Important as the Idea. Loved the Story of How She Had to Bribe Her Toddler with M&Ms to Potty-Train Her for Childcare. Inspiring Read!" Tweet. *Twitter*, May 7, 2021. https://twitter.com/RoKhanna/status/1390654952230596611.

Romano, Aja. "Justice League's Snyder Cut Saga Reminds Us Which Fans' Voices Get Heard." *Vox*, March 22, 2021. www.vox.com.

———. "The Internet's Most Beloved Fanfiction Site Is Undergoing a Reckoning." *Vox*, February 26, 2021. www.vox.com.

Rosenberg, Alyssa. "Mike White on Why Men Won't Watch Women on TV." *Slate*, February 28, 2013. https://slate.com.

Ross, Loretta J., and Mary Ann Mauney. "The Changing Faces of White Supremacy." In *Critical White Studies: Looking behind the Mirror*, edited by Richard Delgado and Jean Stefancic, 552–57. Philadelphia: Temple University Press, 1997.

Rouse, Lauren. "Voltron: Legendary Defender and Compulsory Able-Bodiedness." In *Dis/Ability in Media, Law, and History: Intersectional, Embodied, AND Socially Constructed?*, edited by Micky Lee, Frank Rudy Cooper, and Patricia Reeve, 1st edition., 150–61. Abingdon, Oxon, UK: Routledge, 2022.

Rouse, Lauren, and Mel Stanfill. "Fan Demographics on Archive of Our Own." *Flow*, February 22, 2023. www.flowjournal.org.

Rubin, Gayle S. "Thinking Sex: Notes for a Radical Theory of the Politics of Sexuality." In *The Lesbian and Gay Studies Reader*, edited by Henry Abelove, Michèle Aina Barale, and David M. Halperin, 3–44. New York: Routledge, 1993.

Rufo, Christopher F. "@ConceptualJames the Goal Is to Have the Public Read Something Crazy in the Newspaper and Immediately Think 'Critical Race Theory.' We Have Decodified the Term and Will Recodify It to Annex the Entire Range of Cultural Constructions That Are Unpopular with Americans." Tweet.

@realchrisrufo (blog), March 15, 2021. https://twitter.com/realchrisrufo/status /1371541044592996352.

———. "@ConceptualJames We Have Successfully Frozen Their Brand—'Critical Race Theory'—into the Public Conversation and Are Steadily Driving up Negative Perceptions. We Will Eventually Turn It Toxic, as We Put All of the Various Cultural Insanities under That Brand Category." Tweet. *@realchrisrufo* (blog), March 15, 2021. https://twitter.com/realchrisrufo/status/1371540368714428416.

Ruiz, Karen. "'Take This Country Back. Load Your Guns and Take to the Streets!' Trump Supporter Who Died at Capitol Riots Was Once an Obama Fan and Attended His Inauguration." *MailOnline*, January 15, 2021, sec. News.

Russo, Julie Levin. "The Queer Politics of Femslash." In *The Routledge Companion to Media Fandom*, edited by Melissa A. Click and Suzanne Scott, 164–55. New York: Routledge, 2017.

Ryan, Maureen. "What TV Can Learn from 'The 100' Mess." *Variety* (blog), March 14, 2016. http://variety.com/2016/tv/opinion/the-100-lexa-jason-rothenberg -1201729110/.

Salter, Anastasia, and Bridget Blodgett. *Toxic Geek Masculinity in Media: Sexism, Trolling, and Identity Policing*. New York: Palgrave Macmillan, 2017.

Salter, Anastasia, and Mel Stanfill. *A Portrait of the Auteur as Fanboy: The Construction of Authorship in Transmedia Franchises*. Jackson: University Press of Mississippi, 2020.

———. "Understanding Digital Culture: Humanist Lenses for Internet Research." Workshop, Orlando, Florida, 2020. https://digitalculture.cah.ucf.edu/.

Salter, Michael. "From Geek Masculinity to Gamergate: The Technological Rationality of Online Abuse." *Crime, Media, Culture* 14, no. 2 (2018): 247–64. https://doi.org/10 .1177/1741659017690893.

Samuels, Allison. "Rachel Dolezal's True Lies." *Vanity Fair*, July 19, 2015. www.vanityfair .com.

Sands, Geneva. "White Supremacists Remain Deadliest US Terror Threat, Homeland Security Report Says." *CNN*, October 6, 2020. www.cnn.com.

Sandvoss, Cornel. "The Politics of Against: Political Participation, Anti-Fandom, and Populism." In *Anti-Fandom: Dislike and Hate in the Digital Age*, edited by Melissa A. Click, 125–46. New York: New York University Press, 2019.

———. "Toward an Understanding of Political Enthusiasm as Media Fandom: Blogging, Fan Productivity, and Affect in American Politics." *Participations: Journal of Audience and Reception Studies* 10 (2013): 252–96.

———. *Fans: The Mirror of Consumption*. Malden, MA: Polity, 2005.

Sandvoss, Cornel, Jonathan Gray, and C. Lee Harrington. "Introduction: Why Still Study Fans?" In *Fandom, Second Edition: Identities and Communities in a Mediated World*, edited by Jonathan Gray, Cornel Sandvoss, and C. Lee Harrington, 2nd edition, 1–26. New York: New York University Press, 2017.

Savran, David. *Taking It like a Man: White Masculinity, Masochism, and Contemporary American Culture*. Princeton, NJ: Princeton University Press, 1998.

Schmidt, Lisa. "Monstrous Melodrama: Expanding the Scope of Melodramatic Identification to Interpret Negative Fan Responses to 'Supernatural.'" *Transformative
Works and Cultures* 4 (2010). https://doi.org/10.3983/twc.2010.0152.

"Schools Have Become Cesspools for Radical Thought." *Ingraham Angle.* Fox News,
July 5, 2021.

Schroeder, Pete. "Warren: U.S. Government Needs to Confront Crypto Threats 'Head
On.'" *Reuters*, June 9, 2021, sec. Technology. www.reuters.com.

Scodari, Christine. "'Nyota Uhura Is Not a White Girl': Gender, Intersectionality, and
Star Trek 2009's Alternate Romantic Universes." *Feminist Media Studies* 12, no. 3
(2012): 335–51. https://doi.org/10.1080/14680777.2011.615605.

———. "Resistance Re-Examined: Gender, Fan Practices, and Science Fiction Television." *Popular Communication* 1, no. 2 (2003): 111–30. https://doi.org/10.1207
/S15405710PC0102_3.

Scott, Suzanne. *Fake Geek Girls: Fandom, Gender, and the Convergence Culture Industry.* New York: New York University Press, 2019.

———. "Towards a Theory of Producer/Fan Trolling." *Participations: Journal of Audience and Reception Studies* 15, no. 1 (2018): 143–59.

———. "Fangirls in Refrigerators: The Politics of (in)Visibility in Comic Book Culture."
Transformative Works and Cultures 13 (2013).

Serwer, Adam. "The Fight over the 1619 Project Is Not about the Facts." *The Atlantic*,
December 23, 2019. www.theatlantic.com.

Seymour, Jessica. "Racebending and Prosumer Fanart Practices in Harry Potter Fandom." In *A Companion to Fandom and Fan Studies*, edited by Paul Booth, 333–48.
Oxford, UK: Wiley-Blackwell, 2018.

Shapiro, Ben. "Facts, Episode 3: Is Fascism Right-Wing?" *Ben.* Accessed October 9,
2022. https://www.youtube.com/channel/UCnQC_G5Xsjhp9fEJKuIcrSw.

"The 1619 Project." *New York Times* August 14, 2019, sec. Magazine. www.nytimes.com.

Smith, David. "How Did Republicans Turn Critical Race Theory into a Winning
Electoral Issue?" *The Guardian*, November 3, 2021, sec. US news. www.theguardian
.com.

Smith, Jennifer, Emily Goodin, and Megan Sheets. "Hunt for the MAGA Cop Killer:
Feds Launch Murder Probe into Death of Trump-Supporting Capitol Cop Who
Was 'Hit over the Head with a Fire Extinguisher' as Hundreds of Officers Line the
Streets in Tribute and Capitol Flags Fly at Half-Staff." *MailOnline*, January 8, 2021,
sec. News.

Stabile, Carol A. "Conspiracy or Consensus? Reconsidering the Moral Panic." *Journal of Communication Inquiry* 25, no. 3 (2001): 258–78. https://doi.org/10.1177
/0196859901025003005.

Stanfill, Mel. *Rock This Way: Cultural Constructions of Musical Legitimacy.* Ann Arbor:
University of Michigan Press, 2023.

———. "Introduction: The Reactionary in the Fan and the Fan in the Reactionary." *Television & New Media* 21, no. 2 (2020): 123–34. https://doi.org/10.1177
/1527476419879912.

———. *Exploiting Fandom: How the Media Industry Seeks to Manipulate Fans*. Iowa City: University of Iowa Press, 2019.

———. "Fans of Color in Femslash." *Transformative Works and Cultures* 29 (2019). https://doi.org/10.3983/twc.2019.1528.

———. "The Unbearable Whiteness of Fandom and Fan Studies." In *A Companion to Fandom and Fan Studies*, edited by Paul Booth, 305–17. Oxford, UK: Wiley-Blackwell, 2018.

———. "The Fan Fiction Gold Rush, Generational Turnover, and the Battle for Fandom's Soul." In *The Routledge Companion to Media Fandom*, edited by Melissa A. Click and Suzanne Scott, 77–85. New York: Routledge, 2017.

———. "From #LGBTFansDeserveBetter to the Clexa Youth: *The 100* and Youth Audiences." Paper presented at the conference of the Children's Literature Association, Tampa, FL, June 22–24, 2017.

———. "'They're Losers, but I Know Better': Intra-Fandom Stereotyping and the Normalization of the Fan Subject." *Critical Studies in Media Communication* 20, no. 2 (2013): 117–34. https://doi.org/10.1080/15295036.2012.755053.

———. "Doing Fandom, (Mis)Doing Whiteness: Heteronormativity, Racialization, and the Discursive Construction of Fandom." *Transformative Works and Cultures* 8 (2011). https://doi.org/10.3983/twc.2011.0256.

Stasi, Mafalda. "The Toy Soldiers from Leeds: The Slash Palimpsest." In *Fan Fiction and Fan Communities in the Age of the Internet: New Essays*, edited by Karen Hellekson and Kristina Busse, 115–33. Jefferson, NC: McFarland, 2006.

Stein, Louisa Ellen. *Millennial Fandom: Television Audiences in the Transmedia Age.* Iowa City: University of Iowa Press, 2015.

"Steven Crowder's Twitter Monthly Stats (Social Blade Twitter Statistics)." Accessed October 8, 2022. https://socialblade.com/twitter/user/scrowder/monthly.

Summers, Kate. "Adult Reading Habits and Preferences in Relation to Gender Differences." *Reference & User Services Quarterly* 52, no. 3 (March 22, 2013): 243–49. https://doi.org/10.5860/rusq.52.3.3319.

Tarvin, Emily. "YouTube Fandom Names in Channel Communities and Branding." *Transformative Works and Cultures* 36 (2021). https://doi.org/10.3983/twc.2021.1879.

Tarvin, Emily, and Mel Stanfill. "'YouTube's Predator Problem': Platform Moderation as Governance-Washing, and User Resistance." *Convergence* 28, no. 3 (2022): 822–37. https://doi.org/10.1177/13548565211066490.

"'The Tea Party to the 10th Power': Trumpworld Bets Big on Critical Race Theory." *Politico*, June 23, 2021.

Ted Cruz [@tedcruz]. "Goya Is a Staple of Cuban Food. My Grandparents Ate Goya Black Beans Twice a Day for Nearly 90 Years. And Now the Left Is Trying to Cancel Hispanic Culture and Silence Free Speech. #BuyGoya." Tweet. *Twitter*, July 10, 2020. https://twitter.com/tedcruz/status/1281679899607142400.

Theodoropoulou, Vivi. "The Anti-Fan within the Fan: Awe and Envy in Sport Fandom." In *Fandom: Identities and Communities in a Mediated World*, edited by

Jonathan Gray, Cornel Sandvoss, and C. Lee Harrington, 316–27. New York: New York University Press, 2007.

"Tlaib Calls to Defund Immigration Agencies." *Fox Business Tonight.* Fox News, July 8, 2021.

Tobin, Ben, and Emma Austin. "'Gun Girl' Claims a Riot at Ohio University, but Her Old Adversary at UK Isn't Buying It." *The Courier-Journal* (Louisville, KY), January 13, 2020. Accessed October 9, 2022. www.courier-journal.com.

Tosenberger, Catherine. "'The Epic Love Story of Sam and Dean': 'Supernatural,' Queer Readings, and the Romance of Incestuous Fan Fiction." *Transformative Works and Cultures* 1 (2008). https://doi.org/10.3983/twc.v1i0.30.

"Tragedy of Trump on Show." *West Australian,* January 8, 2021, 2nd edition, sec. MAI.

The Trevor Project. "The Trevor Project | For Young LGBTQ Lives." Accessed September 11, 2022. www.thetrevorproject.org.

Trice, Michael, and Liza Potts. "Building Dark Patterns into Platforms: How Gamer-Gate Perturbed Twitter's User Experience." *Present Tense* 6, no. 3 (2018).

Tufekci, Zeynep. *Twitter and Tear Gas: The Power and Fragility of Networked Protest.* Reprint edition. New Haven, CT: Yale University Press, 2018.

Turk, Tisha. "Interdisciplinarity in Fan Studies." In *A Companion to Fandom and Fan Studies,* edited by Paul Booth, 539–51. Oxford, UK: Wiley-Blackwell, 2018.

Tushnet, Rebecca. "'I'm a Lawyer, Not an Ethnographer, Jim': Textual Poachers and Fair Use." *Journal of Fandom Studies* 2, no. 1 (2014): 21–30. https://doi.org/10.1386/jfs .2.1.21_1.

TWC Editor. "What Is an Anti? Exploring a Key Term and Contemporary Debates." *Transformative Works and Cultures* 37 (2022). https://doi.org/10.3983/twc.2022.2277.

———. "Pattern Recognition: A Dialogue on Racism in Fan Communities." *Transformative Works and Cultures* 3 (2009). https://doi.org/10.3983/twc.2009.0172.

"Uncovering Who Is Driving the Fight against Critical Race Theory in Schools." *NPR Fresh Air.* NPR, June 24, 2021.

Urban Dictionary. "Urban Dictionary: Senpai." Accessed November 4, 2023. www .urbandictionary.com.

Vance, Carole S. "Negotiating Sex and Gender in the Attorney General's Commission on Pornography." In *The Gender/Sexuality Reader: Culture, History, Political Economy,* 440–52. New York: Routledge, 1997.

"Vote to Advance Sweeping Voting Rights Bill Fails to Overcome GOP Filibuster." *Don Lemon Tonight.* CNN, June 22, 2021.

Vought, Russell. Training in the Federal Government, M-20-34. Memorandum for the Heads of Executive Departments and Agencies, September 4, 2020. www .whitehouse.gov.

Waggoner, Erin B. "Bury Your Gays and Social Media Fan Response: Television, LGBTQ Representation, and Communitarian Ethics." *Journal of Homosexuality* 65, no. 13 (2018): 1877–91. https://doi.org/10.1080/00918369.2017.1391015.

Walker, Rob. "The Shifting Symbolism of the Gadsden Flag." *New Yorker,* October 2, 2016. www.newyorker.com.

"Walther Arms, Inc.," March 28, 2017. https://www.facebook.com.

Wanzo, Rebecca. "African American Acafandom and Other Strangers: New Genealogies of Fan Studies." *Transformative Works and Cultures* 20 (2015).

Warner, Kristen J. "(Black Female) Fans Strike Back: The Emergence of the Iris West Defense Squad." In *The Routledge Companion to Media Fandom*, edited by Melissa A. Click and Suzanne Scott, 253–61. New York: Routledge, 2017.

———. "ABC's Scandal and Black Women's Fandom." In *Cupcakes, Pinterest, and Ladyporn: Feminized Popular Culture in the Early Twenty-First Century*, edited by Elana Levine, 32–50. Urbana: University of Illinois Press, 2015.

———. "If Loving Olitz Is Wrong, I Don't Wanna Be Right." *Black Scholar* 45, no. 1 (2015): 16–20. https://doi.org/10.1080/00064246.2014.997599.

Waysdorf, Abby. "Placing Fandom: Reflections on Film Tourism." In *Locating Imagination in Popular Culture: Place, Tourism, and Belonging*, edited by Nicky van Es, Stijn Reijnders, Leonieke Bolderman, and Abby Waysdorf, 1st edition, 283–96. New York: Routledge, 2020.

Weber, Shannon. "What's Wrong with Be(Com)Ing Queer? Biological Determinism as Discursive Queer Hegemony." *Sexualities* 15, no. 5–6 (2012): 679–701. https://doi.org/10.1177/1363460712446275.

Wei, John. "Iron Man in Chinese Boys' Love Fandom: A Story Untold." *Transformative Works and Cultures* 17 (2014). https://doi.org/10.3983/twc.2014.0561.

Wellman, David. "Minstrel Shows, Affirmative Action Talk, and Angry White Men: Marking Racial Otherness in the 1990s." In *Displacing Whiteness: Essays in Social and Cultural Criticism*, edited by Ruth Frankenberg, 311–32. Durham, NC: Duke University Press, 1997.

"We're Not Gay, We Just Love Each Other." Fanlore. Accessed July 2, 2023. https://fanlore.org/wiki.

Williams, Zoe. "The Saturday Interview: Stuart Hall." *The Guardian*, February 11, 2012, sec. From the Guardian. www.theguardian.com.

Willis, Ika. "Keeping Promises to Queer Children: Making Space (for Mary Sue) at Hogwarts." In *Fan Fiction and Fan Communities in the Age of the Internet: New Essays*, edited by Karen Hellekson and Kristina Busse, 153–70. Jefferson, NC: McFarland, 2006.

Wilson, Angel. "How One Fanfic Is Breaking AO3 (and Fandom)." *The Geekiary*, February 10, 2021. https://thegeekiary.com.

Wilson, Jason. "Playing with Politics: Political Fans and Twitter Faking in Post-Broadcast Democracy." *Convergence: The International Journal of Research into New Media Technologies* 17, no. 4 (2011): 445–61. https://doi.org/10.1177/1354856511414348.

Wilson, Katie. "Red Pillers, Sad Puppies, and Gamergaters: The State of Male Privilege in Internet Fan Communities." In *A Companion to Fandom and Fan Studies*, edited by Paul Booth, 431–46. Oxford, UK: Wiley-Blackwell, 2018.

Winter, Rachel. "Fanon Bernie Sanders: Political Real Person Fan Fiction and the Construction of a Candidate." *Transformative Works and Cultures* 32 (2020). https://doi.org/10.3983/twc.2020.1679.

Winter, Rachel, Steve Scheinert, Mel Stanfill, Anastasia Salter, Olivia B. Newton, Jihye Song, Stephen Fiore, William Rand, and Ivan Garibay. "A Taxonomy of User Actions on Social Networking Sites." In *Proceedings of the 31st ACM Conference on Hypertext and Social Media*, 233–34. Virtual Event, USA: ACM, 2020. https://doi.org/10.1145/3372923.3404808.

Wofford, Taylor. "Is GamerGate about Media Ethics or Harassing Women? Harassment, the Data Shows." *Newsweek*, October 25, 2014. www.newsweek.com.

Woledge, Elizabeth. "Intimatopia: Genre Intersections between Slash and the Mainstream." In *Fan Fiction and Fan Communities in the Age of the Internet: New Essays*, edited by Karen Hellekson and Kristina Busse, 97–114. Jefferson, NC: McFarland, 2006.

Woo, Benjamin. "The Invisible Bag of Holding: Whiteness and Media Fandom." In *The Routledge Companion to Media Fandom*, edited by Melissa A. Click and Suzanne Scott, 245–52. New York: Routledge, 2017.

"Words We're Watching: 'Streisand Effect.'" Merriam-Webster, accessed October 16, 2022. www.merriam-webster.com.

Yang, Ling, and Hongwei Bao. "Queerly Intimate: Friends, Fans, and Affective Communication in a Super Girl Fan Fiction Community." *Cultural Studies* 26, no. 6 (2012): 842–71. https://doi.org/10.1080/09502386.2012.679286.

Yodovich, Neta. "'A Little Costumed Girl at a Sci-Fi Convention': Boundary Work as a Main Destigmatization Strategy among Women Fans." *Women's Studies in Communication* 39, no. 3 (2016): 289–307. https://doi.org/10.1080/07491409.2016.1193781.

Young, Helen. "Race in Online Fantasy Fandom: Whiteness on Westeros.Org." *Continuum* 28, no. 5 (September 3, 2014): 737–47. https://doi.org/10.1080/10304312.2014.941331.

Young, Jock. "Moral Panics and the Transgressive Other." *Crime, Media, Culture* 7, no. 3 (2011): 245–58. https://doi.org/10.1177/1741659011417604.

Zengerle, Jason. "Can the Black Rifle Coffee Company Become the Starbucks of the Right?" *New York Times*, July 14, 2021, sec. Magazine. www.nytimes.com.

Zoellner, Danielle. "'Gun Girl' Kaitlin Bennett Accused of Making Anti-Semitic Statements in Leaked Messages." *The Independent*, April 17, 2020. www.independent.co.uk.

Zoonen, Liesbet van. "Popular Culture as Political Communication: An Introduction." *Javnost—The Public* 7, no. 2 (2000): 5–17. https://doi.org/10.1080/13183222.2000.11008740.

INDEX

absolutism, authors and, 112

activism: advertisers' relation to, 87–88; consumption and, 131–32; fan-tagonism relation to, 95; harassment compared to, 177; media industries relation to, 84; men's rights, 19, 40, 176; against Rothenberg, 86–87

advertisers: activism relation to, 87–88; on YouTube, 129

advocacy, 105–6; fan fiction as, 108; for representation, 107–8; shipping as, 112

affective attachments, 1, 58

"African American Acafandom and Other Strangers" (Wanzo), 17

Alexander, Leigh, 88

Allington, Daniel, 78

Alpha/Beta/Omega stories, 67

alt-right, 192n59; Gamergate relation to, 13; racism and, 154–55; toxic fandom relation to, 14; "us" and "them" mentality in, 28; victim identity and, 40, 169–70

Amell, Stephen, 79

American culture, 110

Analytics-Qualified Qualitative Analysis, 20

Anderson, Becky, 7

Anderson, Karrin Vasby, 52

anger campaign, 89–91, 92–95, 100

AntConc, 46

anti-antis, 23, 105; antis compared to, 120, 126–27; BLM relation to, 122, 124; censorship relation to, 117–19; consent and, 115–16; DNI for, 119–20; fan fiction relation to, 112–13; pleasure relation to, 116–17, 126; racism relation to, 121

antiestablishment beliefs, 57

Antifa, 168, 214n84

antifandom, 3, 14–15, 102; CRT as, 24; in electoral politics, 47; in Gamergate, 19; Tea Party as, 45; of Warren, 21, 44, 45, 47–48, 50, 57–58, 60–61

antifanon, CRT as, 153, 159, 165, 172

antis, 23, 102–3, 181; anti-antis compared to, 120, 126–27; censorship relation to, 117; DNI for, 119; fan fiction relation to, 115, 116, 177; harassment relation to, 114–15; pedophilia relation to, 109–10; racism relation to, 121–22; sexuality relation to, 111, 112, 126; on Twitter, 104–5

anti-trans rhetoric, 111–12

Anti Wars, 102, 103, 111, 115–16, 173, 185; cultural contestation in, 125; morality in, 178; racism relation to, 119, 126; sexuality relation to, 120; underage sex relation to, 208n67

Antos, Heather, 26

Archive of Our Own (AO3), 173; femslash on, 76; mega-tagging on, 8–11, 12, 176; mpreg on, 69–70; Stucky on, 65, 67–68; tags on, 116, 191n57; women on, 200n17

argumentation, description as, 38–39

Arrow (TV series), 79

attachments: affective, 1, 58; emotional, 44; in politics, 21–22; to victim identity, 180; to whiteness, 24, 152, 158, 171, 172

authority, Comicsgate relation to, 35–36, 37–38

populism, 15, 57

pornography, 34; feminism relation to, 111

Potts, Liza, 89

power relations, 4, 20, 24, 180–81; in electoral politics, 48; parasocial relationships relation to, 184; in political rivalry, 45; racism and, 74; sexuality and, 111; in slash fiction, 75; Stucky and, 67–68

Proctor, William, 2, 3

progressiveness, 62, 64; antiestablishment beliefs compared to, 57; of Warren, 53–54

progressive toxicity, 3

progressivism, 119; intersectionality and, 126

Puar, Jasbir, 69

QAnon Shaman, 6–7

queerbaiting, 92, 94, 177; *The 100* and, 82–84; visibility and, 77–78

queer identity, 63; conservatism relation to, 148–49

queerness: in fan fiction, 65; nonnormativity compared to, 64; slash fiction relation to, 179

queer people, 31, 173

queer representation, in comics, 31

queer space, fandom as, 62

queer theory, 4

queer women, femslash relation to, 77, 80

Quinn, Zoë, 189n1

Rabid Puppies, 16, 175

RaceFail '09, 123

racial formation, 153

racial inequality, 155

racialized violence, 98

racial stereotypes, in fan fiction, 124

racism, 17–18, 56, 196n39, 206n22; alt-right and, 154–55; antis relation to, 121–22; Anti Wars relation to, 119, 126;

Comicsgate relation to, 30, 41; CRT relation to, 155–56, 163, 177; as evil, 160; in fiction, 120–21, 123–24; in *The 100*, 98–100; sexuality and, 125, 126; in slash fiction, 72–74; structural, 166; systemic, 157, 161, 165, 168; whiteness relation to, 167

radicalization: marginalization relation to, 175–76; stereotypes relation to, 16; whiteness and, 170–71

rape, 110, 111

reactionary backlash, to *Batgirl*, 25

reactionary culture, 1–2, 13–15, 19

reactionary fandom, 2, 26

reactionary politics, 2, 4, 26, 39; Comicsgate relation to, 42; popular culture relation to, 15

reality, fiction compared to, 113

regulation, of cryptocurrency, 56–57

Reid, Robin Anne, 65

#ReleaseTheSnyderCut, 82

representation, 105–6, 107–8

Rico, Andrew Ryan, 18

right-wing buzzwords, 55–56, 60, 141, 159–60

right-wing populism, 15

Rittenhouse, Kyle, 123

Ross, Loretta J., 170

Rothenberg, Jason, 22, 82, 83, 101, 181; activism against, 86–87; anger campaign against, 89–91, 92–95; threats toward, 95–98; toxic fandom toward, 84, 85; on Twitter, 88–90, 100

Rouse, Lauren, 102

Rubin, Gayle S., 109–10, 112, 114

Rufo, Christopher, 150, 152, 156

Russo, Julie Levin, 18, 63–64, 77

Sad Puppies, 16, 175

Salter, Anastasia, 14, 16, 28, 169–70, 179

Salter, Michael, 101

same-sex romances, 18, 206n29. *See also* homosexuality

ABOUT THE AUTHOR

MEL STANFILL is Associate Professor with a joint appointment in the Texts and Technology Program and the Department of English at the University of Central Florida. Stanfill is the author of three books, including *Rock This Way: Cultural Constructions of Musical Legitimacy* (2023).